No Place Like Home in a New City

No Place like Home in a New City

Anti-Urbanism and Life in Nairobi

Bettina Ng'weno

UNIVERSITY OF CALIFORNIA PRESS

University of California Press
Oakland, California

Suggested citation: Ng'weno, B. *No Place Like Home in a New City: Anti-Urbanism and Life in Nairobi*. Oakland: University of California Press, 2025. DOI: https://doi.org/10.1525/luminos.245

Library of Congress Cataloging-in-Publication Data

Names: Ng'weno, Bettina, author.
Title: No place like home in a new city : anti-urbanism and life in Nairobi / Bettina Ng'weno.
Description: Oakland, California : University of California Press, [2025] | Includes bibliographical references and index.
Identifiers: LCCN 2025003767 (print) | LCCN 2025003768 (ebook) | ISBN 9780520423206 (hardback) | ISBN 9780520421219 (paperback) | ISBN 9780520421226 (ebook)
Subjects: LCSH: City planning—Kenya—Nairobi. | City dwellers—Kenya—Nairobi—Social conditions—21st century.
Classification: LCC HT169.K4 N356 2025 (print) | LCC HT169.K4 (ebook) | DDC 967.62/504—dc23/eng/20250212

LC record available at https://lccn.loc.gov/2025003767
LC ebook record available at https://lccn.loc.gov/2025003768

GPSR Authorized Representative: Easy Access System Europe, Mustamäe tee 50, 10621 Tallinn, Estonia, gpsr.requests@easproject.com

34 33 32 31 30 29 28 27 26 25
10 9 8 7 6 5 4 3 2 1

This book is dedicated to my father,
Hilary Ng'weno

And to all of you
who also love being from Nairobi

CONTENTS

List of Illustrations ix
Acknowledgments xi

Introduction: Dawn *1*

1. The Rain at Home *17*

2. Growing Old in a New City *33*

3. One Hundred Years of Segregation *51*

4. Dancing to the Sound of Nairobi *69*

5. Remnant of a Green City in the Sun *87*

6. Remains of an Unrealized Yesterday *107*

7. Place of Sweet Water *129*

8. No Place Like Home *150*

Epilogue: Civil Twilight *167*

Notes *173*
Bibliography *193*
General Index *209*

ILLUSTRATIONS

MAPS

1. Nairobi's neighborhoods   *2*
2. Nairobi's municipal boundaries   *59*
3. Elevations and rivers of Nairobi   *130*

FIGURES

 1. View of Nairobi   *5*
 2. Nairobi residents at City Park   *20*
 3. Construction work in Upper Hill   *34*
 4. Hilary Ng'weno and family, 1957   *38*
 5. Downtown Nairobi   *46*
 6. Kaloleni Social Hall   *73*
 7. City Park   *88*
 8. City Park bandstand   *96*
 9. Joseph and Sheila Murumbi's graves   *108*
10. Commonwealth war graves   *112*
11. Joseph Murumbi Peace Memorial Sculpture Garden   *116*
12. Sign to Pio Gama Pinto's grave   *118*
13. Pio Gama Pinto's grave   *119*
14. Mass graves, City Park Cemetery   *123*
15. Kibagare River   *131*
16. Riparian area demolitions   *134*

17. Garbage buildup in Nairobi river   144
18. Kibagare River in flood   147
19. Bulldozers in Upper Hill   157
20. My father's walking route   170

ACKNOWLEDGMENTS

This book would not have been possible without the help, support, and encouragement of family, friends, and colleagues. They are more numerous than I can thank here individually, as so many people helped in so many ways. Sadly, a fair number of the people whom I spoke to for this book have gone too early to join the ancestors. I am eternally grateful for the time they took to talk with me about their youth in Nairobi. I do not name all those who helped me by name for confidentiality reasons, but please know I am thanking you personally.

This project percolated while I worked for Aga Khan University (AKU) in Nairobi. I thank my colleagues at the Faculty of Arts and Sciences for thinking with me and entertaining my explorations around the city. In addition, as I crisscrossed Nairobi just to get to work at AKU, I learned to navigate a city undergoing rapid transformation. In particular, I thank Michael Karinga and Sheila Ochugboju. Our conversations during my time at AKU and afterward, when working on the film project *Last Dance in Kaloleni*, illuminated new ideas of the city and put me in contact with many people. I also thank Peter Kariuki, whose keen eye still finds new things in Nairobi streets.

While working at AKU in 2011 I joined the community organization Friends of City Park. This book owes a tremendous debt to the generosity, expertise, and hard work of its volunteers and employees, who not only corrected and commented on numerous versions of my chapters on City Park but were constant allies in struggles for environmental and social justice in Nairobi. I learned so much from you. You helped me see that the impossible was possible with constant, informed, detailed hard work. What I got right in this book is due to your care and attention. The mistakes are my own.

The film project *Last Dance in Kaloleni* broadened my understanding of the Railways, generational change, music, and time. I particularly thank those who so kindly worked with me on this project, especially Njane Mugambi and family, Chao Tayiana Maina, Clara Shuma, James Makau Nzioka, Lawrence Kiiru, Christine Olale Tantuo, and Neha Manoj Shah, as well as my aunts, uncles, cousins, and extended family in Nairobi and Funyula, and the many people who so generously answered my questions about their lives in 1950s Nairobi (including ML, DA, GW, HBN, and HJO in Nairobi; NM in Mbitini; SW, AO, MOO, and GW in Funyula; and SMO and Cpt. O in Kisumu).

In Nairobi I was blessed with an intellectual community including Yvonne Owuor, Ngala Chome, Garnette Oluoch Olunya, Joyce Nyairo, Bill Odidi, Kaithe Kiiru, Wambui Mwangi, Peter Odhiambo, Shem Migot-Adholla, Muthoni Likimani, Parselelo Kantai, Radha Upadhyaya, Susan Moenga, and Warris Vianni, as well as friends and family who made me rethink my work. I acknowledge Steven Oundo, Julia Kunguru, Leonard Obura Aloo, Angela Ondari, Joe Muganda, Jerry Riley, Jonathon Fox, Sophia Skoda, Chris Groom, and Peter Usher, who provided information and help with networks and thinking. I owe very special thanks to Yasmin Madhani and to Makanda Kioko for their friendship and their constant support for, intellectual engagement with, and excitement at my project. And a grateful shout-out to Pauline Groom, who encouraged me to find and speak in my own voice.

Part of the process of finding my voice was an email to around a hundred friends regarding things I found interesting going on in Nairobi and Kenya. This book is a product of conversations with that group, who indulged me, challenged me, and asked me questions. Thank you for your input and contributions.

I wrote parts of this book in Nairobi, Hawaii, and California. In Hawaii I thank Sidney Westly for her friendship, hospitality, and remembrances of Nairobi, and Toby Miller for the best writing retreat possible. I especially thank Ayesha Nibbe and David Henkin for encouraging me to go to Hawaii and for offering stimulating ideas, health remedies, and constant support. To have the peace of mind to write, I also need peace of body, which I found in two activities I love—Hawaiian outrigger canoe paddling and flamenco. I am particularly grateful to the 2022 and 2023 Lanikai Canoe Club women's novice crew and of course to my flamenco crew, with Jimmy Kay Ramos in Sacramento and Punta-Tacón in Davis. Thanks to everyone for the encouragement and support—and guess what, I finally finished! In California I particularly thank Leanna Sinibaldi for her supportive friendship and Lina Gamboa for all the gentle pushes to finish.

I am grateful to my Department of African American and African Studies at the University of California, Davis, for their constant support. I am also grateful to the wonderful community of researchers and thinkers in the Mellon research initiative Reimagining Indian Ocean Worlds. I thank all the participants in that initiative for the openness, generosity of thought, and generative comments on works in progress, and in particular, the graduate students for their fresh ideas and inquiring minds. I can't imagine better people to think with. I also thank other graduate students I worked with over the long decade of completing this work, and specifically Seon-Hye Moon for her kindness and help towards the end. I had many wonderful conversations and discussions with academic and artistic friends who helped shape and sharpen my ideas, including Cristiana Giordano, Nidhi Mahajan, Kathleen Coll, Lok Siu, Espelencia Baptiste, Ekwa Msangi, Peggy Brunache, Carlos Andres Barragan, Ingrid Lagos, Silvia Soto, Jamila Moore-Pewu, Joella Bitters, Sonja M. Sonnenburg, Andrea Dooley, Nicole Ranganath, Zoila Mendoza, Tony Dumas, Julia Alejandra Morales Fontanilla, Adrian Yen, Mark Jerng, Jake Culbertson, Ayanda Manqoyi, Christian Alvarado, and Genesis Lara. I never tire of talking to and thinking with you. I am grateful to Kimberly Nettles-Barcelon for encouraging me not to shy away from including my family in my work. Importantly, this book would not have been completed without the wonderful input of Ishani Saraf, William F. Stafford, and Anuj Vaidya, the best writing group ever.

At the University of California Press I thank Kate Marshall for her guidance and help through the publication process and acknowledge Bill Nelson for the beautiful maps and Erika Búky for careful copyediting. I also acknowledge the challenging and stimulating comments of the peer reviewers: Awet T. Weldemichael, Wale Adebanwi, and an anonymous reviewer. I thank and credit you for making this a much better book. I continue to think with the ideas you brought up.

I got editorial help from Elena Abbott at a time when I was struggling with illness. Her kindness, consideration, specific and detailed help, and constant enthusiasm for my project enabled me to push through and keep working. I am so grateful to have worked with her. She had the amazing ability of guiding me through my own mazes back to the track I wanted to be on. Thank you so much, Elena.

Finally, I thank my family, near and far. This is their story as much as mine. I would like to express my gratitude to my father, Hilary Ng'weno, for the many conversations about Muthurwa, Nairobi, the Railways, music, film, and family, and for his constantly inquiring mind, which enabled him to get so much done. He always felt an urgency about telling stories of our space and home. I thank my mother, Fleur Ng'weno, and my sister, Amolo Ng'weno, for their constant engagement with the book—the questions, the ideas, the information, and the enthusiasm. I could not have done it without you.

Introduction

Dawn

All of Anna's neighbors have gone, and with them her livelihood as a tailor and her social connections.[1] In March 2020, President Uhuru Kenyatta placed restrictions on movement in and out of the city of Nairobi to control the spread of COVID-19. When he lifted those restrictions in July 2020, people left Nairobi with all their belongings, desperately trying to return to families and communities in the countryside before the city might once again become a containment zone. Anna is one of the few remaining tenants in the neighborhood of Jericho, a working-class government housing estate developed in 1961, just before Kenya became independent.[2] There is an eerie silence here now. The exodus was massive.

Of course, although thousands of city residents left during the pandemic, many remained. Some, whose jobs remained secure, did not have to leave. Some entrepreneurs found that their businesses were unaffected or even boosted by the pandemic. Others struggled to maintain their occupations and lives in the city. And still others, like Anna, had nowhere else to go. Her story is not unusual. Jericho is home to residents who inherited their houses from their parents and grandparents. They have no country home to "return" to.

Less than six months after Kenyatta lifted the movement restrictions, the residents of Jericho faced an exodus of another kind. Anna and her neighbors were informed by the government that their neighborhood was scheduled for demolition and redevelopment. Still reeling from the economic fallout of COVID, where were they to go?

Since its start as a depot for the East African Railways and Harbours in the early twentieth century, Nairobi has been seen as a city of temporary migrants. Most everyone comes from somewhere else—not just the colonial administrators who planned the city but also the workers, builders, traders, entertainers, and

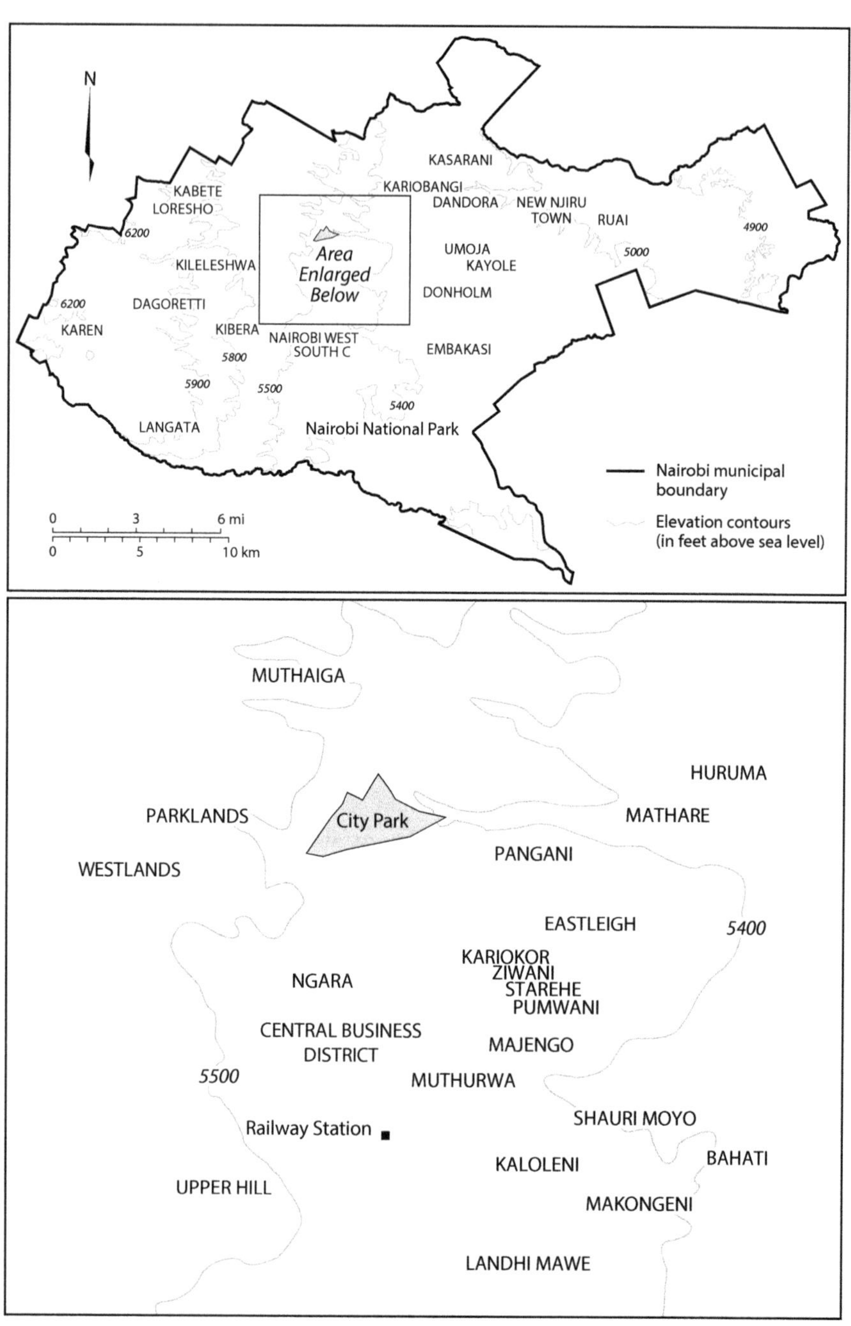

MAP 1. Nairobi's neighborhoods.

professionals who were drawn in from other parts of the country and from across the Indian Ocean. Most of these people were not meant to stay. They were there only to build a new modern city. Once that was done, they were expected to return to the countryside or to Asia, lest their continuing presence contaminate the city's newness and modernity. Indeed, in Nairobi, as in other cities around the world, urban planning, policy, laws, and administration have been geared toward maintaining some people as temporary residents in order to make the city a permanent home for others.

I refer to these practices as *anti-urbanism*. Anti-urbanism is a form of urbanism—a form of knowing, imagining, planning, designing, and administering cities. As its organizing principle, anti-urbanism maintains that the majority of people cannot, should not, and must not be permanent residents of a city. It is a refusal of the idea that the city is home.

Nevertheless, more and more "temporary" people—like Anna—see Nairobi as home. In the obsession of planners, politicians, and scholars with the newness and modernity of Nairobi, we easily forget just how long these residents have been living in the city, and we overlook the practices they have engaged in to make the city their own. This book is for and about the residents who claim Nairobi as home.

THE PROBLEM OF NAIROBI AS HOME

In this book I address anti-urbanism and its long-term consequences for city life by focusing on a problem I call "Nairobi as home." First I ask why considering the city as home should be a problem. How have ideologies of time and space—implemented through policies, laws, practices, and designs—made it impossible, in principle and practice, for residents to call Nairobi home? How are these ideologies and their practical manifestations reflected in the built environment and the dynamics of rapid demolition and reconstruction? How have residents contested this problem? And finally, what approaches can we use to investigate and discuss this denial of the city as home in Nairobi and elsewhere?

This book tells the story of what kind of city emerged from the structuring and restructuring of housing in specific sections of Nairobi. It is about the place-making practices and dreams that different Nairobi residents have made visible and tangible: the ways they live in, talk about, use, repurpose, and make urban space. It argues that users, as well as planners, dream cities into being and transform city spaces to meet their needs. Throughout, it illuminates how people in Nairobi have challenged and adapted to changing urban spaces.

I started researching this book between 2011 and 2013, when trying to commute five kilometers to work across Nairobi, the city of my birth, amid massive road construction. When I went to work on any given day, I did not know if I would be able to travel back on the same road. Since then I have collected expansive ethnographic material on Nairobi, including archival data, newspapers, memoirs, court cases, title deeds, maps, interviews, family experiences, and memories. I have amassed extensive data from participant-observation in public urban planning, community and stakeholder meetings, meetings to discuss the city master plan, and meetings with the Kenya Urban Roads Authority (KURA). I have taken long walks and drives along Nairobi's streets and spent eleven years as a volunteer with the organization Friends of City Park. And, of course, I have years of experience growing up and living in Nairobi.

As an anthropologist I am interested in the way the quotidian makes city life and cities. I also pay attention to the distribution of power that shapes both the everyday and the extraordinary aspects of city life. In examining the built and natural environment of Nairobi, I illustrate the various ways anti-urbanism is structured and manifested—and how it is challenged. I examine different neighborhoods, geographic features, built environments, and activities to depict the consequences of the assumption that the city cannot be home for the vast majority of its inhabitants.

I have been guided by my long-term relationship with the city as much as by an anthropological or geographical research perspective. As a third-generation Nairobian in my fifties, from a family in which multiple generations of relatives worked for the Railways, I am interested in understanding permanence and aging in a city that is constantly under renewal. Having lived through some of the processes of renewal, I am also interested in what it feels like to be in a space of constant, rapid, and intermittent change, which has become the norm in contemporary cities in much of the world.

Cities striving to be modern use anti-urbanism as a foundational ideology for their urbanism. Anti-urbanism is the process by which cities pursue modernity through the control of needed but unwanted populations. The people who are needed to create and maintain "modern," "futuristic," "world-class," or "global" cities are not always wanted in these spaces once they are built. The cities were not made for them. This contradiction is managed by anti-urbanism articulated in law, policy, practice, and design.

Often scholars and nonscholars alike lament a lack of planning in Nairobi and other African cities.[3] People complain that certain settlements or even the whole city is unplanned. They complain that the Nairobi master plan has not been updated since the 1970s. I argue, rather, that the simultaneous development of town planning and colonial experimentation and administration are actually part of the enduring problems of Nairobi and other cities that grew out of a colonial context. Rather than being peripheral to urban planning, Africa and Asia were central to its reimagining and development.[4] To illuminate these historical and geographical connections, this book considers Nairobi as a global city.[5] It is connected to the rest of the world, but it has its own specific character, flavors, histories, and attitudes.

FIGURE 1. A view of Nairobi from Lavington, in the western part of the city. Photo by author.

In addition, this book considers how foreign and local investment in infrastructure, industry, and housing under neoliberal governance is transforming urban landscapes.[6] Because anti-urbanism dictates what is and should be permanent or impermanent in the city, we need approaches that elucidate the ramifications of concepts of time and space in these new urban dynamics. The anthropologist Jane Guyer argues that perhaps the contemporary moment is best comprehended through intimate ethnography, which she describes as a walk through the city to observe everyday life in flux.[7] Such ethnography seeks to understand the dreams, aspirations, imaginaries, and perceptions that allow residents to claim the city on their own terms.[8] But I believe we must also look at the way these dynamics shape the lives of the needed but unwanted residents.

Making the city home is a process shaped by narratives of the past, the visions of public intellectuals, moral ideologies governing how people should be in the city, and power negotiations.[9] Ideas about cities do not always overlap with the reality, and these disparities give rise to new readings and renderings of the city. According to urban scholars, how we think about cities is influenced by our understandings of and projections about specific regions as sites of innovation and change.[10] I argue that these ideas are built on colonial foundations that distinguish temporally as well as spatially between town and country, between urban and rural, and between racialized spaces within cities—placing some in the future and relegating others to the past. These dynamics have material consequences for life in the city.

I offer a view into Nairobi that is rarely considered—that of long-term residents like Anna and my family. I hope through these experiences, I can get to the often erased, disparaged, and denied experience of seeking permanence in the face of newness—the possibility of Nairobi as home for those who already call it home. The perspective of the long-term resident also shows how the city has changed—a view that can be lost in readings of the city that look only forward and never back. This *longue durée* view also allows me to consider other changes that affect everyday life in Nairobi, such as climate change, and gives me a vantage from which to look back at past dreams of the future city.

No Place like Home in a New City is about the ways that anti-urbanism structured and structures Nairobi, but it is also about the feelings, experiences, and challenges of making a home in a city that was not built for you.[11] Through their mundane practices, long-term residents have imagined alternatives to an urbanism based on colonial racial foundations, one that did not want them. Their refusal of the economic, legal, administrative, and political structures that try to relegate them elsewhere challenges colonial and postcolonial policies of anti-urbanism; they have envisioned and tried to realize other ways of being urban. They have created alternative urban spaces and futures—what we might call "imaginaries of otherwise."

ANTI-URBANISM

In Kenya and across Africa, colonial administrations categorized territory in racial and ethnic terms.[12] The scholarship of colonial-era planning typically focuses on both the racial segregation and the spatial inequality that resulted.[13] I argue that racial segregation is ordered by placement in time (the assignment of temporality) as a way of justifying placement in space. This idea is dependent on the notion that not everyone is living in or sharing the same time.[14] Rather, some of us are in and of the past, and others are in and of the future. African residents are framed as temporary, and the city as modern but lacking history.[15] Anti-urbanism wields this ideology of impermanence against people understood as existing in a backward past.[16]

Cities were characterized as cosmopolitan, modern, chaotic, unruly places in need of control and order, in contrast to the monoracial, ethnic, cultural, traditional purity ascribed to the African countryside. This contrast rendered cities themselves out of place in Africa, and their inhabitants out of place in cities.[17] Moreover, in a vision that cast the city as the aspirational future of the countryside, cities became temporally separated from the rest of the country.[18] This framing also temporally separated parts of the city, with some areas considered modern and other backward, some gentrifying while others stagnated. As colonial governments sought to build European cities with temporary African workers, they divided Africans' time in the city into three episodes: arrival in the city to work; working in the city; and leaving the city on retirement or termination of employment.

This dynamic is one of the long-lasting products of colonial racialized thinking. The demand for labor created needed but unwanted urban populations who were young and predominantly male. Even today Nairobi has few elderly residents. However, it has few children as well.[19] This pattern has had large social effects and generated keen scholarly, social, and political interest in youth in Africa and its cities.[20] Too often, while according to youth the qualities of agility, flexibility and creativity, such observers also project in their analysis an insecure temporality, a distaste for idleness, an obsession with productivity, a demand for economic success, and a fear of violence or moral decay. All of this, I argue, arises out of the anti-urbanist belief that the city is intended for those who are employed.

These anti-urbanist ideologies are ingrained in popular culture. For instance, the Kenyan film *Nairobi Half Life* narrates the entry into the city of a young rural African man who must adjust to a cold, cruel, and alienating urban life.[21] The protagonist is depicted as being both lost in the city and lost to his "real" home in the countryside. In the South African film *Tsotsi*, the protagonist is a violent, disaffected, unfeeling youth, lost to society and without community. He is "humanized" after finding a baby in the backseat of a car he has stolen.[22] The title of the film, *Tsotsi*, which means a young street thug, gangster, or urban delinquent, reflects the film's intense anti-urbanism. In these cinematic depictions of African urban spaces, the disaffected youth (depicted as neither productive nor reproductive), if male, turns violent, and if female, turns to prostitution.

Anti-urbanism dictates whether and how people should live in the city. It concerns time as much as space. It creates impermanence through structures and practices that lead to segregation, removals, and neglect of people and infrastructure. As a structuring ideology, anti-urbanism is evident in a city's layout, buildings, amenities, and the services and practices of bureaucrats, as well as in residents' efforts to establish a permanent presence in the city and official responses to those efforts. Anti-urbanism is most evident in the way demolition is used as a form of urban governance.

Although they do not frame their understanding of cities in terms of anti-urbanism, a number of scholars of urban Africa make reference to anti-urban regimes and discourses or describe practices I would term anti-urban.[23] For instance, in *Street Archives and City Life*, a study of migrants to Dar es Salaam, the historian Emily Callaci refers to socialist-era Tanzania as "having one of the most anti-urban political regimes on the planet."[24] Her study demonstrates the postcolonial attachment to anti-urbanism, by which the "out of place" urban resident is cast as lost, a failure, and a traitor to the socialist state. She argues that the socialist state's anti-urbanist discourse blamed the migrant for any failure to prosper in the city, rather than acknowledging the state's failure to provide for citizens' welfare. Similarly, David Morton's *Age of Concrete*, a study of Maputo, the capital of Mozambique (formerly Lourenço Marques), is concerned with colonial and postcolonial (socialist) anti-urbanism. It demonstrates the fight against impermanence, down to the level of materials (like concrete or reed) used to build houses. The unflinching persistence of anti-urbanism in Mozambique, including ownership laws, pass laws, segregation, and moral critique, challenges Callaci's assertion about socialist-era Tanzania's being the most anti-urbanist regime on the planet, as does the example of Nairobi.

If anti-urbanism creates forced impermanence, we can juxtapose it with forms of urbanism designed to enable residents to escape the city. Scholars of urban planning have long been concerned about how modern industrial cities dehumanize their occupants with an absence of spaces of community and sociality.[25] In Europe and United States, industrial urban spaces, with their congested housing, pollution, poverty, and diversity produced a distaste for the city among the very planners who once extolled it as the pinnacle of modernity and efficiency. As Achille Mbembe and Sarah Nuttall observe, South African cities like Johannesburg have also been read as "part of the antiurban ideology that has consistently perceived the industrial city, in particular, as a cesspool of vice."[26] The industrial city came to be seen as a modernity gone wrong. This antipathy influenced urban planning and policy in the twentieth century.

Steven Conn, in *Americans Against the City*, argues that this perception of the modern industrial city gave rise to a form of urbanism that was inherently anti-urban.[27] City planners mobilized a longstanding and deep antipathy toward cities and a romantic view of the countryside. This attitude was in part a reaction to industrialization and demographic shifts, including the influx of immigrants and the Great Migration of rural African Americans, that swelled the population of cities and changed their socioeconomic and ethnic composition. With features such as suburbs, these planners tried to create the "ideal village" within the city (or on its outskirts) that was homogeneous and separate from the urban population. Urban density, diversity, and public space were thus cast as problematic. The concept of the garden city can be seen as an effort to incorporate the imagined good of the country within urban spaces.

This reading of anti-urbanism, which is about understanding the city as dehumanizing, evil, dangerous, corrupted, asocial, full of vice, and otherwise dysfunctional, is different from my approach. Moreover, unlike many discussions of anti-urbanism in other parts of the world, I do not focus on the industrial city. Rather, I focus on how modernist notions of the city have rendered some residents temporary in order to make others permanent. I address the attitudes and tactics intended to keep people out of cities or limit their time there.

In Conn's example, US planners and policy makers were trying to produce a countryside within the city and isolate unwanted urban populations. Their policies and designs were intended to shelter privileged residents from the negative aspects of the city. In contrast, in Africa, and indeed in other parts of the once-colonized world, planners and policy makers aimed to create a humanized, modern ideal of the city in part by restricting access to it. Indeed, the American anti-urbanism referenced by Conn was built on top of decades of government policy that relegated Native peoples of the Americas to rural spaces that were thought to be backward and out of time.

The anti-urbanism that this book addresses is primarily concerned with how temporality and spatiality are assigned to people and places in a way that negates the possibility of their being at home in the city. While garden cities in Europe such as Letchworth and Welwyn near London and Augusta, Georgia, in the United States allowed the wealthy urban and predominantly white population to escape the industrialized city, in the colonies garden cities served to restrict colonized peoples and the poor from cities.[28] Here I am interested in who is kept out of the city; who is rendered temporary and by what means; and what the consequences are for everyone in the city. I contend that the city cannot be humanized without recognizing and challenging this foundational and persistent anti-urbanism.

Rather than associating anti-urbanism with a specific regime, discourse, or historical phenomenon (such as a socialist regime) and thus limiting it to a particular time or place, I position it as a concept and ideology underlying the production of all cities that strive to be modern. An important part of anti-urbanism is the contrast between the modern city and its residents and the traditional/backward countryside and residents.

ANTI-URBANISM ACROSS COLONIAL AND POSTCOLONIAL DIVIDES

While most scholars of urban Africa have pointed out how colonial urban segregation has extended into postcolonial life, they address it as a predominantly spatial problem.[29] In South Africa, scholars examine policies and practices that excluded Africans from urban centers and segregated them into specific spaces, and the consequences for the current functioning of South African cities.[30] The environmental and policy scientist Ambe J. Njoh would argue that similar practices obtained in the former French colonies of West Africa, which have inherited city spaces that were designed to modernize, segregate, dominate, and experiment.[31] I address segregation as a problem of time as much as one of space. Anti-urbanism creates and depends on impermanence to justify placement. Such impermanence can be, and has been, attached to social categories beyond race, such as gender, class, religion, and migrant status.

Impermanence facilitates anti-urbanism's persistence beyond political changes such as national independence, changes of government, or majority rule. Segregation is a form of impermanence used to deal with needed but unwanted urban populations. It creates a holding space before more permanent removal. Segregated spaces have been used to manage populations categorized as "native," "detribalized native," "Asian," and "poor," rendering them temporary.[32] I argue that we should think of these colonial classifications as categories of time and space rather than as identities.

Whether anti-urbanism took the postcolonial form of apartheid in South Africa, segregation in Zambia and French West Africa, socialism in Tanzania and Mozambique, nationalism in Ghana, or gender in Gabon, the basic ideology of anti-urbanism has far-reaching consequences for how cities are imagined, peopled, claimed, and lived in.[33] In particular, both state and civil organizations have set out to regulate and police how out-of-place-people can be in the city or to return them to their "correct place."[34] Such ideas have shaped the design and constructions of cities, city infrastructures, national politics, and land policy.

To understand the consequences of anti-urbanism for Nairobi, I look at two aspects of the city: its geographic layout and the efforts of its long-term residents to make Nairobi home. The layout of the city demonstrates the enduring structural effects of anti-urbanism. Long-term residents (as opposed to migrants) make visible the persistence of anti-urbanism and struggles against it.

Chapters 1–3 and 5 look at how anti-urbanism structures the layout, housing, and inequality of Nairobi. The geographic layout of the city demonstrates the enduring anti-urbanist design against which efforts to create permanence exist, as well as the way the natural topography interacts with anti-urbanism under new conditions such as climate change. Throughout the book, and particularly in chapters 2, 7 and 8, I examine the role of demolition as a tool of anti-urbanist governance. I also look at the ways that people have made the city their own through family, dance and music, advocacy, ancestors, and memory.

In looking at anti-urbanism, I posit new ways of thinking about the social and structural dynamics of Nairobi and the categories used to narrate its stories. Since part of the rationale for displacing people is the proximity of housing to rivers, I also look at how the category of *riparian* has become a tool of anti-urbanism. Throughout the book I use the concepts of *remnant, microcosm, remains, unremembered, family, ancestral, dreams, home* and *the perfect storm* to challenge such displacement and anti-urbanist structuring and to imagine a city beyond and besides anti-urbanism.

This book challenges anti-urbanism by asking, What are the consequences for residents, and for the life of the city, of refusing the possibility of the Nairobi as home?

GROWING OLD IN A NEW CITY

My father, Hilary Ng'weno, was always adamant that he was from Nairobi. He reacted angrily to an article in the local newspapers that listed him as a famous son of Busia County, a predominantly rural county in western Kenya. As he slapped down the newspaper in annoyance, I teased him, asking, "What is the big deal?" After all, in our family, we had always called the space where my grandparents lived "home." The shorthand term indicated the space of our extended family, in Funyula in Busia County and immediately across the border in Uganda. We would ask family members in Nairobi, "Is anyone going home? Can you take this with you when you go?" We would say, "We can't visit Auntie or Uncle today, as they have traveled home." Yet my father was not born in Busia County; in fact, he spent less than a year of his life there. This "home" was not a place he belonged to in the way he felt he belonged to Nairobi.

But his protest also spoke to something more. The newspaper article was one of a series of articles focusing on different counties in Kenya, trying to make the process of political and administrative decentralization—referred to as *devolution*—legible to the general public after a change to the national constitution in 2010. The articles chose different famous people to personalize each county. The profiles were organized around political affiliation, cultural background, ethnicity, and language. When I asked my father what the big deal was, he was not amused. He angrily replied, "Who will they list for Nairobi County?"

My father's anger was not a denial or rejection of Busia but rather a reaction to being erased from Nairobi—racially, ethnically, and personally. It was a protest against anti-urbanism, its continued power to affect his life, and what he read as its dangers for the future. When he asked who would represent Nairobi, he was worried about the consequences of the answer. This was not the first or last such protest I heard from him. I found myself protesting similarly as a facet of my own identification with the city. It was part of the impetus to write this book.

Unwanted long-term residents, like my father, hold the keys to questions about anti-urbanism in Nairobi and other cities. Rejecting the adage (and colonial dream) that as people age and are no longer productive, they return to the countryside, this book investigates engagement with the city at different stages in life that allow for generational continuity and change. I ask how the experiences and contributions of long-term residents highlight leisure and rest along with labor at any age. In light of this, how can we understand impermanence, idleness, productivity, economic success, and violence or moral decay, not to mention agility, flexibility, and creativity in the context of aging? These residents' weariness, their success and failure, and their perseverance and persistence, as well as their reactions to change, have much to tell us about the modern city.

However, my interest in long-term residents in Nairobi is not an argument about the inherited colonial framing of legitimacy through narratives of origin, or the moral framing of longevity as a form of seniority. Nor is it about ownership or other framings of space as property, or the notion of legitimacy through productivity. Rather, it is a call for a new framing of cities and belonging that can include permanence along with newness; a conception that cities are full of people who are entitled to be there simply because they *are* there; a vision that can include dreams, futures, and places not designed by experts but created through practices of care, advocacy, and protest. It can include both the living and the dead and adapt to a changing climate.

Most Nairobi residents today are migrants who came to the city as adults. Nevertheless, I challenge assumptions that everyone in the city is a migrant, and I interrogate the consequences of such thinking for life in Nairobi. The experiences of long-term residents provide a vantage from which to critique the colonial and consequent postcolonial constructions of time and space that deny the possibility of the city as home.

As a concept, *home* can encompass many ideas: a dwelling, the place you go when you have nowhere else to go, a place of belonging, a place to call your own, a place of relatives, a place of marriage, a place of ancestors, a multigenerational place, a place you constructed, a ritually sanctioned space, a place you return to, a place where you go to die, a place you go after death, a place of permanence, of security, of peace. Home can be a place of moral, customary, and legal rights; a place of acceptance, foundations, and belonging; and the place you are from even if you are not there anymore.

Yet none of these versions of home are necessarily legitimate, sufficient, or correct. Rather, these multiple conceptions of *home* challenge the idea posed by antiurbanism that for some populations, the city can never be home. In the face of the idea that I can't be home here, I can't be from here, I can't belong here, and I can't remain here, I echo my father's insistence that he was from Nairobi and that he had made it home. What kinds of spaces are created when they are explicitly defined as *not* home? And for whom are they created?

In conversation with prior studies that have focused on migrants, new arrivals, and those who have left cities, an examination of long-term residents and their understanding of home can build a broader, fuller, more complex idea of cities like Nairobi.[35] Such an approach must take into account the effects of the narratives we tell about cities, relate different neighborhoods to each other, and account for changes in culture, society, politics, and climate. It must blur the boundaries between urban and rural. Most importantly it must call for forms of urban policy and governance that speak to and for the dynamic, complex, and enduring urban populations who live in the city, with the aim to build just, acceptable, humane urban futures.

Nairobi cries out for a new urbanism and other ways of imagining the city. More generally, Nairobi makes us question how we should think of cities in the face of rapid spatial and temporal shifts. How do we think of city life when the rate of change leaves us unable to drive the same route to and from work on any given day? How should the rapid transformations occurring in much of the developing world today change the way we might think of cities in general?

What questions do we need to ask of Nairobi today to understand or shape the Nairobi of the future?

AT HOME IN AN ORDINARY CITY

Contemporary Nairobi is full of changing places, like Anna's neighborhood of Jericho. Being in Nairobi and many other African and Asian cities involves experiencing the simultaneous demolition and reconstruction of the city.[36] The dialectic between the two can be read as an example of a struggle over the temporality and spatiality defining the city.[37] The struggle is waged among residents, inhabitants, planners, investors, politicians, and the environment. The changes draw on an anti-urbanist framing of African cities: cities lacking history, with only temporary inhabitants, provide the perfect tabula rasa for futuristic narratives of new cities, infrastructure projects, and urban planning.

Among the methods through which these futures are realized, the most important is demolition. Demolition features in every chapter of this book. It is the foundation upon which housing, race, and urban belonging are built in Nairobi. Initiated during the colonial period as a tool of governance that rearranged both time and space, demolition is used today to sustain the conception of the city as a blank slate whose residents are out of place. Most important to this conceptualization is the implicit claim that as people out of place, city inhabitants can never be rendered homeless: they always have a home to return to, provided that they go back where they belong, in the countryside.[38] This constructed lack of belonging to the city has devastating consequences not only for policy and life but also for notions of time and space.

Although demolitions have paved the way for successive production of "modern" and "desirable" change since the colonial period, the terms on which they are now enacted are quite different.[39] Demolition, as the precursor of new construction, is often sold to the inhabitants of the cities, and to and by international investors, as a reconfiguration of temporality (becoming modern) and spatiality (becoming global) in an international arena.[40] The blinding light of the future city that illuminates plans, advertising, and infrastructure expenditure obscures the more mundane city of the present.[41]

One legacy of colonialism is that African cities are often thought of, both locally and abroad, as derivative of other places.[42] Even their architecture is understood as copied from other places. In *Ordinary Cities: Between Modernity and Development*, the urban geographer Jennifer Robinson pushes back against framing some cities as global and the rest as derivative or local. Rather she posits each city as ordinary. In concert with Robinson, the urban theorist Abdou Maliq Simone, the anthropologist Filip De Boeck, and the geographer David McDonald all ask us to conceptualize African cities and their African inhabitants in all their specificity as spaces through which to think about cities more generally.[43] Focusing on long-term Nairobi residents' dreams and practices brings the global and local into productive conversation.

By positioning Nairobi as emblematic of contemporary global urban dynamics, I reject the peripheral positioning of most African cities in literature on urban spaces.[44] In so doing, I build on Robinson's call to frame all cities as ordinary. I have set out to decenter Europe and America in the discussion of global cities and urbanity, and Chinese cities, Dubai, and Singapore in the discussion of newness, modernity, and change.[45] Nairobi is a prime example of global urban transformation because of its combination of colonial heritage, nation building, neoliberal governance, recent intensive real estate investment, and international funding of infrastructure projects. These transformations, which are taking place around the world, demand a rethinking of existing notions of cities—a rethinking that can reckon with anti-urbanism and its long-term consequences.

African cities lay bare the colonial and racial logics underlying these global urban transformations. Indeed, city planning as a discipline grew up hand in hand with colonialism.[46] For instance, in the twentieth century, the idea of a "garden city" reflected a union of city planning and colonialism (see chapter 5). As Liora Bigon argues, the garden city concept in Africa was built on ethnoracial, sanitary, and segregationist discourses aimed at suppressing African housing, tropical vegetation, and African urbanity—in other words, anti-urbanism.[47] Bigon shows that colonial territories were used as experimental sites for circulating, spreading, adapting, and revising planning ideas and practices. Anthony D. King, a sociologist and historian of global urbanism, demonstrates how the training of urban planners in the United Kingdom created a circulation of ideas and practices between and through metropole and colonies.[48] The process continues today, with development projects in Africa incorporating ideas and personnel from Japan and China.[49] Colonial cities can thus be considered laboratories of modernity.[50]

As Moore-Pewu makes clear, anti-urbanism is a widespread and multifaceted phenomenon not sufficiently captured by terms such as *gentrification, redevelopment,* or *postindustrial.*[51] This book opens up a space from which to understand city change from the point of view of people whose lives have always been affected by it: those for whom the city was not built, but who nevertheless in multiple ways have built the city.

Claiming the city, through lived practice, in court cases, and in popular culture and media, requires us to think about how new forms relate to older forms, how new occupants relate to older occupants, how new streets relate to older streets, how new dreams relate to old dreams, and how these cities relate to each other and the rest of the world.[52] Most importantly, we must ask what kinds of stories are told about, by, through, and from these cities. African cities ask for, and make possible, a reexamination of ideas of self and belonging, histories, claims, and rights, imagined futures, forms of sociality and politics, aesthetics and sensibilities, languages and discourses, location and locality, ecology and climate, and relations to other places, both near and far.

There is a need for a new form of urbanism, a decolonized urbanism that leaves behind demolition as a standard tool of governance, and one that can imagine a contemporary resident as not just a worker but also a child, an old person, a person at leisure, a disabled person, and an ancestor, one that can reimagine a green city for a changing climate, and, most importantly, can imagine that city as home.

THE RAILWAY AND THE RIVER

Three truisms are often repeated about Nairobi: first, that it started as a stop on the railway line between the coast and Lake Victoria; second, that it is name means "the place of cool (or sweet) water;" and finally, that it was branded the Green City in the Sun. These truisms speak to the geographic location and layout of the city as well as the layout of this book. The cool, drinkable, permanent water made it a good stop on caravan routes. Later the water and the forest provided fuel for the Railways' steam engines. The purchase by Railways executives of substantial land on speculation added to the greenery of the city. The streams running through the city created valleys and hills that influenced the construction of the railway line and the layout of roads and neighborhoods. We could say that the water brought the Railways, and the Railways created the green city in the sun.[53]

We can use Nairobi's geographic features to think about the *longue durée* city and about change. The rivers and the Railways brought things to, through, and from the city. They are the foundations on which the city was built and the scaffolding by which it has been shaped. They tell stories of Nairobi's change in their effects, their own change, and the objects they move.

The cool waters of Nairobi as they descended out of the hills and met flat land formed a swamp that was believed to be unhealthy, and which therefore drove the direction of housing construction. Colonial policy reserved housing in the city's higher elevations for Europeans, away from the swamps—and from "native" populations. Thus, the rivers both attracted people to the city and divided it. The Railways similarly brought people to Nairobi but divided the city. The Railways and rivers demand we look across city neighborhoods and cultures to understand how these different parts of the city are related to each other. [54]

The Railways attracted workers to Nairobi with the prospect of long-term, unionized, pensionable employment and permanent housing. These benefits allowed workers and their families to build identities, futures, and a presence in the city without the evictions, disruptions, or displacements faced by most other African inhabitants of the city. Before Kenya became independent in 1963, the Railways provided the majority of Nairobi's formal housing for Africans, with as many as ten thousand bedsitters (single-room housing units) built by 1959.[55] They allowed workers a sense of cosmopolitan international life, connecting East

Africa internally and abroad. Worker's children could be born in clinics and attend school without disruptions. It gave them a secure presence in the city.

Like Nairobi, I am a child of the Railways. Not only did I grow up to the sound of trains passing our house in Nairobi, but our whole family was shaped by my grandfather's decision to come to Nairobi in the 1930s to work as a train driver. The Railways shaped the trajectory of our family from relative poverty to educated middle class, from rural to urban Nairobi people. They brought my rural grandparents to the city. They afforded my father an education at some of Kenya's top schools, which led him to study at Harvard in the late 1950s, and it provided for train journeys between Nairobi and Mombasa on school vacations, enlivened by the chance of meeting relatives still working with the Railways. This book is about the spaces of Nairobi, the Railways, the rivers, the parks, the times, music, and people that made all that possible—that made me, an urban child of independent Kenya, possible.

1

The Rain at Home

In the early 1980s I found myself waiting in the chief's office in Makadara, an old neighborhood of Nairobi. I was there to get my newly mandated national identification card. Kenyan citizens over sixteen now had to have ID cards that "proved" their citizenship and thus their right to work.[1]

In those days there were very few chiefs' offices in Nairobi. They were a hangover from colonial rule, associated with the governance of rural, not urban, spaces.[2] The 1912 Native Authority Ordinance set up "chiefs" under the provincial administration to collect taxes, oversee customary law, maintain law and order, and implement colonial policy in the countryside.[3] From 1919 onward, Africans over the age of sixteen were required to register at the district government office, providing their name, administrative district and location, tribe, and employment.[4] Chiefs then issued a *kipande* (identification document) that enabled them to both track and ensure a constant supply of labor for the colonial project. The 1930 Native Tribunal Ordinance increased the chief's power of arbitration.[5] Chiefs were seen as intermediaries between the colonial state and Africans, mediating the supply of labor and land.[6] They also symbolized the power exercised by old men over younger men and women.

During the colonial period and for some time afterward, only sections of Nairobi once known as "native locations" had chief's offices, as Africans were restricted to living in these areas. After Independence in 1963, the structure of the chief's office was maintained. From 1971 its authority was expanded to include overseeing the ownership, distribution, and management of land.[7] With the introduction of the national ID system in 1978, every Kenyan had to interact with the chief's office, even urban Africans outside the old native locations.

Because chief's offices in Nairobi were limited to native locations, the lines at Makadara were endless. The long ID application form asked for my constituency, my location, my sublocation, and my area (designations that make sense only to the state) as well as ancestry, tribe, clan, and the birthplaces of my parents and grandparents. I needed to confirm information with my father, but traveling back home to Upper Hill would have taken forever, and I would have lost my place in the line, where I had already been waiting hours in the hot sun.

When I finally got inside, a bureaucrat recognized my last name and appointed himself my helper. He guided me to a pay phone where I could call my father for more details. To help me, he got on the phone himself. I heard him ask my father, "Is it raining at home?" This question was meant to establish common tribal affiliation and spatial bonding, with "home" alluding not to my parents' house in Upper Hill but to the place in western Kenya to which our family name apparently linked us. Although my father often used the word in the same sense, when faced by a functionary of the state he rebuffed this inquiry by replying, "But you can see for yourself by looking out of the window if it is raining."

Although my form listed my birthplace and address as well as my father's birthplace and address in Nairobi, the bureaucrat's confusion was evident. This answer did not fit the correct order of things. To those who found themselves in the rural institution of the chief's office, Nairobi could not be home.[8] The problem of the rain at home was not incidental to this particular bureaucrat, nor to me. Rather it is a problem set up by the idea that Nairobi could not, and should not, be home to someone with my last name—or any other African last name, for that matter.

This story is one of countless such encounters with government functionaries who have the power to determine identity, city design, and policy. The chief's office certifies citizenship and belonging in Kenya. I was coming to get a card that attested my "proper" place and identity in the eyes of the state. If I had followed the wishes of my helper at the chief's office and agreed to say I came from somewhere else, the state would be able to banish me there, as they often did to quell student riots in Nairobi when I was growing up. Protesting university students were sent "home" and had to report to their chief's office every week, to keep them in the countryside.

Rustication, or banishment to the countryside, is an example of anti-urbanism, the ideology behind urban governance, urban planning, and demolitions. It designates some people, and not others, as out of place and disposable. The ideology of anti-urbanism and its repeated confirmation by government functionaries in practice and policy determine how urban development and gentrification processes unfold.

As legend has it, Nairobi started as a stop on the railway—the first stop after the long climb inland from the coast where the water was fresh rather than alkaline. It was declared the first colonial royal charter city in 1950, followed by Singapore in 1951. Royal charter cities had legal standing independent from the rest of the colony and the right to self-government. From the start, Nairobi was conceived of by planners and government officials as a colonial town whose only permanent inhabitants were white European settlers. All others in the town were at the service of these settlers, and ordinances, regulations, policies, and laws were enacted to create and maintain the appearance of a European city and white supremacy.[9]

Paradoxically, many visitors to Nairobi today proclaim their distaste not for its danger or dirt, but rather for what they see as its "European" character: its high-rise buildings, its paved streets, its fast pace, its organization, its formal English, its attire, its traffic, and of course its disinterest in anything beyond its borders. For them this is not the "real" Africa—a stereotype itself constituted through colonial discourse and practices. This complaint is also echoed at times by residents, and especially by their rural counterparts, in a nostalgia for the life they left behind and for a pristine, unspoiled Africa of colonial dreams.

These stereotypes of what cities, and Africa, should look, feel, and sound like are part of a colonial and postcolonial anti-urbanism that positions urban spaces in Africa as modern and thus outside Africa—and also, ironically, as the pinnacle of rural Africa's aspirations. The future is displaced to a "modern" space that is rendered European. Typical of this thinking, James Smart, a European resident of Nairobi, could write in 1951 that "expanding Nairobi stepped out of 1949 into its Charter Year to gather to itself, in the words of the pioneers, 'the first traditions of *a land which has not memory yet.'"[10]

This characterization of Nairobi as European did not sit well with the majority of the city's population, who were never European.[11] The designation of Nairobi as a royal charter city was greeted not with jubilation but with widespread protests by both African and Asian residents, who felt that the new status of the city was a ploy to grab land and remove them from the city.[12] Strikes were organized in response to the detention of Fred Kubai and Makan Singh, leaders of the East African Trade Union Confederation (EATUC), who protested the new designation.[13]

The EATUC, founded on May 1, 1949, called for better work and living conditions, along with national independence. The strikes brought together the employed and the unemployed, industry workers and service workers, political groups and the underclass, the young and the old of Nairobi. Within a week the strikes had spread to all of Kenya's main towns.[14] The strikers called for freedom for workers, freedom for Africans throughout East Africa, the release of their leaders, free accommodation or housing allowances, sick leave, an increased minimum wage, the abolition of race-based wage structures, and the abolition of the *kipande* system.[15] This civil unrest of the new city was one example of resistance to the idea that Nairobi was, or should be, a European city and an effort to disrupt the racial definitions and footprint of the city. It also demonstrated the close connections between housing, work, self-determination, race, and the status of Nairobi as a city.

FIGURE 2. Nairobi residents at the City Park bandstand. Photo by author.

This chapter takes as its premise that the multiracial (African and Asian) protest against royal charter city status was a protest against displacement, an attempt to claim the city as not just European but also African and Asian. It forces us to consider other readings of the city, other lives and aspirations not reflected in official policy, plans, or regulations. It demonstrates that people felt these ideas were worth fighting over.

The structuring of Nairobi was guided by ideas of personhood, time, and space that can be grouped around four overlapping and interrelated themes: the "native question;" the question of detribalization; the Asian question; and the question of the poor. The resulting arrangement of space and people, of infrastructures and industry, of work, leisure, reproduction, and time itself, continue to structure Nairobi today and thus determine the city's prosperity, poverty, and inequality as well.

POPULATING NAIROBI

A little over 120 years ago, the space that was to become the city of Nairobi consisted of forested hills separated from the savanna by permanent freshwater rivers. As the names for the city (from Enkare Nyirobi, Maasai for "place of cool water") and some of its neighborhoods indicate, it was a meeting place of at least four cultural groups—the Athi, the Maasai, the Kamba, and the Kikuyu.[16] In the

1700s, Kikuyu farmers moved south toward the forested areas, acquiring cultivation rights from the Athi or the Maasai through payments in cattle. The Kamba had lived in the plains to the east.[17] These different communities had different land relations, including pastoralism, farming, and hunting and gathering. The communities were also mobile: Kikuyu farmers took over Athi hunting and gathering lands, and Maasai moved across vast territories. For these groups, the forest lands represented boundaries as well as a meeting place. This is perhaps the reason why no settlement existed when Nairobi became a railway depot.

Nevertheless, Nairobi grew quickly from a small, tented railway camp in 1899 to a town of six thousand inhabitants, with housing and sanitation problems, by 1902.[18] It was also a stop on caravan routes to the interior of the country. Nairobi hosted Muslim settlements and peripheral villages such as those at Pangani, Mji wa Mombasa, Mji wa Maskini, Kangemi, Kawangware, and Kileleshwa.[19] Within a few years, these settlements were occupied by Kikuyu, Kamba, Luo, Maasai, Luhya, Nyamwezi, Baganda, Nandi, Kipsigis, Bajunis, Sukuma, and coast peoples, as some of the village names indicate.[20]

Because of its freshwater and forested hinterland, Nairobi became an important stop on the railway line. In 1907 it became the capital of the East African Protectorate and in 1920 the capital of the Crown Colony of Kenya.[21] The Railways transformed the demography of Nairobi, first, by creating a permanent settlement; second, by bringing in workers from other regions of Kenya and abroad; third, by creating a commercial center that attracted local and foreign traders; and fourth, by making it the hub of connections to the rest of the country. How the resulting population was distributed in the city was dependent on the ideologies of the colonial administration and settlers.

Colonial administrations sought to build Nairobi as a European city with temporary African workers.[22] The European population of the city was brought by the Railways, as laborers, administrators and suppliers, and by the colonial administration. European commerce came to rely heavily on the Railways, which connected rural farmers to markets in Kenya and abroad. As a sign of British imperial power, the rail line was also instrumental in attracting European settlers to Kenya. It features extensively in pleas and advertisements to that effect. Besides the British, who made up the majority of the European population, the Railways also brought Afrikaners from South Africa, Italians, and Greeks.

Although some Asians were already living in East Africa when the British arrived, the majority came during the latter part of the nineteenth century, accompanying the inward move of the British. Asian East Africans are most famous for their work in building the railway line from Mombasa to Lake Victoria from 1896 to 1901. Most came from Gujarat, Sindh, Punjab, Bombay, and Goa in today's India and Pakistan, but others came from Iran and Afghanistan. Not all worked as Railways laborers; some were suppliers and financiers to the Railways, as well as traders and bankers.

As the rail line ran westward from coastal Kenya toward Uganda, its path affected people from the coast and Lake Victoria regions in addition to the Maasai, Kikuyu, and Kamba populations of Nairobi. Particularly affected were people from western Kenya, predominantly Luo and Luhya near Lake Victoria, and Swahili, Taita, and people from the coastal settlement of Freretown (occupied by the descendants of formerly enslaved Africans returned from India). The colonial administration recruited men from Sudan, Somalia, and India (Punjab) for the military, as well as people from India (particularly Goa) and the Seychelles as administrators and office workers.

In addition, traders from the surrounding areas (Kikuyu, Maasai, and Kamba) and from farther afield (Somali and Swahili) brought agricultural products, livestock, and crafts to trade in the city.[23] With time, traders of all kinds and races were supplying food, materials, and imports to the growing population of Nairobi. In the past fifty years, as Nairobi has become an international hub for aid work around Africa and the headquarters of the United Nations Environment Program (UNEP) and United Nations Human Settlements Program (UN-Habitat), it has attracted many international residents. Whichever way you look at it, for the past 120 years, migrant populations have vastly outnumbered people born in the vicinity of Nairobi. At Independence, fewer than 3 percent of the 300,000 residents of Nairobi were born in the city.[24] Today, although this proportion is gradually increasing, its 4.3 million inhabitants were mostly born elsewhere.

Nairobi, then, has always been both racially and ethnically diverse. The effort to create a European city demanded policies that controlled this diversity while maintaining the supply of labor for building the city. This created a category of necessary but unwanted residents. These same populations were, and are, needed to provide maintenance and services for those for whom the city was built. As in other cities around the world, they are managed in two ways—temporal and spatial.

The temporal solution is to create and mandate impermanence, limiting residence in the city to productive populations. Single male workers are ideal temporary residents; children and the elderly are relegated to the countryside. In Nairobi this practice is reflected in the forms of housing created by institutions like the Railways. "Housing estates" consisting of barrack housing for laborers or single rooms for domestic workers were located in "native locations" a short distance from the Railways.

When residents cease to be useful (whether because they are unemployed, retired, or dead), they must return to the countryside. Africans and Asians could not even be buried in colonial Nairobi unless they were designated as "detribalized," with military affiliations (see chapter 5).

The spatial solution is segregation. In Nairobi, this was enacted through policies of containment and rustication. Containment designated certain places in the city, like native locations, where Africans could reside. Rustication removed unwanted populations, including most women, from the city to the countryside (and thereby shored up the power of rural male chiefs). Segregation between the rural and the urban was enforced through pass laws. Those who could not prove employment by displaying a *kipande* could not reside in the city. Within the city, services and privileges such as electricity and sanitation were restricted to specific groups of people.

While transport, trade, and colonial governance drew a wide variety of people to Nairobi, anti-urbanism determined who could stay, for how long, in what parts of the city, and under what conditions.[25]

THE NATIVE QUESTION

By the time the British established colonies in East Africa, colonialism as an idea had been refined in the Americas, Australia, and Asia through theories of human development that included degeneration, evolution, social Darwinism, and scientific racism.[26] These theories engage time and space in different ways. Degeneration theories posit that people, cultures, and societies are in a process of moving backward and getting worse. However, those in colder climates and at higher elevations and latitudes degenerate more slowly than those in more tropical climes. Thus the rate of degeneration is determined by the environment, and the passage of time is uneven across geographical space. As people move through space, their rate of degeneration changes. Darwin's idea of evolution radically challenged this idea by positing a constant process of change for the better. Rather than moving backward or degenerating, organisms adapt to a changing environment. This adaptation came to be seen as progress or betterment.

Social Darwinism and scientific racism combine ideas from both degeneration theories (especially the uneven passage of time across space) and evolution theories (as applied to societies rather than to biology) to arrange human societies hierarchically by civilization. Social Darwinism posited that power structures and societies were on a biological evolutionary continuum. In scientific racism, scientists in physical anthropology, psychology, criminology, and genetics, along with physicians and naturalists, sought to correlate biological traits with social deviance. In these theories civilizations were placed on an evolutionary ladder, the rungs of which were determined by geography. Adherents of such theories argued that progress could be achieved through reforming "unfit" groups or preventing them from reproducing.[27]

Colonial uptake of social Darwinism and scientific racism produced geographies of civilizations whose occupants' relationship to time was dependent on geography and race. As people moved through space they were thought to move through time. Some places, and therefore some people, were considered modern and others backward, some of the future and some of the past, some in the process of evolving and some evolved. In Kenya these ideas were first articulated by colonial governments as a modernizing mission—a mission of bringing the land and the people into modernity. Today these ideas undergird concepts and policies of progress or development.[28]

Europeans positioned themselves in a dynamic process of forward progress and others in a timeless, static existence.[29] Essential to this modernizing project were the conceptual connection between time, space, and people, and the distinction between the "native" and all others. Colonialism has justified itself around the globe by characterizing local inhabitants as incapable, childlike, and unable to rule themselves—or as savage, barbarous, backward, lazy, and primitive.[30]

By the application of this logic, colonial subjects became conscripts of modernity—unwilling participants in a temporal project not of their making, shaped by and obligated to live according to the terms of the colonizers.[31] In addition, non-Europeans were often slotted into the path of progress in a way that suited the vision and ambitions of the colonizers. For instance, the British government initially considered Indian traders agents of "civilization and progress" by virtue of their participation in capitalism: they created African markets and African consumers. Thus in the 1890s Indian traders and laborers were central to the modernizing mission of the British in Kenya. However, by the 1920s the colonial idea of East Africa as the "America of the Hindus," as an Indian settlement, was being met with protests from European settlers who wanted Kenya to be a "White man's country," and the presence of Asians became a liability.[32]

By 1902 the colonial government sought to control the population of Kenya, and Nairobi in particular, through laws that enacted racial segregation on four scales: at the levels of the country, the city, specific buildings, and sections of buildings. Their aim was to demonstrate and maintain white supremacy. Kenya often looked to the Cape Colony, in South Africa, for experience in managing Africans, and many colonial officials in Kenya were from, or trained in, South Africa.[33]

At the country level, British colonialism was based on the idea of assigning everyone to their correct place. Africans should be relegated to rural ethnic reserves (land reserved for specific ethnic groups, such as the Digo or Kikuyu) or territories (land held in trust for pastoralists such as the Maasai, often referred to as Maasailand). This spatial segregation was also in effect a temporal one, distinguishing the "modern" from the "primitive," "backward," and "traditional." It was realized through the 1902 Crown Lands Ordinance, which, in addition to creating native reserves, aimed to provide land for European settlement. Under the ordinance, any land considered to be unoccupied became Crown land, available for transfer to Europeans.[34] As the legal scholar Hastings Okoth-Ogendo puts it, these measures effectively made Africans "tenants of the Crown."[35] Pass laws, like the Vagrancy Acts of 1902, 1922, and 1949, restricted movement to Nairobi from the countryside. Africans without *kipande* were "repatriated" or "returned" to the countryside.[36]

From the beginning of colonial governance in Nairobi, settlers argued for freehold property rights in lands allocated to them by the Crown (outright private ownership of land, freely transferable on an open market) rather than leasehold (land rented from the state for a set period, with possible limitations on transfer). In part to prevent the capital-rich Asian population from buying up the land, they also wanted areas of land to be reserved for different races, excluding Indians from European areas and limiting Africans to native reserves. In 1908 the Native Lands Trust and Crown Lands (Amendment) Ordinance decisively reserved the highlands of Kenya for Europeans only (hence the label "White Highlands").[37] The Crown Lands Ordinance of 1925 extended the 1902 ordinance and empowered the administration to grant rural land to white settlers on 999-year leases.[38]

To quell European agrarian settlers' fears of competition from Asians, the Crown Lands Ordinances and their amendments barred Asians from buying land or settling in the highlands.[39] In 1923, however, the colonial administration allowed Indian farming settlements in some lowland areas. As a result of their largely being restricted to urban areas, Asian Kenyans are some of the oldest permanent residents of Nairobi. At the height of their population, just before Independence in 1962, they constituted more than 35 percent of Nairobi's population.[40] Today, although more than 50 percent of Asian Kenyans still live in Nairobi, they make up less than 1 percent of the city's population.[41]

Property laws in colonial Kenya were thus designed to uphold colonial racial regimes to benefit and protect white settlers. Through racialized laws, Africans were restricted *from* cities, while Asians were restricted *to* urban areas.[42] Despite these forms of spatial segregation, the colonial government, and in particular the Railways, needed African workers in the cities. To resolve the contradiction of Africans' presence in the cities, it was understood to be temporary, lasting only as long as their employment did.

RESIDENTIAL AREAS AND LOCATIONS

Within the city of Nairobi space was organized hierarchically by race and class. In 1905 the Land Committee for the East Africa Protectorate recommended segregating racial groups. The Townships (Public Heath, Segregation of Races) Rules empowered the governor to reserve areas for "European residential; Asiatic residential; locations for 'Asiatics of the working classes'; 'native' locations; commercial areas for Europeans and or Asiatics (but not natives) and open spaces."[43]

Here it is important to distinguish between the concepts of residential areas and locations. Residential areas were called townships or municipalities. Townships were self-governing areas reserved for permanent settlement. They were provided with services such as water, electricity, sanitary and garbage services, hospitals, and schools.[44] Locations, by contrast, were reserved for the temporary settlement of African or Asian working classes with limited or no services. The "native locations," for instance, were sites that provided temporary housing for African urban laborers. There were no African housing estates in townships. Of the native locations, the Railway estates offered the best housing.

This property regime discriminated by class as well as race. Locations were for the working classes. Residential areas were intended to house businessmen, managers, traders, financiers, suppliers to the Railways, and landowners. Residential areas had freehold property, while locations were owned by state or private employers. Europeans and some "Asiatics" qualified as residents. But since no Africans could be imagined as traders or businessmen, and their economic activities were deemed illegal, neither could they be imagined as residents. The time and space permitted them in the city were contingent on their employment.

In Nairobi, if you were African or Asian, the township rules effectively controlled where you lived, the kind of job you might have, the level you could rise to in a job, the legality of your commerce, your mobility around town, which school you could attend, what hospital would treat you, your access to electricity, sewage, and water services, and the kind of health care you could receive.

The concept of the "native" was produced in a tense relationship between city and country, where the city was racialized as European and the country as African. The city was also characterized as modern and the countryside as premodern, or the city as of the future and the countryside of the past. As a designated resident of the countryside, the native existed in a timeless, unchanging, tribal past. This concept of *native* is built on the concept of *tribe* as a totally self-contained social world frozen in time and space, unable to change. The native in the city was thus both out of place and out of time.

It was this conceptualization of the native that my father confronted when he refused to answer the question from the chief's office about the rain at home. Even in the 1980s, the chief's office itself was only slowly shaking off the heritage of the "native administration." It is this temporality of the "native" that simultaneously makes it impossible for Nairobi to be home and (as I argue in chapter 8) makes it impossible to be counted as homeless in Nairobi.

THE QUESTION OF DETRIBALIZATION

The colonial category of "native" does not lock people into place so much as it locks them into time. People who ventured out of their "proper" place also moved through time (and, logically, those who "returned" to the rural areas retreated in time). Only settlers could travel across space while completely maintaining their position in time. They also had the power to imbue space with new temporalities. European rural settlers were seen as bringing modernity to the countryside, rather than being pulled by the countryside back into static, tribal past.[45]

Because tribe was the foundation of native time and space, natives who moved into European spaces were considered "detribalized" if they remained long enough.[46] This was both a goal and a problem for the colonial administration. Churches, schools, work, and the colonial administration in general aimed to change the native into a compliant worker under the power of chiefs, priests, teachers, bosses, and colonial police. Those who became too modern—a union member, a student who questioned authority, a breakaway African church pastor, a female street vendor, or an advocate for liberation—were faulted for being lost, unable to cope with modernity, and out of place and time. This issue of detribalization always involved the seesaw of revolt and compliance that is written onto the urban subject in Nairobi.

Colonial governments blamed urban, "detribalized" natives for two of the major Kenyan nationalist revolts: the Thuku riots of 1922 and the Mau Mau of 1952–58.[47] Young, urban men were criticized as being lost, corrupted, inappropriately modern, and out of touch with tradition. In 1921, Harry Thuku, a government clerk, helped found the Young Kikuyu Association, which became the multiethnic East African Association a month later. It was predominantly made up of young, urban, self-employed Kikuyu men. To the colonial administration, Harry Thuku, proficient in English, articulate, Christian, and an advocate for the recognition of African land ownership through awarding titles, exemplified all that was wrong (and powerful) about the "detribalized native." The association campaigned against the *kipande* system, hut and poll taxes (which could lead to dispossession), oppression by tribal police and chiefs, and the forced labor of women and girls.[48] Women were thus some of Thuku's strongest supporters, and they, under Mary Muthoni Nyanjiru, led the protest after his arrest in 1922.

The anti-urban myth of the native (and the potential dangers of detribalization) is one that endures today in everyday expressions and conversations about city and country, as well as in social and political processes such as burials.[49] Like the concepts of tribe and native, detribalization is an ideology of time and space that has been mobilized for the control of populations rather than a reflection of the lived experience of people in or outside the city.

The colonial administration understood and governed religious affiliation as a temporal issue. Christian and Muslim Africans, especially from outside Kenya, were not considered to be native. Rather they were considered either detribalized or immigrant races. These included Christian and Muslim Nubians, Somalis, Swahili, and Seychellois, as well as people from Freretown in coastal Kenya, all of whom were early inhabitants of Nairobi.[50] Being Muslim or Christian removed tribal temporality, thus allowing for a different idea of impermanence.

Space for the needed but unwanted populations in the city was established through segregation not only of housing, social spaces, and work, but even cemeteries. In the 1948 map of segregated Nairobi, four areas stood out specifically because they were *not* restricted by race: the mortuary, the mental hospital at Mathare, the racecourse, and City Park.[51] The cemeteries of the city, however, were segregated. Africans who died in the city were expected to be buried in the countryside or outside city limits. Neither in retirement nor in death could they occupy space in the city. The only cemeteries available for the burial of Africans in Nairobi were for "detribalized natives" in the Detribalized Native Cemetery in Nairobi West (which was then outside the city's boundary) and the African military cemeteries at Kariokor, Kibera, and Lang'ata, of which only the first was within the colonial city limits. They served Muslim or Christian "detribalized natives" or immigrant Africans.

Land allocation, in principle, was one way to situate out-of-place people in the temporal and spatial framework of Nairobi. As discussed in chapter 8, one of the few allocations of land to Africans was to "detribalized" Nubian Sudanese soldiers. In 1902, the colonial government designated 4,197 acres just outside the city limits as a military reserve so that the soldiers would be within easy access for service.[52] The new occupants called it Kibra (Kibera), Nubian for "forest." At Independence, the Nubian community remained on the land instead of being repatriated to Sudan, and Kibera was incorporated into the city in 1963. Not until 2017, however, were Nubian land rights in Kibera recognized by the Kenyan government, and by then the allocated land had shrunk to 288 acres.[53]

UNHYGIENIC SPACE, UNHYGIENIC PEOPLE

The new disciplines of public health, sanitation, immigration, and urban planning gained global prominence in the early part of the twentieth century. They were powerful tools for shaping urban populations in keeping with ambitions to modernize. Throughout North and South America these sciences were used as rationales for removing, segregating, and controlling poor, Black, Indigenous, or non–northern European immigrant populations in ways that still affect the layout of most large cities on these continents to today.[54]

Africa was no exception to this global trend. In Nairobi, public health policies ostensibly for controlling malaria supported the segregation of out-of-place populations and helped make these populations temporary. The historian Goodwin Murunga argues that these policies were "meant to protect Europeans from the dangers allegedly posed by the Indian and African presence," effectively making Europeans the rightful occupants of cities.[55] Between 1902 and 1926, starting with the demolition of the Indian Bazaar in 1902 and followed by malarial control measures, public health was a main excuse for the displacement of successful Asian or African businesses and settlements in Nairobi.[56]

In spite of laws restricting land ownership and residency, the colonial government was unable to maintain legal restrictions on land ownership because of the financial power of the early Asian population of Nairobi. The main businesses in Nairobi were run by Asians.[57] As early as 1903, Asian traders, railway suppliers, and financiers were able to offer better terms for purchasing freehold land than Europeans were.[58] For instance, Alibhai Mulla Jeevanjee, a railway supplier and

Indian businessman, purchased his first plots in Nairobi from the Railways in 1900, some of which he rented to Europeans and the government.

The colonial government attempted to prevent these kinds of sales through legal restrictions on land alienation, including prohibitions proposed by a Nairobi Committee in 1905, the Nairobi Chamber of Commerce in 1910, and public health studies such as the *Nairobi Sanitary Commission Report* and the *Simpson Report* of 1913.[59] These prohibitions targeted Asians who were making significant inroads in the European business areas. The 1913 Public Health Ordinance made race the basis of town planning in Nairobi.[60]

The water that made Nairobi an advantageous location for the Railways was considered a public health hazard by the colonial administration. Despite its high elevation, part of the city was located on what was termed a "malarial swamp."[61] While indeed the flat, poorly drained area of black cotton soils in the southeastern part of the city was once a papyrus-filled swamp, it was not until the arrival of the Railways that the swamp became malarial.[62]

Prior to the 1900s malaria was absent from the highlands around Nairobi.[63] Consequently, few people had immunity against the disease. Both the forest and the papyrus restricted the breeding of *A. gambiae*, the main species of mosquito that carries malaria in Kenya.[64] The forest shade prevented mosquitoes from breeding in pools. Papyrus emits oils that form a thin layer on the water's surface, preventing mosquito larvae from breathing. As the forest was consumed for locomotive fuel and cleared for agriculture and settlement, however, conditions became ripe for mosquito breeding.

The mosquitoes, and malaria itself, were brought into the area by train, truck, car, and oxcart, along with the migration of people from lower elevations. The arrival of malaria hit the local populations hard.[65] There were epidemics of malaria in Nairobi in 1913, 1922, 1926, 1935, and 1940. The highest incidences of the disease occurred during the long rains, between March and May.

The epidemic of 1926 increased efforts to control malaria in the city and in particular to protect the white colonial administrators. The government mandated the draining of swamps, the planting of eucalyptus trees to dry out the soil, and the relocation of the European population to the hills at a distance from the lowlands—and from African and Asian children, who were thought to carry the disease.[66] Domestic workers in European households had to live a certain distance from the main house on the compound and were not allowed to have their children living with them. Most government housing was already set up as bachelor barracks, without spaces for children. Cities became progressively segregated by age and gender as well as by race.[67]

There was both a horizontal and a vertical separation of populations in Nairobi, with European populations on the hills and African populations on the flat lands, buffered by an Asian residential zone and green space.[68] These mandates concentrated African and Asian populations in areas that were densely populated and on swampy ground—creating the perfect conditions for malaria epidemics. While house spacing, sanitation, ditches, and paved roads were mandated for the hills, no such provisions applied to the plains. The African and Asian populations thus bore the brunt of the malaria epidemics and, as a consequence, were blamed for the disease.

Public health, and malarial control in particular, had an enormous effect on the form and location of segregation in Nairobi, controlling where people could live, at what density and in what kinds of structures, and for how long. The combination of urban planning with public health measures was a founding element of anti-urbanism ideology and policy.

HOUSING TEMPORARY PEOPLE

By 1923 the government's ideas of legal segregation had begun to change. There was a consensus that commercial segregation should be discontinued, but disagreement over residential segregation held up all sales of township plots. In 1923 it was concluded that "in the view of the competent medical authorities that, as a sanitation measure, segregation of Europeans and Asiatics is not absolutely essential for the preservation of the health of the community." This decision did not apply outside townships, however, and thus did not end segregation for those in "locations," particularly Africans. The 1923 *Kenya Gazette* stipulated that residential quarters of natives should be separated from those of "immigrant races." Specifically, "in the case of individual natives, such as servants, strict segregation would be unworkable: but it is important that, when areas have been fixed in townships for native residence, those areas should be regarded as definitely set aside for the use of natives, and no encroachment thereon by non-African races should be permitted."[69]

Housing has always been a problem in Nairobi. Although housing was provided for company workers and domestic servants (but not their children), people who were self-employed (e.g., women market vendors) and those employed by individuals outside of domestic service, (e.g., safari porters, guards, or construction crews) were rarely provided with accommodation and thus rented rooms in the city. As Louise White points out in her study of prostitution in early Nairobi, many of the first landlords were women who worked in prostitution and ran boardinghouses as well.[70]

It was only after World War II, with a need to house war veterans and concern about urban unrest, that housing for African families was built in Nairobi. The new housing estates of Ziwani, Starehe, and Kaloleni were based on the British garden city design (see chapter 6). These estates, however, were intended only for those in formal government employment.

The urban historians Aurora Martin and Pauline Bezemer delineate two planning phases in Nairobi's public housing: the *landhi* concept (1918–29) and the garden city model (1929–48).[71] The first, exemplified by Muthurwa housing estate, was barrack-style, high-density housing intended for single men, with communal kitchens and toilet facilities. This design, copied from Indian Railway housing, was also built to house mine workers in Rhodesia and South Africa in the early 1900s.[72] The second, exemplified by Kaloleni, was lower-density housing intended for nuclear families, with shops, schools, and open spaces, influenced by the British garden city concept and replicated in cities such as Lusaka in Northern Rhodesia (now Zambia) and Kumasi in the Gold Coast (Ghana), built starting in the 1940s. According to Martin and Bezemer, the garden city concept was only "firstly and fully realized in the Ziwani (1939–1942) and Starehe (1942–1946) estates and afterwards concluded in the 'model' settlement Kaloleni (1943–1948)."[73]

De facto and de jure housing segregation resulted in considerable movement of people to new parts of the city. It also created social divisions between townships and locations, highlands and lowlands, the west and the east, and the wet and the dry parts of Nairobi. Anti-urbanism as an ideology effectively determined the demographic layout of the city, incorporating altitude, hydrology, cardinal directions, health, race, and class into town planning and policy. These spaces reflected gradients not only of altitude and rainfall but also of population density, greenery, and services. As Nairobi developed, policies for managing gender, trade, and labor as well as race combined to produce an anti-urban housing landscape that was not only inadequate and substandard but also intended to exclude women, children, the elderly, and the poor from the city.

After Independence in 1963, the constructs of "native" and "detribalized native" had to change, as the category of "settler" against which they were constructed ceased to exist. But instead of disappearing, they morphed to reflect class while still maintaining the racially based spatial organization of the city. This remained true even as the city territory expanded ninefold at Independence. The new boundaries incorporated areas such as Lang'ata, Buruburu, Huruma, Komarock, Runda, Gigiri, Kibera, and Kangemi, which were rural lands with unstable peri-urban populations, along with farmers and herders. Anti-urbanism privileged some racial and ethnic groups at the expense of others, forming class divisions along the way. One example is the steady acquisition of Maasai land that fell inside and near the new city boundaries. This started in the 1950s with the Swynnerton plan, which aimed to modernize agriculture in part through enclosure of pastoral lands. When I was a child, Maasai cattle grazed in large sections of Lang'ata and Southlands within Nairobi. Some of this land was owned by the Maasai politician John Keen and was made accessible to Maasai herders. Keen and others (mainly non-Maasai) came to own the land through the privatization of group ranches that carried on from the 1950s through the 1990s. These privatization programs pitted communal land ownership and pastoralism against private land ownership and modernity. The Maasai way of life was seen as antithetical to modernity and the city, and therefore the Maasai had to be removed. (In a challenge to the anti-urbanism that displaced them from their grazing lands, even today Maasai cattle are brought in to graze in the streets, verges, parks, and green spaces of southern Nairobi during droughts or failure of the rains.)

In the colonial city, gender, age, class and ethnicity facilitated anti-urbanism articulated through the control of race; in the postcolonial city, race, gender, age and ethnicity facilitated anti-urbanism articulated through the control of class. The racial spatialization of the city had enduring economic and social consequences. It made most people in Nairobi temporary inhabitants, refusing them a home in the city.

Although about 8 percent of Kenya's population lives in Nairobi, few of its residents, politicians, or planners have ever thought of it as home . In fact, it was a hundred years before Nairobi had a mayor who was actually born in the city. For most residents, memories and histories are displaced, associated with somewhere else. For Nairobi, as for many cities in East Africa, there are only very modern dreams of a future yet to be realized. This dynamic engenders the oft-asked question, "Where is your home?"

In 1987, in reaction to a drawn-out court battle over the burial place of the lawyer S. M Otieno, my father stated, "Bury me in Lang'ata," to emphasize his urban roots, his wish to remain in the city, and to declare Nairobi his home—to establish continuity between the past, the present, and the future. Lang'ata Cemetery was built in 1958 outside the Nairobi city limits as a place to bury Africans who died in Nairobi. Once the city boundaries were expanded, Lang'ata became the first cemetery for African burials in Nairobi other than the military cemeteries. It remains the only cemetery open to the general public in Nairobi. Little did my father know that less than ten years after his declaration, Lang'ata cemetery would be declared full. Even so, bodies have been arriving there for burial every day for almost thirty years, as there is nowhere else in the city for them to go. No new cemeteries have been built since 1958, even though the city population has increased fifteenfold. Today you can have only temporary burials at Lang'ata, as the space will be needed again for someone else who has nowhere else to go. The threads of anti-urbanism entangle the dead as much as the living, rendering them temporary even as they remain in the city.

2

Growing Old in a New City

In 2012 our neighbors came to see us, beside themselves with worry, holding a map in their hands. They said, "They plan to build a road through our houses."

It is hard to describe the panic and anxiety their words induced. This was the house where my parents had lived for forty-three years, where my sister and I grew up. It was home in a way no other place on earth could be home, with all its memories. There was a booming, hollow sound in my head, as if all else had ceased to be present. This house was inhabited by friends and families we grew up with. Their curtains were still on the windows, their traces left behind. Every time we talked of this house, we talked of them, of how this house became our house and our home. This house, these trees, this place. I wrote in my field notes:

> I tried to think but could not.
> I tried to sleep but could not.
> I tried to stop the constriction in my chest,
> With zinc and vitamin C and all sort of herbal remedies,
> But could not.
> I tried to imagine leaving and having no place to return to,
> And could not.
> I tried to imagine where else my parents could live in Nairobi,
> And could not.
> I tried to work but could not.
> I tried to plan but could not.
> I tried to breathe but could not.
> I tried, I tried . . .

Because Nairobi is so new and growing newer every day, the old parts of the city and their long-term residents are below the radar of most Kenyans. Nairobi is

FIGURE 3. Construction work in Upper Hill. Photo by author.

defined by constant construction and reconstruction of structures, buildings, neighborhoods, roads, and enclosed spaces. The glass and concrete of high-rise buildings, tin roofs, overpasses, new roads, and treeless sidewalks concentrate the sun like magnifying lenses that smolder rather than dazzle. This is Nairobi, the (not so) green city in the sun, in all its modern, bustling splendor.

Once imagined as a colonial city to which Africans had limited access, Nairobi is now envisioned as a "world-class African metropolis," according to the Nairobi Metro 2030 strategy. Yet today, as the city transforms into a metropolitan county, more and more people have lived their whole lives in Nairobi and see it as home. In the inaugural county governor's race of 2012, candidates were eager to state that they were "born and bred" in Nairobi, no matter their age or ethnicity. Still, the Nairobi where they were born and bred is not the one where they live today. Not only have the neighborhoods changed, but the candidates have changed neighborhoods. Many who did well for themselves—aided by government programs of the post-Independence period, like Africanization, which aimed to restrict public employment and commerce to citizens, and by the rapid growth of the city and country—moved to wealthier, once exclusively European neighborhoods. Today, their old neighborhoods are scheduled for demolition or already demolished.

Kaloleni is a neighborhood where salaried workers in Nairobi once dreamed of living. It was once home to the former presidents Mwai Kibaki of Kenya and Milton Obote of Uganda, was well as to the father of US President Barack Obama. Today, Kaloleni has faded into decay, government neglect, and obscurity, forming part of the inner-city area now called Eastlands.

But not everyone has moved. In the decades after Independence, the Kenya government's ability to provide services and infrastructure declined as a result of global economic shocks. The fiscal shortfall, due to the oil shock in the 1970s and amplified by the structural-adjustment economic policies mandated by international aid agencies in the 1980s, meant that Kenya could not meet its financial obligations, let alone realize new dreams.[1] These obligations included pension payments to workers. Many retired Railways and Nairobi City Council workers and their descendants found themselves bound to the city in ways their ancestors were not. They could not afford to travel "home" to the countryside for holidays. The candidates for the governor's race in 2012 were appealing to this new urban population.

As I pondered the destruction of my childhood home, I was moved by the candidates' appeal to those who were born and bred in Nairobi. Landless and poor, my grandfather moved from western Kenya to the city in the 1930s. He worked for the Railways for almost twenty-five years, raising his seven children in the ten-by-ten-foot confines of African railway workers' housing in Muthurwa, at the center of the city. All but one of my paternal aunts and uncles were born there, and many still live in Nairobi. Their world was a multilingual one dominated by Swahili, the common language of the Railways. My grandfather, like so many others before him, returned to the countryside on retirement and became a farmer for the first time.

My father lived almost all his life within a two-kilometer radius from where he was born in Nairobi, except for his college years in the United States. For those like him, there is no journey home. They are already there. Yet even though it is their home, today's Nairobi is strange to them, as it has undergone too many recent additions and extensions to keep track of.

What does it mean to grow old in such a rapidly changing city? What does it mean to have no other home? What conflicts of urban imaginaries and ways of being manifest between the dreams and aspirations of planners and the needs and dreams of long-term residents? This chapter explores lives lived in the oldest parts of Nairobi to understand the fragility and dynamics of making a city home in the face of anti-urbanism.

This is not a journey into an idyllic past. After all, who really wants to live in a ten-by-ten-foot room with eight other people? Or with a dirt road next to the house, whose dust causes asthma attacks, and stains clean laundry set out to dry? This is not the stuff of nostalgia. Rather it is a journey into the city yet to come: the city that always exists beyond its own reality, a modern city of someone else's dreams.

What futures do long-term African residents imagine for Nairobi, and how have they transformed the city in efforts to realize those dreams? How do current changes feel to them in light of those dreams and years in the city? This chapter looks at the ways in which Africans in Railways housing created lives that transcended the boundaries set for them by colonial plans, and how they changed spaces to suit their imagination of the city, a city that was theirs—African and modern; a city of family, children, schools, leisure, and work; a city that was home. These imaginaries and claims to the city still butt up against new plans for Nairobi that also do not accommodate children, aging, generational change, or permanence. In the footsteps of those who imagined the city before me, I write here about what could have been, not what was.

THE RAILWAY CITY

Many years after it ceased to resound for miles across the city, the *king'ora* (siren) that demarcated the shifts of Railways workers remains a defining memory of life in the native locations of Nairobi. A quintessential tool of colonialism, which controlled both labor and time, the *king'ora* shaped life beyond the rail yards and was accorded multiple names in local languages. Friends who grew up in nearby housing estates remember hearing the *king'ora* as late as the 1980s.[2] One Railways worker recalled, "You could hear it as far away as Kibera."[3] It held the power to shape everyday life and to create a working class from the 1930s onward.

The first planned African housing in Nairobi, Muthurwa, was constructed by the East African Railways & Harbours near the shunting yards on what became known as Landhies Road.[4] The word *landhi* itself came from India and referred to the houses of railway workers.[5] Because they provided long-term, stable working conditions and housing that distinguished their residents from much of the rest of the city, Railways settlements enable insight into a population who, unusually for urban Africans, enjoyed a degree of permanence.

For the Railways, reliable, trained and long-term labor was essential. In this respect it differed fundamentally from the rest of government and European residents, who considered urban Africans as short-term and expendable labor. The Railways thus created unique urban spaces. The vast majority of Railways workers (85 percent) spent all or nearly all their working lives with the company, and only 5 percent ever broke service with the Railways.[6] The average term of employment was twenty-five years. Nevertheless, the barrack-style housing in Muthurwa was designed for unmarried men.

The housing was intended to promote efficiency by housing workers close to their work sites. This focus on efficiency was reflected even in the settlement's lighting. Because trains operated both night and day, the estates were lit by streetlights to enable night-shift workers to get to work. My father remembers the brightness of the night sky in Nairobi, in contrast to that of the countryside. Yet the Railways did not see fit to provide electric light in workers' rooms.

Although the design of Railways housing did not acknowledge the existence of workers' families, it was forced to accommodate them: the Kenya-Uganda Railway began building dispensaries and maternity clinic facilities for its employees as far back as 1908.[7] So many children were born at the Railways clinic in Nairobi that when my grandmother experienced complications with her pregnancy and had to go to Pumwani Maternity Hospital to give birth to my father, he acquired the nickname Majengo, after the neighborhood where he was born, outside the Railways compound. With all these births, Railways neighborhoods in East Africa differed in gender and age ratios from other urban spaces: as in the countryside, children made up about 50 percent of the residents.[8] As time passed, the Railways provided a variety of services, including clinics, nursery and primary schools, adult education, postal services, and welfare services. Its housing facilities operated as a city within a city.

A PLACE OF CHILDREN

Because many railway workers were unmarried men, some women living in workers' housing took on extra domestic responsibilities: my grandmother ended up feeding upwards of twenty men every day. These men were relatives, fellow clansmen, or people from the same region of western Kenya or eastern Uganda. She also had seven children of her own to feed, as well as friends of theirs who did not have female relatives in the city. Although tradition dictated that elders should eat before children, my grandmother was adamant that the children should eat before the adults did. My aunt remembers that my grandmother ordered all children to come home immediately on hearing the *king'ora* to be served their midday meal, giving them a ten-minute head start over the men, who had to walk back from the rail yards to Muthurwa for lunch.[9] Thus the children too were disciplined by the clock of industrial labor.

From at least the late 1930s, my family and many others in Muthurwa and other Railway estates transformed the company's bachelor quarters into family accommodations. Employees were expected to share rooms: for a man to live in his own room or with his wife, he had to have worked for the Railways for a certain number of years (around six) and to have reached a certain grade of employment. By 1938, when my father was born, my grandfather had enough seniority to be allocated a room to share with his wife.

Although city planners conceived of Africans in Nairobi as laborers, and single male laborers at that, the Railways residential estates in the 1950s were known in Luo as *ka jonyuol*, the place of children.[10] But family life was constrained, disrupted, and reshaped by the logics of colonial industry and racial understanding. My father recalled that to reduce the crowding in their single room, the oldest

FIGURE 4. My father, Hilary Ng'weno (middle, standing) with his parents on either side and siblings, uncle, aunt, and cousin, 1957.

three boys would spend their days at home and their nights with an uncle, my grandmother's brother, who also worked for the Railways. They slept under their uncle's bed. Other people (both men and women) talk about coming to Nairobi as children in the 1940s and staying with male relatives in Railways housing.[11] Many unmarried men brought up children of their relatives. So there were many more men and children than women in Railways compounds. The Railways provided access to schools and clinics; it supplied milk rations during World War II, as well as amenities unknown to many others, like films, gardens, and parks.

The novelist Muthoni Likimani bears witness in her autobiography and novels to the presence by the 1950s of Africans who knew no other home than Nairobi.[12] Yet it was only in the late 1940s that the colonial government, worried about urban tensions, started to think about constructing urban accommodations for families. Believing that male workers would be more controllable with their families present and dependent on them, they made efforts to create a "respectable working class" through social welfare programs for dependent wives and children.[13] In preparation for Nairobi's becoming a city in 1950, in 1948 these ideas become incorporated into a city master plan, titled *Nairobi Master Plan for a Colonial City*.

While some children were born in Nairobi, others were sent by their parents or came of their own volition. One of the children who ate at my grandmother's house had been sent to Nairobi at the age of eight and lived with his unmarried uncle until he went to college. When my grandmother had twins, a girl of thirteen came from her countryside village to help her look after them for a year. When she returned to the countryside, she quickly grew dissatisfied and got into a fight with her mother. She decided to return to the city and, at fourteen, boarded a train by herself for the twelve-hour journey to Nairobi.[14] There she lived with my great-uncle until he could find a suitable spouse for her.

Putting male relatives in the position of raising children changed kinship norms and refused the dictates of colonial respectability. The girl my great-uncle looked after finally married a man about ten years her senior, who had fought in Burma during World War II and now worked for the Railways. She recalls the classes and services set up in the 1950s to produce "good wives" and contented married workers, like cooking, sewing, sanitation, and adult literacy classes, although she took no interest in them. She set the terms of her "modern" life in the city, challenging colonial efforts at a singular idea of urban domesticity.

Growing up in Railways spaces allowed children to form identities linked with the city. Although conceiving of themselves as part of a defined and enclosed group, Railways children went exploring in the farther reaches of the city. As one of my father's childhood friends put it, one form of discovery on these expeditions was eating the leftovers from restaurants—an encounter with exotic tastes like peaches, as well as supplementary sources of food.[15] My father often tells of riding the buses simply because he could, and it made him feel like someone, like an urbanite. He and friends would ride to Dagoretti, at one end of the line, back through Lavington to Westlands and Waiyaki Way on another side of the city, and then back to the center, taking in the sights as they went.[16]

The Railways created not only a demographically distinctive space but also a novel linguistic space. In the polyglot Railways community, Swahili became the common language of childhood communication. On arriving at Mang'u, a national secondary boarding school, my father and a friend of his felt they stood out from the other students.[17] Although they were both ethnically Samia, they did not talk to each other in Samia. As a result, other children at the school could not figure out where these two boys were "from." Finally, when asked why they only spoke Swahili, the friend replied, "We are not from the countryside. Those are not our issues or interests. We are from the city." And being from the city conveyed all sorts of benefits. They were the youngest children in the school, not because they were exceptionally smart but because their education had not been interrupted by farming duties or the violence and displacement of the Emergency and associated struggles.[18]

Not only was the Railways a cosmopolitan place with a strong lingua franca, it was also a place that enjoyed globally popular forms of entertainment. As a child I remember going to movies often with my father, who developed a love for cinema during his childhood. He remembered exchanging his World War II milk ration with my grandfather for twenty-five cents, which he spent on going to films and riding buses around town. Cinema was so much part of his life that if he missed a film in Muthurwa he would leave the Railway compounds to see it at Pumwani Memorial Hall. However, the films were not simply entertainment: newsreels and documentaries served as colonial propaganda that promoted the British war effort and later imperial enterprises, and Westerns were vehicles for racial ideas.[19]

The children watching these films developed ideas of identity and associations that distinguished them from people in the countryside. When I was growing up in Nairobi, to disparage some action or person as "totally country," we would use the term *miro* in Sheng (Nairobi creole). My father claims that this term originated in the cinemas of Nairobi as far back as the 1940s. British propaganda newsreels that played before the featured films would open with a collage of images of Zulu dances called *Mirrors of Africa*. These images, which did not reflect any particular ethnic or rural group in Kenya, struck the urban kids as a portrayal of an Africa they did not belong to—a rural one. Thus the English word *mirrors* evolved into *miro*, meaning something or someone not urban. As my father explained, "A *miro* was a fellow from the countryside—better yet, a fellow in the city who behaved like he was a country bumpkin, a fellow without finesse, one who hadn't yet come to terms with town life."[20]

The colonial administration made every effort, through law and policy as well as urban planning and architecture, to prevent children in Nairobi. However, Africans working for the Railways transformed their bachelor housing into a place of children who grew up with a sense of stability, community, and family, and an urban identity. Their presence itself was a challenge to colonial anti-urbanism. It was also tangible evidence of other dreams for the city—dreams that included generational continuity and increased opportunity, dreams with an urban future. Dreams of how to be modern, dreams of family. Some of these dreams became political dreams, ways of imagining desired futures. These children grew up imagining another city, a Nairobi shaped by their own sensibilities rather than just colonial ones.

Nairobi achieved city status in 1950 through a royal charter. This achievement is recorded in a British newsreel film of the time called *Nairobi*, made by the Colonial Film Unit. The short film starts with cars coming into the city from the countryside and ends with them leaving the city. Thus it portrays a city not lived in but worked in. The people who live there do not count. With its promise of wide roads for wealthy commuters and Nairobi's current obsession with traffic, the film could have been made today.

Absent from the film, however, are the protests and boycotts by African and Asian workers over Nairobi's new status. The East African Trade Union Confederation (EATUC) organized a boycott of civic celebrations of Nairobi's Charter Day on March 30, 1950.[21] The items boycotted—beer, cigarettes, and buses—were all under the control of the colonial government. They were also distinctively urban. The protesters saw Nairobi's city status as enabling a land grab and displacement.

This boycott addressed a number of issues that had already been faced by those living in Muthurwa. Residents had changed their housing to include families and changed their families to include children. They had traveled the city to explore its extent and dynamics and in order to belong. They were accorded advantages in schools and services that enabled them to prosper in the long-term. They lived in and explored a cosmopolitan modern space full of dreams, fantasies, connections with distant places, music, and dance. Although they were always under the discipline of both wage labor and colonialism, they lived their lives beyond these constraints, shaping the city to their tastes. They demanded more.

In the rebuilding of Nairobi to accommodate the new ideal of workers with families, the municipal government built the Kaloleni estate in 1945. Among its amenities was a huge social hall. Again, this space was transformed by residents to meet their own desires. Kaloleni came to be a center for politics, dance, and music. It housed a number of future East African politicians and presidents. It was also instrumental in organizing the Charter Day boycotts and later transforming those boycotts into larger protests. Long-term residents protested the new vision of their city that did not fit with what they dreamed of or had built. Sixty years later, the poor and the working class are still protesting new developments under similar fears of displacement and the takeover of valuable land.

THE RAILWAY CITY REVISED

In 2010 twelve petitioners, filing on behalf of 359 others, took the Kenya Railways Staff Retirement Benefit Scheme, the Kenya Railways Corporation, and the attorney general of Kenya to court over their eviction from the residential estate of Muthurwa.[22] Their petition drew on the 2010 National Constitution, demanding adequate and accessible housing, dignity, and human rights. The evictions were handled very badly, marked by inadequate notice, the cutting off of water and sanitary services, violence, and intimidation. The court case not only challenged these measures but raised the question of what happened to all the people who were born, grew up, and lived in the old Railways housing once their labor was used up.

The first petitioner, Satrose Ayuma, exemplified the problem of growing old in a new city. The petition states that Ayuma was born in Muthurwa, grew up there, married there, lost her husband there, and raises children there. Like many others, she had no other home. Although the petition does not mention her parents, it seems likely they were born in Muthurwa too; after all, when Ayuma was born in 1960, people had been living there for at least thirty years. Now, at age fifty-five, Ayuma had to find another place to call home.

Involving a scheme that sought to sell off the land to finance the pension scheme, the case indirectly pitted pensioners living in Muthurwa against the nine thousand or so other pensioners no longer living in Muthurwa or other Railways housing. As a result of increasing local government debt during the 1990s and

2000s, service provision suffered.[23] From 2000 the central government created different entities to fund and deliver local services. In 2006 the Kenya Railways Corporation established the Kenya Railways Staff Retirement Benefits Scheme to pay retired workers' pensions. However, the scheme inherited liabilities estimated at 12.6 billion Kenya shillings (Ksh). To compensate for these liabilities, Railways land and other assets valued at Ksh 12.4 billion were designated for sale to fund the pensions of retired Railways workers. On paper, this arrangement made the Kenya Railways Staff Retirement Benefits Scheme the "largest and most highly funded pension plan in the country," as the *Daily Nation* reported.[24] However, as most of the assets were not liquid and were vulnerable to embezzlement, pensions went unpaid, and multiple suits have been brought against the scheme for the nonpayment of pensions from 2007 to 2018.

The assets included seventy-two acres of the Muthurwa housing estate, put up for sale in 2006. The sale took time, and the rapidly increasing prices of land contributed to the delay, as prices rose while deals were being negotiated. In 2012, the land was valued by the selling agents at US\$ 3.6 million.[25] However, land prices in Nairobi are among the fastest appreciating in the world.[26] In 2014 land in the central business district (CBD), which now includes Muthurwa, was priced at US\$3.75 million per acre.[27] Thus the value of the land increased seventy-two-fold in just two years. In 2025 the same land would be worth US \$6.7 million per acre, or US \$495 million in total. In comparison to these property prices, what is the value of the dignity, human rights, and adequate housing petitioned for in the lawsuit?

Ayuma's life of impoverishment and declining support reflects the trajectory of Kenya from 1980 through 2000. Nairobi's transformation from newly chartered royal city to chaotic city makes Muthurwa hard to recognize today. The Railways housing still exists, but open spaces have been built over. A market separates the housing from the social hall, and a bus stop crowds the other side. In 2019 each house was marked with an X targeting it for demolition. Mathews Tuikong, the chief executive of the Kenya Railways Retirement Benefits Scheme, stated that "the houses in Muthurwa Estate have been condemned because they are an eyesore."[28]

According to an anonymous post on the blog MaVulture, "If you were raised in Muthurwa in the 1960s and went back there today, you would think you had died and gone to hell. The term decay does not even begin to describe what became of this once clean and orderly working-class Railway town." The author recalls childhoods with good schools, fields to play in, and things to discover, and the ever-present amusement of the trains. The collapse of the Railways in the 1990s and various economic shocks until 2000 transformed Muthurwa from a place of movies, dances, education, and children into a place of dirt, danger, and dilapidated housing. The post goes on, "The place bears exactly no resemblance to the orderly estate that belonged to Kenya Railways decades ago. In economic terms, it is vibrant. But in social terms, it is dead and beyond decay. It is like a river so heavily polluted with industrial effluent that it cannot support any life."[29]

But just as the colonial city that was not intended to sustain families yet became a place of children, even in this period of neglect residents strove to make something else of the space. Muthurwa was also known as Dallas after the Dallas Boxing Club, which met at the Muthurwa Social Hall and produced Kenya's finest boxers, including the 1988 Olympic gold medalist Robert Wangila (born in Nairobi in 1967). During the 1980s and 1990s, Kenyan boxers excelled in international competitions. Kenya Railways, along with big government employers such as Kenya Breweries, the post office, the police, and the prison system took pride in having boxing teams.

With structural adjustment, some of these fully or partially government-owned corporations (parastatals) were privatized, and they reduced their support for boxing. Both the sport and the spaces that nurtured it, like the social hall, fell into decline. Meanwhile, in an effort to accommodate street vendors evicted from the CBD in 2006, the government of Kenya and the Nairobi City Council constructed a market at Muthurwa on Railways land. This was the event that sparked the protests in Muthurwa. The market lay between the housing estate and its social hall, disrupting historical links. Muruthwa residents, worried about security and the collapse of their community, petitioned the government in 2006 to spare the social hall, and the government initially agreed.[30] However, in 2008, residents were again blocked from accessing the hall, as it was being used by a construction company. Later, banks were opened in it. Protests from the community and demands to restore it to use as a sporting facility arose once more. The fight continues today.

The community dreams of a social hall with "active indoor recreational amenities such as pugilism, karate, judo, tae-kwan-do, weightlifting and others."[31] The government also has sporting dreams, which take the form of stadiums as part of a branding campaign, articulated in the Nairobi urban development master plan.[32] This plan is based on the policy document *Nairobi Metro 2030: A World-Class African Metropolis*, a comprehensive and thoughtful document that outlines possibilities for the city that seem to reflect the dreams of its long-term residents. These include "good quality housing, adequate, accessible and high-quality facilities and a healthy, safe and lively environment so that those who work in the metropolitan area together with their families can enjoy the best possible standard of living."[33] Nevertheless, the transformation of this vision into the master plan for the city leaves much to be desired. Indeed, as the urban scholars Samuel Owuor and T. Mbatia argue, a wide distance between vision and implementation is a long-held tradition in Nairobi city planning.[34]

The 2014 master plan was unveiled by the new governor of Nairobi, Evans Kidero. (Kidero, although he campaigned as a resident born and bred in Nairobi, worked for much of his life outside the city and built a rural home.) In many ways the 2014 plan echoes the 1948 plan, with the same aims of modernization that facilitates the movement of the elite in and out of the city, and with little regard for or belief in the existence of the long-term Nairobi resident. The new master plan was first and foremost concerned with traffic congestion and the coordination of commuter traffic to and from the city center. It included a proposal to refinance the Kenya Railway Corporation by creating a "Railway City" that would facilitate the removal of "unnecessary" functions from the CBD.[35]

Also referred to as Golf City, this development was to be built on the Kenya Railways Golf Club, a golf course for Railways staff built in 1922 that runs along the main highway in Nairobi, Uhuru Highway, dividing the Upper Hill area from the CBD with a refreshing swath of green. In 2008, together with the Kenya Railways Staff Retirement Benefits Scheme, the Kenya Railways Corporation sought investors to develop the land into "a 5-star hotel, a modern 4-star hotel with state-of-the-art conference facilities, exclusive cottages, an international quality 9-hole golf course and a huge shopping mall with sufficient parking lots."[36] Although stalled for a while by a lawsuit brought by a Chinese company over noncompliance with a contract, the project exemplifies the current emphasis on hotels, high-end housing, and shopping malls in Nairobi's development. The government expected to earn about Ksh 1 billion (US$10 million) in annual lease fees from this US $2 billion project, which also includes developing other "Railway City" complexes in Mombasa and Kisumu.[37]

In December 2016, trees were felled to initiate this project, described as the second most expensive development in Kenyan history (after the controversial Standard Gauge Railway, or SGR). Lost to the "sufficient" parking lots was any space for children, the working class, or the retired workers who once filled the area.

As an ongoing project, by 2020, the Nairobi Railway City (NRC) was being marketed by Bayside Realty with a promise to "transform Nairobi into the greatest international city."[38] They described the project plan with the futuristic superlative language now common in neoliberal development projects, replete with invocations of competitiveness, monumentalism, commodification, modernization, securitization, future projection, and internationalization. And of course, traffic. A six-minute promotional 2020 video depicts the project as moving Nairobi from the past into the future, with shopping, international business, modern food markets, synergy with the university—and improved traffic flow. Interestingly, the plan for Railway City now includes promises of a park and green space, connections with the neighborhoods of Upper Hill and Eastlands, and a "Kenya Railway Cultural center for all citizens."

Railway City is now a joint project between the Kenyan and British governments, with UK funding of £80 million to develop 425 acres of *"prime underutilized* land within the Central Business District."[39] The Kenya Railways Corporation emphasizes that "since early 2020 the UK Government has funded a team of urban development experts to provide relevant Kenyan government agencies involved in taking forward NRC with technical support that has included a review of the master plan, land due diligence, identification of priority projects, a feasibility study and detailed design and associated engineering and costing of the first priority project, a new central Railway Station at the Center of Nairobi City Center." The new design is supposed to be designed for everyone, or as we like to say in Kenya, "for all walks of life."[40]

Yet there is little reference in the plan to children, leisure, or history, and still less to the dreams of family and community highlighted by Satrose Ayuma in her petition. There is no reference to generational change and no concept of long-term housing a convenient distance from work, or a place to retire once you have grown old.

THE CITY YET TO COME: NAIROBI

In his late seventies, my father walked daily through the streets of downtown Nairobi seeing no other people his age. Passers-by saw him as a foreigner, surprised that he should speak Swahili with no traceable accent. He looked urban, but his age told them he could not be; someone as old as he was must have come from somewhere else. Who was this unusual elderly, urban person? What does it mean for people like my father to be perceived as foreign in a place where they have resided longer than anyone around them?

If I think of areas of Nairobi where the elderly, those over seventy, are a common sight, I realize they are sharply defined by race. The first neighborhood that comes to mind is Parklands. Almost all the elderly people there are Asian Kenyans—a group that probably constitutes the majority of the city's visible elderly. In neighborhoods like Karen, Lang'ata, and Westlands, the elderly tend to be European Kenyans. Although Asians and Europeans are tiny minority populations in Kenya, elderly people in these groups far outnumber the African elderly population in Nairobi. In a city of 4.3 million residents in 2019, there were only 3,563 people my parents' age or older, a substantial proportion of whom were European or Asian Kenyans.[41]

The elderly are a small percentage of Kenya's population as a whole, and disproportionately few of them live in urban areas: those over 65 in 2019 made up 3.9 percent of the Kenyan population, but 4.5 percent of the rural population, and only 1.3 percent of the urban.[42] However, the number of middle-aged and graying African people in Nairobi is growing. When I was a child, we rarely knew other children's grandparents, who mostly lived in the countryside. Today, grandparents and grandchildren reside in the same city. Yet neither the elderly nor the children are provided for in housing complexes. Even housing developments built around golf courses, with gyms and mainly decorative "swimming" pools, lack children's playgrounds. Children end up playing in the parking lots. Nairobi's housing is still designed for that single worker of the 1930s: temporary, childless, and young. It continues to embody colonial ideas about labor and African humanity—that is, anti-urbanist ideas.

FIGURE 5. Downtown Nairobi. Photo by author.

Today, some twenty-five to thirty years after the initial economic restructuring mandated by the World Bank, new dynamics are again rapidly changing the experience of life in Nairobi. These changes are premised on construction rather than decay. They are narrated as growth and rebirth and look to China for inspiration. As in other African cities, such as Douala, Accra, and Cape Town, new plans are being made for Nairobi and new visions created.[43]

The urban theorist AbdouMaliq Simone observes that

urban development attempts to resolutely settle the question of how things within the city get articulated once and for all. . . . Yet, because this objective and its subsequent results do not often effectively engage local histories in recognizable ways, such trajectories of urban development face a particular conundrum. . . . There are two senses of time in operation. In other words, a city is full of memories about what has taken place in the past, and those memories also include a certain amount of imagination—of hopes and dreams that the city would have been a certain kind of place, but one that never seemed to reach fruition. These imaginations have never fully gone away, as the city remains a place of dreams, present and past, of bits and pieces of ways of doing things that never really had enough time or support to fully implant themselves.[44]

According to Jane Guyer, LaRay Denzer, and Adigun Agbaje, the disconnect with local histories makes daily life a "struggle with rapid, chronic, seemingly directionless and uncontrolled change."[45]

To the anthropologist David Scott this is part of a postcolonial predicament in which the present is made up of "futures past," or dreams that are no longer "ours to imagine, let alone seek after and inhabit." Thus, the futures we once imagined for Nairobi can no longer be articulated. For Scott, understanding the fraught relationship between the horizon of expectation (what was hoped for) and the space of experience (what is) enables us to make sense of a shift from a moment "when the future appears guaranteed by the present to one in which it seems undermined by it."[46] How are we to think about memories and dreams, the people who hold them, and the emotions they elicit in the context of change? What does it mean to grow old as these horizons shift?

If Nairobi was designed as a city of laborers, then we should not be surprised that there is no space for people who can no longer work. Nevertheless, today's cities want to be known for sustainability, and not for volatility, instability, or insecurity. The Urban scholar Vanessa Watson argues that in calling a city "world-class" or "modern," planners exercise a symbolic power that "involves the production of narratives promoting the city and addressed to global elites; it also implies a concern with the importance of a city in relation to other cities rather than the extent to which it functions for its citizens."[47] We must ask, then, if a city cannot sustain an aging population and multiple generations, is it sustainable? What is the effect of failing to attend to the horizon of expectations over and over again?

For Simone, "cityness also includes a sense that behind the present moment there is another time operating, other things taking place, unfolding, waiting, getting ready or slipping away, and that we know only a fragment of what is taking place."[48] For most of Nairobi's population, the city has two temporal aspects: the near future and the city yet to come. It is not a city of the present or the past. It is defined by its newness.

For lifelong residents, this new city operates on yet another different temporality, one that includes the past and the horizons of expectations that past elicits. These memories and visions are rarely considered when planning the new city. Yet they speak to a city that people love to experience and know, a city that may once have transformed their lives for the better, a city teeming with children and spaces for children, a city where workers had lives beyond their work, a city of mixtures and diversity, a city of recreation and leisure as well as a city of work, struggle, and challenge.

Guyer and colleagues, like Simone, analyze a present characterized by and experienced as uncertainty.[49] I started this chapter by trying to illustrate the *feeling* of imminent displacement from a place called home. In the case against evictions in Muthurwa, the anxiety of the first petitioner, Satrose Ayuma, is palpable. She says: "I am in a state of anguish since my meager income can only sustain my cost of living within Muthurwa Estate." What matters to her is "its vicinity to schools, hospitals, and other social amenities where my children learn and its proximity to my workplace." The judge of the case allowed the evictions but demanded that they be done in a dignified manner. The ruling recognized the roots of her anguish, declaring, "Wherever and whenever evictions occur, they are extremely traumatic. They cause physical, psychological, and emotional distress and they entail losses of means of economic sustenance and increase impoverishment."[50]

I recorded my own reactions to the possible loss of home in my field notes:

This place may one day be beautiful, but we will not live here anymore, and no warnings or effort seems to be made to soften that process. I have thought about the gentrification of Nairobi and the scramble for land downtown. I have thought about what it means to be in the way of progress. I have felt it in my chest. While I railed against the efforts to demolish old residential estates in downtown Nairobi for some time now, until I saw that map I did not know how it *feels*. And imagine, we are so much better off than others. All the people in old railway pension housing that are scheduled for demolition. They will find nowhere in this new city to live. And why can't this new city be for them as well? Why should these elderly people who call this city home move? Why can't they be incorporated in the new development?

> Yes, I know how it feels,
> Like an asthma attack.
> The fist wrenching the air out of your chest,
> The sudden constriction of breath,
> The difficulty in breathing,
> The lightness of your head for lack of oxygen.
> Yes, I know how it feels,
> Like a racing heart,
> And a mind with no focus.

Yet I have *no idea* how it feels, there,
Where life is more fragile,
And choices are fewer,
And years longer.

LOST IN THE CITY THAT USED TO BE NAIROBI

"You are so lost" is a common expression in Kenya. It can mean I haven't seen you in a long time. It can mean we are out of touch. It can mean you have changed. It is most often used if you have been away for a long time. But in Nairobi anybody who has been away for some time can become so lost, both figuratively and actually. Familiar landscapes no longer look the same. Every Christmas we used to host a family potluck lunch. Because we are a big family, forty or so relatives would come and celebrate in the backyard each year. As the years passed and the houses around us gave way to offices and high-rise apartments or were taken out by road construction, on arrival my cousins would say that they were almost lost coming home, to the place they had known all their lives.

It is a very strange feeling to be lost in the place where you grew up because it has changed so much. This feeling could be summed up by what Glenn Albrecht and colleagues call *solastalgia*, a kind of psychoterratic illness, or ecological grief or anxiety.[51] Solastalgia was recently conceptualized to account for the distress caused by profound environmental change for those who are not displaced but continue to live in the changed environments, in particular environments transformed through climate change or mining. Also described as the homesickness you have when you are still at home, solastalgia is an indication of a mismatch between the people living in a changed environment and the change itself. One can imagine it as an unsettling, a feeling of being no longer at ease. You become so lost.

To be lost, however, implies that you were once found. You were situated on ground that was familiar, defined by the social and cultural meanings and relationships embedded in the landscapes by you, by the generations before you, and by experiences and memories. It is ground made familiar through, and in spite of, change wrought by your hands and the hands of those known to you. You were located. You were at home. To be lost means to be detached from that home, to be untethered.

To be no longer at ease, to use the words of Chinua Achebe, implies that you were once at ease.[52] You were in a place where things made sense, including change—a place where you knew and understood the environment around you. The social theorist Andreas Huyssen dismisses any facile notion of being at ease as a dream of modernism.[53] Yet perhaps we could conceive of being at ease not as imagining "some golden age of stability and permanence" but rather as the attempt "to secure some continuity within time, to provide some extension of lived space within which we can breathe and move."[54] To be at ease, then, is not to be in a static time where nothing changes, but to be in a temporal, environmental, political, and social context where change makes sense, has a manageable pace and scale, and has a foreseeable horizon of expectation. Change itself is not the problem. Rather the distress arises from the scale, speed, and finality of the change; the disregard of the longevity, effort, and relevance of prior attempts at place making; and the lack of alternatives for remaking new places, whether by age, class, race, or cultural background.

Solastalgia sees change as unwelcome and a cause of emotional stress and distress. At the heart of the distress is a the lack of power to direct, affect, or even participate in the change taking place, a change that can in brief moments undo years of sedimented place making. Like nostalgia, which reimagines lost places and pasts in a rosy light, the sense of impotence and loss produced by unwelcome change can make a landscape precious, sacred, or culturally significant even if it was not originally seen as such. An ordinary, not very interesting but familiar street in Nairobi can become home in ways it never used to be.

Current processes of urban development build on and reinforce anti-urbanist designs, enhancing the pull of both the future and the past. Long-term employees of the Railways could think of themselves as those who sought to change the city in order to make it home. Making Nairobi home, whatever that might involve—raising children in the city, riding a bus, changing families, bringing a lawsuit to remain in place—is a challenge to the anti-urbanism ideology that insists the city can't be home. Yet this challenge falters in the face of rapid urban development that residents have little control over.

3

One Hundred Years of Segregation

In 2017 I was sitting listening to the public relations officer for the Kenya Urban Roads Authority (KURA) tell me that he couldn't say for sure whether a road would go through my house, but he couldn't say it wouldn't, either. He leaned back in his fancy chair behind a desk in an office built to impress. He told me about his own home in the countryside, about his respect for my parents, about all the buildings KURA had already knocked down around the city, and about the financial district it hoped to create where I and my parents were living. He omitted to mention what would happen to the owners and residents of the demolished houses or to consider the futility of building a financial district in this age of virtual finance.

He dismissed my anxiety and stress. After all, my parents' house was located in an area of rapidly rising house prices. He advised us to sell and "move to Muthaiga or Karen." He assumed that we aspired to be able to live in one of these wealthy, well-serviced neighborhoods. Wasn't that everyone's dream? Much to his shock, I replied, "I don't know about you, but I refuse to live in ethnic or racial enclaves." He protested, saying, "Other people live there as well," but his tone lacked conviction.

This conversation reflects the persistence of anti-urbanism in Nairobi. The public relations officer talked of his rural home while contemplating the demolition of our urban home. He was not of the city and had no emotional attachment to it. Rather, he understood the city from a class and financial perspective, one in which land represented money and nothing else—in which one part of the city was interchangeable with another, depending only on the price. The anti-urbanist view assumes that temporary city dwellers will and must move.

When space is equated with money, the notion of home is left out, and the relationship between class and the value of land is entangled with ideas of racial or ethnic belonging. The KURA officer could not easily deny that Karen and Muthaiga are racial enclaves. These dynamics prompt us to ask, In what ways have class and ethnicity come to replace race in structuring Nairobi's spatiality and temporality?

Class structures and their attendant property values have been built on colonial racial foundations, replicating the exclusions and disparities of the colonial city and extending anti-urbanism into postcolonial policy, administration and law. This chapter looks at efforts by wealthier Asians and Africans to mobilize class and race in efforts to flee the colonial constraints of "locations" and their lack of services (see chapter 1). After Independence, Africans mobilized race against Asians to gain access to neighborhoods segregated by wealth and class. Both struggles reflected a quest for permanence and an effort to escape parts of the city that would only ever be seen as temporary. The making of a middle class (or more bluntly, a wealthy class) was thus always a racial project, one that guided the politics and polices after Independence as it did during the colonial period.

THE ASIAN QUESTION

Between 2011 and 2013 I worked for Aga Khan University, which is located in Parklands, in northeastern Nairobi. One day the university hosted a public talk by Natalie Sham about urban design, titled "A Walk Through Parklands." Most of the people who attended were residents of Parklands. Many were also contractors, architects, and urban planners. More than half the audience was Nairobians of Asian descent. As the presenter talked about the problems of roads, design, and how to create neighborhoods on a human scale, residents brought up their issues and concerns. Toward the end of the discussion, a contractor in a deep blue turban stood up and said, "Who are we kidding? The real issue is that this neighborhood is segregated and has been for a hundred years."

At the time, I was struck that the person who brought up the segregated nature of Parklands was Asian, as the exclusionary nature of Parklands is often downplayed, but I am increasingly more interested in his framing of the problem. Was his assertion even true?

While Parklands is understood as an Asian neighborhood today, it did not start off that way. The movement of Asians to Parklands can be explained only through other movements, which pull people from other neighborhoods into the story: Africans out of Pangani, Asians out of Eastleigh, and Somalis out of Ngara. These movements also include the westward shift of Asian residents and the eastward shift of African residents. The moving forces included class and efforts to escape class-based locations. All this movement occurred in the shadow of colonial efforts to regulate race and class. Asian movement west to Parklands led to yet another shift: the exodus of white residents.

The process through which Parklands became Asian involves interacting dynamics of race and class in the organization of space. While class became the more powerful force after Independence, the two were always linked, and either one could be invoked in an effort to escape tacit and overt segregation in Nairobi. Class and race are structured on top of and through the categories of "native," "detribalized native," migrant (nonsettler), and settler. All these categories have temporal associations. Native and settler are permanent, one rural and the other urban. Detribalized native and migrant are both temporary but urban—one local (African) and one foreign (primarily Asian). Both are out of place.

The story of how Parklands became a predominantly Asian neighborhood reflects a history of struggle against categorization, a struggle for permanence, and a flight from impermanence. It also reflects the inextricable link between class and race in the organization of Nairobi.

Some of the first racial rearrangements of the city stemmed from concern with the vibrancy of commerce in areas that were predominantly African and Asian. The Indian Bazaar, located at the center of Nairobi, was built on land owned by the tycoon A. M. Jeevanjee, who supplied the Railways with provisions.[1] It provided commercial spaces as well as housing for a cosmopolitan array of city residents. However, in an effort to blunt the economic impact of Indian trade in the Bazaar, the colonial government created Eastleigh Township in 1921 under the pretext of protecting public health. The argument was that the Indian Bazaar, one of the earliest commercial and residential quarters in colonial Nairobi and a melting pot of classes, ethnicities, races, and genders, was a reservoir of disease—in particular plague—because of overcrowding.[2] Eastleigh Township, which was an amalgamation of Egerton Estate, Nairobi East Township, and the areas known as Egerton, Eastleigh, and Eastleigh Extensions, now became a "location" for Asian artisans.[3]

The effort to make Eastleigh Asian ran into difficulties involving the property-owning Somalis already living in Nairobi East. For the colonial government, and for the Somalis themselves, natives and Somalis were distinct categories. Somalis actively constructed themselves as nonnatives by taking advantage of ordinances that excepted them from native status.[4] As the Nairobi East Township consisted of freehold property with no restrictions on sale (among nonnatives), Somalis were able to purchase land there, aided by income from their occupations as clerks, interpreters, and soldiers for the colonial state.

Although Eastleigh was designated as a township, the government did not extend services to it, thus effectively rendering it a "location."[5] Locations, as opposed to residential areas and townships, were considered temporary, lacked services such as electricity and running water, and were reserved for the working classes. As a result, higher-class Asians refused to settle there. Their reaction exemplifies the process by which racial segregation turns into class segregation: wealthier Asians distinguished themselves from poorer Asians by asserting the right to live elsewhere.

Initially, "elsewhere" was an area near City Park called Pangani. Situated on the Mathare River on the edge of the Karura Forest, Pangani had started out as a settlement of safari workers, who were not provided with housing or steady employment, and of administrative guards from Tanganyika, especially Nyamwezi people.[6] It had been developed as a lodging area for Africans by 1902 and was the largest and most cosmopolitan of the early African settlements in Nairobi, with extensive urban amenities. By 1920 single women were prominent property owners in Pangani, offering accommodation to migrant workers and travelers.[7] The area had a strong Muslim character and hosted three mosques (Kikuyu, Luo/Luhya, and Kamba).

As part of the response to malaria outbreaks in the 1920s, the colonial government displaced the African proprietors of Pangani in order to create a buffer zone of Asians between African and European settlements. These African proprietors were offered lifelong term leases in a new area near Pumwani (in the lower, flatter part of the city). While many refused, some 220 people, predominantly women, took up residence and ownership in the new estate, which became known as Shauri Moyo ("take heart") in remembrance of their displacement.[8] The Asian presence in Pangani survives through ethnic sports clubs, such as the Patel Club, and the Goan Institute.

The incoming Asians replaced Somalis who had previously lived in Ngara, between Pangani and Parklands. In turn, Somalis replaced Asians in Eastleigh. This movement was encouraged by the government, as it solved the problem of Somali camels too close to European settlement. Before 1923, Somalis used to bring their cattle and camels through Ngara. My father remembers seeing the camels during his childhood in the 1940s and '50s. The Somalis started butcheries and supplied meat to Nairobi's growing population. However, the European residents of Parklands, who did not want livestock nearby, backed the displacement of Somalis to Eastleigh. In the 1930s and '40s Eastleigh became the main area of Somali settlement in Nairobi. Somalis rented houses from Asian landowners and later bought land.[9]

Meanwhile, wealthier Asians started to move farther west, from Pangani to Ngara, and to buy land in Parklands. Asian landlords used money from their rental properties in Eastleigh to purchase property in Ngara and later in Parklands. Some of the iconic features of Ngara, like the Digamber Jain Mumukshu Mandal, a Jain temple, were built in the 1950s.[10]

The relationship between Pangani and Eastleigh, Somalis and Asians, was thus rooted in efforts to escape "locations" and the class associations they engendered. They were part of an attempt to escape being temporary, and thus, to escape the designation of native or migrant.

While the move to Pangani by Asians in the 1930s and '40s was encouraged by the colonial administration, the move farther west to Parklands was not. In fact, it took a lawsuit by the medical doctor A. C. L. de Souza for non-Europeans to be allowed to live in Parklands.

A. C. L. DE SOUZA AND THE ASIAN TRANSFORMATION OF PARKLANDS

A. C. L. de Souza came to Kenya from Goa in 1915 as a government medical officer. In 1919 he opened a private practice with his wife, Mary, who was also a doctor.[11] He founded the Goan Overseas Association in 1927. He also served as an editor of *The Goan Voice*, started a school, and became a city councilor. In 1934 he became a member of the Legislative Council of Kenya (LegCo).[12]

In 1924 De Souza sued to be able to live on land that he had purchased in Parklands. He had been able to buy this freehold property, but residential restrictions had prevented him from living there. A 1923 white paper on "the Asian Question," as it was termed in the *Kenya Gazette*, set the terms by which Asians might be incorporated into the colony. It lifted racial segregation between Asian and Europeans in commercial areas but was silent about restrictions on residential areas. De Souza took advantage of this vagueness and in 1924 brought a legal challenge to Nairobi's racial-segregation laws.

The lawsuit came on the heels of the 1922 Thuku riots in Nairobi. A surge in African nationalism led to the founding of the first major African political organizations, Afro-Asian political mobilizations, and the first major African nationalist rebellion.[13] The Thuku riots' multiethnic and multiracial makeup caused the administration to be more attuned to other racial and class claims in its efforts to divide protesting populations.

As a Goan, de Souza fell into an in-between category in the eyes of the colonial administration. As Christian Indians with Portuguese citizenship, Goans were difficult for the colonial administration to classify.[14] For most administrative purposes, Portuguese were not classified as European—and Goans were not classified as Asian. Thus in the eyes of the state, and perhaps colonial society, de Souza was neither properly Indian nor properly European. Perhaps it was these ambiguities that enabled him to sue to live on his land in Parklands. As a doctor and a former government medical officer, de Souza could also invoke arguments of class, asserting the right to be treated as befitted his income, education, and professional standing. It was his wealth, after all, that had enabled him to buy the property in the first place. The suit was finally settled in his favor in 1928.[15]

As Parklands was near other Asian neighborhoods, Asians with money were quick to buy land in Ngara and Parklands after de Souza won his suit. The railway mogul Jeevanjee had built a house in Ngara, for example, but when his wife came from Karachi to join him in the late 1920s, he bought a ten-acre plot in his wife's name on Second Avenue, Parklands.[16] Wealthy Asians like Jeevanjee strongly opposed segregation based on race and the false rationale of public health. They proposed a class-based commercial and residential organization of the city instead. Scholars like the historian and political analyst Godwin Murunga argue that "subsequent development of the town more or less followed this class-based pattern."[17] I suggest, rather, that it continued to follow a racial form of anti-urbanism retooled as class-based segregation. After the influx of Asians into neighborhoods like Parklands, Europeans left these historically white neighborhoods in protest. Class and race were always interdependent in Nairobi.

Asians moving into Parklands in the 1920s and 1930s transformed the space by refusing to build in a British colonial style. They built more than fifty houses in a new style—Art Deco.[18] Growing up in Nairobi, I always associated these beautiful Art Deco buildings with Asian Kenyans. This manifestation of international modernity declared Asians in Parklands to be part of the future, in contrast with Pangani, Eastleigh, and especially the Indian Bazaar, whose locations relegated them to an impermanent past. Although barely remarked at the time, and hard to find in the legal record, A. C. L. de Souza's suit was transformative. It challenged the racial idea of permanence associated with townships (although it maintained the class association). It set in motion a number of demographic movements and countermovements that rearranged Nairobi. It introduced new architectural styles to the city. But it also unleashed white flight and led to the introduction of racial covenants and caveats in title deeds that reaffirmed segregation in other parts of the city.

CLASS MOBILITY AND WHITE FLIGHT

Frank Morgan, a Seychellois resident of Nairobi, writes of his family's movement to Parklands in *A Reflection of Twelve Decades*. Identifying himself as "coloured," he captures well the racial dynamics of Parklands after the de Souza suit, including the rearticulation of certain Asian locations as African and white flight from Parklands. He writes: "At about this time, 1928, the Municipal Council of Nairobi decided that they required a lot more land on which to build housing for the ever-growing amount of African office workers. So, they decided to take over the whole area of Kariokor, which also included our new house. As a consequence for which, they were willing to give us five acres of land with a similar house at Parklands in the suburbs of Nairobi. This offer greatly pleased my mother and father and they grabbed at it, because Kariokor was coming to have bad memories."[19]

The first housing estate for Africans was built in Kariokor in 1929.[20] Although the Morgan family's movement could be seen as part of an Asian/coloured flight from Kariokor, Morgan represents it as state instigated, with the offer of alternative land in Parklands. Morgan's father was entitled to live in a township (probably because of his class background and high-status state job). Nevertheless, class by itself was not enough to guarantee residence. Morgan explains: "Eventually my father was required to show proof to the government that one of his parents originated from Europe in order to transfer the five acres of derelict land from the Nairobi Municipal Council situated on the fringe of the whites-only zone of First Avenue, Parklands. So, he produced the certificate showing that his grandfather originated from Fayol, Azores [part of Portugal], before they would agree to let him have the land. At the time, my father was also a high official in the Municipality. So, there was really not much that they could do about the situation."[21]

Morgan's father had to point to distant ancestors in order to substantiate his whiteness and Europeanness, which were also contingent on his class and professional position. And the assertion was sufficient for the government, but not for his neighbors. Morgan writes: "In November 1928 we all moved into our new home in Parklands. . . . We had an English neighbor, together with his wife, and they hated their new neighbors. The area was reserved for the whites and we were coloured." These attitudes carried significant threat for Morgan and his family: "One day whilst I was playing with my football in our front garden, the ball accidentally rolled into our English neighbor's piece of very woody land. I struggled across the barbed wire fencing in order to retrieve the ball. The next thing I knew, I heard gunshots and bullets were flying all around me. I got very scared and managed to hide behind a large tree from where I perceived our English neighbor standing on this front porch firing at me." The neighbor had his own ideas about where the Morgan family belonged and sought to enforce them with violence. However, again Morgan's father's class and job status enabled him to respond. "My father and mother had come out running to find out what the commotion was about. After a lot of shouting from the Englishman that I was not allowed on his property he went back into his house, and I raced back with my ball followed by Rex [the dog]. Under the circumstances, my father thought it best to lodge a complaint at the Parklands police station about one mile away and they came over to investigate the incident."[22]

Unwilling to live in the newly mixed neighborhood, the neighbors returned to England. Morgan adds: "In order to avoid further neighbor problems, my father bought the property outright. I do not think that the chap knew who had bought his property."[23]

Morgan's childhood experience highlights the role of both class and race in structuring space in Nairobi. It demonstrates the racism faced by those who moved to Parklands. It shows how the racial category of European had to be stretched to fit the administration's need to enable his family to live there. It demonstrates the tensions between the colonial state and settlers over how best to govern a colony. It shows how the influx of nonwhite immigrant families produced white flight. And Morgan's father buying out his fleeing European neighbors illustrates how economic power facilitated change in the racial makeup of Parklands.

RACIAL COVENANTS AND CONDITIONS
OF INDENTURE

The effects of De Souza's lawsuit were felt as far away as Upper Hill, where they are clearly reflected in the 1993 title deed to my parents' house. First titled in 1905, the land was part of the Uganda Railway Zone, which comprised 331 acres of land leased to a British man, William Henry Smart, on a ninety-nine-year lease. The land then became company land that was subdivided into different private holdings before ending up in the hands of a couple called Oulton in 1955. This particular parcel was reduced to an area of 0.77 acres. On it stood a block of flats consisting of three two-bedroom apartments and three garages, a row of three one-room houses with shared kitchen and bathroom facilities for domestic workers, and a garden. All the successive private owners of the land were European until 1962, when it was bought by a company with Asian owners by the name of Mohan Properties Ltd.

The title deed refers to a 1929 list of "Special Covenants and Conditions contained in the said indenture." The first condition is "not to sell, assign, sublet, part with the possession of, or grant a Power of Attorney over the said premises or any part thereof or any building which may be erected thereon to any person not of pure European descent or to any company or corporation any shareholder or member whereof is not of similar descent." Thus a non-European could not own any stake in the block of flats. The covenant further enjoins the owner "not to use any such dwelling house when erected or permit the same to be used as a place of residence for an Asiatic or African who is not a domestic servant in the service of the tenant or occupier thereof."

Racial covenants and conditions like this make real the temporal and spatial aspects of anti-urbanism. They restrict residence through segregation in ownership as well as tenancy. They bar Africans from living on the property except in the capacity of domestic servants. I found title deeds with similar racial covenants or caveats from other European townships.

All these racial covenants were enacted between 1927–and 1929—that is to say, during or shortly after the De Souza suit. The expansion of the city boundaries to incorporate the European-restricted townships of Muthaiga, Kilimani, Westlands, the Hill (Upper Hill) and Parklands also occurred in 1927.[24]

In 1927 the townships fought to retain self-governance by means of bylaws that included the regulation of property and race.[25] Since the decision in De Souza's case upheld the right of anyone to live on land they could buy, it undid residential segregation by race and effectively replaced it with segregation by class, thereby enabling the intrusion of non-Europeans into previously "European space." In response, Europeans invoked racial covenants in title deeds.

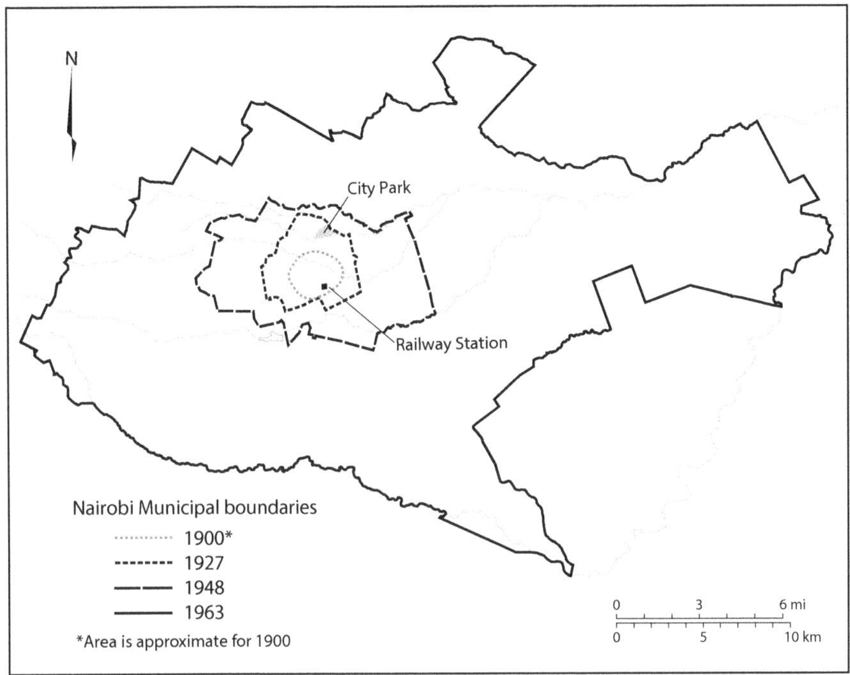

MAP 2. Nairobi's municipal boundaries.

Moody Awori, who served as Kenya's ninth vice president from 2003 to 2008, lived in Nairobi as a young man in the 1950s. He writes in his memoirs about his difficulties in trying to buy a home in Nairobi five years before Independence. His friend Tom Mboya, a prominent Independence-era politician and member of the Legislative Council, had to enlist the help of an Asian friend to buy a plot of land in Lavington in 1958. Awori states that "the house remained in [Mboya's] friend's name until after the last Lancaster House Conference spelt out the timetable for Independence."[26] Though covenants were designed to exclude both "Asiatics" and Africans, Asians in 1958 were able to reside in more parts of the city than Africans.

In 1962 Awori and his wife, Rose, wanted to buy a house in Woodley Estate, a neighborhood developed by the Nairobi Municipal Council for European middle-level bureaucrats. Much like the title deed to my parents' house in Upper Hill, the title deed for this property stipulated that ownership was restricted to persons of pure European descent. However, by then there was a way to override that requirement for someone deemed acceptable. In order to buy the house, Awori had to obtain signed affidavits from all neighbors attesting that they did not object to African neighbors.[27]

The challenge to segregation and impermanence represented by the De Souza suit was answered by white flight and by racial covenants and caveats in title deeds that succeeded in maintaining segregation in the absence of explicit segregation laws. In the 1950s, the maintenance and implementation of these covenants and caveats started to unravel with the exit of Europeans from Kenya due to the Emergency, as well as recognition of the winds of change blowing in urban spaces.

THE QUESTION OF THE POOR

In 1963 Kenya gained independence from British rule following an armed rebellion in the early 1950s in the countryside and civic uprisings and trade union protests in the cities in the later 1950s. The rebellion started as a struggle for land led by the Kenya Land and Freedom Army that became known as the Mau Mau. Many of the participants were veterans of colonial forces in World War II, as were many of those who fought against them as a government paramilitary force called home guards. But many were also urban youths who were characterized as detribalized natives.

Between 1952 and 1958 the colonial government declared a state of emergency in response to the land agitation and anticolonial struggles, known colloquially as the Emergency. The Emergency disrupted life on many levels, wrenching apart families and communities, displacing people, changing ways of life, pulling out men for war. This was particularly true in the immediate surroundings of Nairobi. Among the Kikuyu people it led to a civil war between rebels and loyalists. Emergency policies affected specific areas of the cities, such as Bahati, forcing people to relocate and displacing others to the countryside or detention centers. The British detained and tortured thousands of Africans and a few Asians suspected of participating in the Mau Mau. In Nairobi alone 10 percent of the population was sent to detention centers.[28] After the Emergency, the battle for independence was mainly waged in urban spaces through trade unions.

The final terms of Kenya's constitutional framework and independence were negotiated in three conferences at Lancaster House in London. Independence did not eliminate colonial categories of inclusion and exclusion, such as "native" and "Asian," but rather transformed them to fit a national framework. The "native question" was reformulated as "the question of the poor." The focus on "natives" in the city as needed but unwanted labor shifted to a concern with rural migrants and the spaces they occupied (understood as temporary). The "Asian question" was rearticulated as a question of class and commercial competition.[29] The focus on the incorporation of nonnative racial others became a question of African inclusion in trade and business, with Asians classified as "migrant races" (also understood as temporary). These shifts were facilitated by the ways race and class determined not only where one could live but also salaries and occupations, which in turn affected the demographics of the city.

In the 1930s, the Railways had started to employ educated and skilled Africans in large numbers to save on the expense of European or Asian labor during the Depression. The result was an increase in Nairobi's population.[30] During the 1940s the population more than doubled because of wartime migration of all races into the city, as well as African expulsion from the White Highlands (the highly productive rural areas reserved for white settlement, many of which were near Nairobi).[31] African migrants to the city faced declining living standards, unemployment, low wages, a massive housing shortage, and curfews and influx controls to deal with the resulting unrest.[32]

Nevertheless, Nairobi continued to grow. Its population tripled in the 1950s because of a large expansion of the civil service and the Railways. While the economic and gender historian Claire Robertson describes the 1950s as "a watershed in terms of class formation in Kenya," it was also a time of changing racial and ethnic demographics.[33] My father remembers that when he left to attend Harvard University in 1957, all the government workers he interacted with were European. By the time he returned in 1962, they were mainly African. This shift was due not only to the employment of a larger number of African and Asian workers in the Railways and civil service but also to the white exodus from Kenya during the Emergency and with the approach of Independence.

The upheaval in the countryside around Nairobi during the Emergency, including starvation due to villagization in locations distant from farms, increasing landlessness, conscripted labor, and persecution by chiefs, increased migration into the city. Large numbers of residents (especially Kikuyu, Meru, and Embu) had been expelled from the city, and many urban men were detained in concentration camps. Women took over male roles as traders in the city. In 1958, with the end of the Emergency, thirty thousand men returned to Nairobi from detention, falling into competition with women who had remained in the city as traders.[34]

This competition was exacerbated from 1958, when the colonial administration rewarded male loyalists with exclusive licenses to trade.[35] After 1958 women, other ethnic groups, and nonloyalists were classified as "hawkers" and heavily policed and harassed, practices that were extended after Independence through Nairobi by-laws. Even as late as 2007, with the amendments to the by-laws, the term *hawker* remained, in Marianne Morange's words, "linked to ideas of vagrancy and loitering . . . used by colonial authorities."[36]

The terms *vagrancy* (wandering with no apparent home) and *loitering* (wandering with no apparent purpose) center instability. They combine the idea of being out of place in urban space with the notion of unproductiveness. Vagrancy and loitering laws have been used by governments to extract labor from and police the movements of the poor (they were enacted in many countries following the abolition of slavery). Kenya's Vagrancy Act of 1930 was repealed in 1997 and the vagabond offense in its penal code repealed in 2003.[37] Nevertheless, I know women who were arrested for sitting on their front steps talking to their neighbors at night.

The population increase during the Emergency drastically shifted Nairobi's ethnic makeup. The growing civil service attracted more and more educated people from the Lake Victoria region as well as workers of all kinds from the Nyanza, western, and Ukambani areas of Kenya. Africans in the civil service of the 1950s were predominantly from three ethnic groups—Luo, Luhya, and Kamba—and legal African trade was conducted almost exclusively by Kikuyu men.[38]

In 1962, a year before Independence, Asian Kenyans made up 35 percent of Nairobi's population, as they too had left smaller towns for the city.[39] In that year, only 3 percent of registered companies were owned by Africans, and 98 percent of skilled labor in Nairobi was Asian. To ameliorate the sense of injustice these imbalances created, and to help quell growing tensions over the timing and manner of Independence, the colonial government sought to encourage small-scale African traders. However, the close administrative supervision of these traders hindered rather than facilitated the growth of their ventures. It was hard to establish creditworthiness and deal with building restrictions. Tensions between Asians and Africans increased as a result of disparate access to trade licenses and credit, as well as a tenfold difference in earnings.[40]

REFRAMING THE ASIAN QUESTION AS AFRICANIZATION

As colonialism was a racial project, so too was Independence. In the late 1950s and early 1960s there were extensive debates over whether independent Kenya would be a multiracial nation or an African nation. African nationalism triumphed in the end. Of course, changing the state was a more difficult and complex matter.

Independence in 1963 was supposed to turn the colonial racial setup on its head. The native became the citizen, a subject with modern rights and responsibilities—no longer a person of the past but one of the future. Time now was no longer multifaceted, with some people relegated to the past and some seen as part of the future.

Nevertheless, the countryside remained associated with the past and the city with the future. The newly unified post-Independence understanding of time and space was troubled by the lasting dichotomy of native and detribalized native in Nairobi. Plans and policies governing these old categories were recoded as policies for dealing with the poor, while the old category of Asian was recoded as rich. The categories of detribalized native (urban poor) and Asian (urban rich) remained impermanent, mobile, and illegitimate; the category of native (rural poor) remained permanent, static, and legitimate.[41]

Two major forms of inequality set up by the racialization of space and time became particularly contentious as Independence approached—one rural (land) and one urban (commerce). The rural land problem was partially solved by Kenya's first president, Jomo Kenyatta, who negotiated a loan from the British to buy out European settlers. This allowed for redistribution of land without dispossession (for the settlers)—and created Kenya's first national debt.[42] The postcolonial government used the allocation of new land as one of the tools with which to address racial wealth disparities and meet the demand for land that had fueled the anticolonial struggle.[43]

Inequities in land ownership extended to the city, as most private land in Nairobi was held by Europeans or Asians, whereas most Africans lived on public land. In 1970, 60 percent of the land within the 1948 city boundaries of Nairobi was held by Asian business owners. Although Europeans owned large areas of land, most of it was large residential plots, while Asian-owned plots were characteristically small and high value. The amount of land owned by Africans was very small and subdivided into many small plots, especially in the traditionally African areas of the city. Although they made up 70 percent of the population of Nairobi in 1970, Africans still owned only 9 percent of the privately owned land in the city.[44]

The colonial government had a long history of using land allocation to develop the economy, thereby building individual wealth. European settlers had been allocated hundreds of acres of agricultural land to boost export agriculture, as well as urban allocations to boost trade. Land was later allocated to Asian traders and industrialists, and finally to a very select number of Africans, to boost industry. Allocation of urban land thus built, sustained, and reinforced first a racial and then a class elite.

After Independence, land allocations remained a primary means of rewarding political patronage. The government continued to allocate land titles to private holders. Kenyatta used former settler land as well as Crown land (which became government land) to solidify his support and build alliances.[45] The patronage system continued with the second president of Kenya, Daniel arap Moi.

If Europeans were the face of disparities in land ownership, Asians were the face of disparities in commerce and trade. In the lead-up to Independence Kenyatta argued that peace needed to come with capital, as reflected by the slogan *Uhuru na kazi* ("freedom and work"), and pushed for the Africanization of commerce.[46] Claire Robertson argues that the struggle for Africans to gain entrance into multinational companies and to control smaller businesses was cast in nationalist terms and facilitated by hostility towards Asian merchants.[47]

Just after Independence, two Asian Kenyan politicians of the time, Fitz de Souza (a member of parliament who later became the first deputy speaker of the House) and S. G. Amin, suggested that the government buy out Asian traders, in a manner similar to the buyout of European farmers, to distribute economic opportunity equitably. Yet this proposal proved troublesome. Although willing to provide loans to buy out British farmers, the British government was unwilling to underwrite the buyout of Asian traders, even though many were British subjects. Nor could Asians in Kenya appeal to newly independent India. With no prospects for a loan that would enable an Asian buyout, MP Tom Mboya instead proposed to promote Africanization by restricting licenses for certain types of business, agencies, contracts, and credit in favor of Africans. Implementation was piecemeal and incomplete, but the effect was to place Asians outside the nation, forcing them to prove their citizenship through loosening their hold on retail and trade.[48]

The situation for Asian Kenyans worsened. In 1965 Kenya's most prominent Asian political leader, the freedom fighter Pio Gama Pinto, was assassinated. As a result, in 1966 his friend Joseph Murumbi, who was part Goan, resigned as vice president of Kenya after only seven months in office. In 1967 several Asian Kenyans were deported as business competitors under new trading legislation. The new Kenya Immigration Bill canceled permanent residency certificates and replaced them with work permits. In the same year the Trade Licensing Bill required all businesses to reapply for licenses. Within six months, 18 percent of the Asian community in Kenya, approximately thirty-three thousand people, had left the country; and between 1962 and 1969, a total of fifty thousand Kenyan Asians left, mainly for the United Kingdom.[49]

Fourteen years later, Kenya saw another exodus of Asian Kenyans. In 1982, there was a failed coup attempt in Kenya. During days of chaos and fighting in Nairobi, there were attacks on Asian businesses and houses. Recalling President Idi Amin's 1972 expulsion of Asians from Uganda, many Asian families felt insecure in Kenya. At the same time, the 1980s structural adjustment policies, setting out to reduce protections, tariffs, and other trade barriers, had particularly negative effects on manufacturing in Kenya, an area in which Asian businesses were dominant. Finally, in the multiparty elections that started in 1992, Asians were pressured by all political parties to offer financial support. Kenya thus saw the rise of threats against Asians and growing insecurity for Asian businesses in the 1980s and '90s.

This insecurity was heightened by changes to Kenya's citizenship laws in 1985. Until then there were four ways a person could be considered a citizen of Kenya: by birth in the territory of the country or previous colony, with at least one parent born in the territory; by having a father who was a citizen by birth; by naturalization; and by registration. In 1985, an amendment to the Constitution Act No. 6 changed the criteria for citizenship by birth: a person had to be born in Kenya of parents who were both Kenyan citizens. The aim of this change was to displace Asian and European Kenyans from their businesses and restrict their ability to work and own property in Kenya. It was also a move calculated to exploit general anti-Asian sentiment. This change made a number of Asian Kenyans stateless.[50]

Much like the use of segregation, containment and rustication, the practices of Africanization and citizenship restrictions used space to deal with issues of wealth and class, the dynamics of which had long ago been put into play by colonial, anti-urbanist ideas of race, class, time, and space.

THE EXPANDING CITY

While some Africans made gains in land and home ownership after Independence, the changes in no way met the high demand for housing. From 1962 a shift of another sort—legal, quasi-legal, and illegal—began in areas that had once been native locations, buffer zones, farms, riparian reserves, and forest reserves just outside the city.[51] The expansion of Nairobi's city at Independence incorporated peri-urban and rural peoples and areas like Muthaiga, Kibera, Lang'ata, and the Nairobi National Park. The new boundaries encompassed agricultural, grazing, and "vacant" land.

Areas closest to the city center, within the old boundaries of Nairobi, grew first, as the rights to the properties were clear.[52] Much of the need for housing was first met by Asian businessmen who lived downtown, especially along River Road and in other buffer zones that formed the heart of Nairobi's commercial and Indian residential areas.[53] Many people lived in downtown Nairobi, often above shops. (My parents' first apartment after their marriage was in Pioneer House, right at the center of downtown, with a view over the city from the fourth floor.) Land for housing was also made available by established communities like the Nubian community in Kibera, who had recognized rights to land, and Somalis in Eastleigh who had bought land in prior decades or more recently from Asians leaving the area.

As part of Africanization, successful African traders who could show they had capital and a business proposal were allocated land for industrial development. As a young man, Moody Awori was involved both in business and charitable organizations in Nairobi that benefited from such land allocations, including a plot in Eastlands. In the 1970s Awori started a company that made roof tiles with financing from an Asian Kenyan, Lalit Pandit. Awori went to the Lands Office and asked the commissioner for land in Nairobi's industrial area on which to build a factory. He writes, "Within no time, I left his office with a letter of allotment for a direct allocation of a two-acre plot on Lunga Lunga Road. Within a month I had my title deed."[54]

Awori and Pandit also decided to form a separate property-development company. When they applied for a piece of land in South C, they received "a direct allocation of 30 acres." Finally, when Awori wanted to build a warehouse, he got financing from Continental Finance Company—one of the first African Kenyan finance businesses. He went back to the Lands Office and was "allocated an acre plot."[55] This kind of government support was central to enabling Awori, and other educated, connected Africans with capital (and often with Asian partners or financing), to build industry (and individual wealth) in Nairobi.

Little had changed, however, for the majority of Africans who did not have capital or access to credit. By 1970, most land in the western and northern areas of the city was in private hands (mainly European). In the lower-lying southeastern part of the city, most land was owned by the government.[56] In the buffer-zone areas of Parklands, Ngara, Juja, Eastleigh, and Mathare, more than half the land was Asian owned. Even in the old African locations, little land was owned by Africans.[57] The Nairobi City Council retained ownership of African residential estates and land in locations such as Kaloleni, Mbotela, Makadara, Jerusalem, Donholm, Maringo, and Jericho and parts of Eastleigh, Mathare, and Woodley.[58] And the Railways retained ownership of land in areas such as Muthurwa, Landhi Mawe, and Makongeni. Today all these areas are sites of public-private partnership regeneration projects.

Over the years, the city made concerted efforts to expand housing, which included municipal rental housing schemes. Jerusalem and Jericho were built by the Israeli government in Eastlands between 1961–62 and handed over to the city in the 1970s. Madaraka in Nairobi West was built for African professionals. Housing was also built on the land within the newly expanded city limits, including large tenant-purchase housing schemes such as Buruburu (built between 1974 and 1980 and cofunded by the British Commonwealth Development Corporation) and Nyayo Estate (built between 1999 and 2014 as a project of the National Social Security Fund), which were aimed at the middle class. Site-and-service housing schemes such as those in in Umoja, Huruma, and Kayole were mainly private developments on public or quasi-public land and aimed at the low-income population.[59]

Between 1964 and 1971, land values quadrupled in Nairobi, giving owners a decided financial advantage over renters.[60] Owners were mainly those who had been able to own land during the colonial period—Europeans, Asians, and Somalis and Nubians—as well as the new political and business classes of Africans.

TURUDI MASHAMBANI

Despite the expansion of the city and the provision of additional housing, the post-Independence government of Jomo Kenyatta was decidedly anti-urban. Indeed, Kenyatta adopted the slogan *turudi mashambani* ("let's go back to the rural areas").[61] Intended to promote agricultural development and limit growth, exert political power, and suppress dissent in cities in the 1960s and 1970s, *turudi mashambani* was turned into a government-sponsored song performed by the Mashambani Boys Band. It repeats Kenyatta's refrain, *turudi mashambani*, finishing with *tuijenge Kenya* ("let's build/develop Kenya"). Here, returning to the countryside is equated with building the country, while remaining in the city becomes a form of national betrayal. Notably, the slogan and the song call for people to *return* to the countryside, taking no account of those who were never rural in the first place.

As in socialist Tanzania or Mozambique (see the introduction), the "real" African of Kenyatta's decidedly capitalist dreams remained rural.[62] The countryside was the site of purity and potential, but also of acceptable poverty. The poor in the city were evidence of a failure of modernity. Kenyatta referred to the poorest city dwellers as *ragai*, which, loosely translated, means "lazy" or "useless," and used colonial-era public health laws to evict and rusticate them.[63] This terminology exemplifies the way the poor were treated as the post-Independence version of the "detribalized native." They and their poverty were out of place in the city.

Indeed, the unemployed and the poor became an eyesore and a political liability that challenged the modernity of the city. The sociologist Kinuthia Macharia argues that "from the point of view of those in power, the slums constituted a political (rather than a public health) 'nuisance,' mainly because they were thought to be harboring and/or creating political activists who were supporting the call for the end of the single-party state." Under a government obsessed with maintaining law and order, the demolition tools of anti-urbanism were reinstated with vigor and wrath.[64] Not only were the poor out of place, but, being out of place. they were "detribalized" and criminalized.

As the city expanded eastward, accommodating millions of people and creating vibrant new commercial centers, it occupied what had once been considered a swamp—a flat plain with black cotton soil. The eastward expansion of the city in the 1970s and '80s included the growth of African locations under municipal control, Railways lands that were becoming more and more derelict, green buffer zones, riparian leeways, agricultural lands, rangelands, and unregulated settlements. Much of this land was held by the Nairobi City Council, the Railways, or the government as former Crown land. Some land was bought from farmers, but the majority was not titled. To the north, the city incorporated forests, agricultural land, and some unregulated settlements. To the south, it expanded over Maasai group ranches and grazing lands that were being privatized and subdivided.

Some of the housing expansion was on a small scale, involving add-ons to one-story structures. But the allocation of public land for private development in the 1990s created new landowners in Nairobi. At the end of the Cold War, the government embraced market-oriented neoliberal ideas of privatization and entrepreneurship. Politicians sought to represent Nairobi as an attractive site for global investment through the privatization of services, decentralization, public-private partnerships, and the application of market principles to everyday life.[65] Yet the 1990s were marked by declining resources, soaring inflation, and political change. Corruption flourished, with the political circle of Kenya's second president, Daniel arap Moi, increasingly using public land as a source of patronage assets.[66] Nairobi quickly became a concrete jungle of high-rise tenements.[67] Such structures are often built without official approval and in violation of building regulations. The result is unstable buildings with substandard services and no green spaces or trees (see chapters 5, 7, and 8). The benefits, of course, went to the wealthy.

The blogger, photographer, and urban planner Baraka Mwau describes the rise of tenements in Nairobi as "a form of 'slum upgrading' driven by the private sector."[68] He posits that the transition to tenements came in three forms: on-site conversion of shack structures to tenements; redevelopment schemes such as the site-and-service schemes of the 1980s; and greenfield development on newly subdivided land. However exploitative the housing schemes might have been, they met an urgent demand. Mwau and the town planning consultant Miriam Maina point out that tenements "offer affordable rental housing in convenient locations for the city's low- and middle-income residents," and they are "customized to the tenants' financial capacity and demands, offering varying sizes and typologies."[69] Tenement construction also followed a historical precedent: the ten-by-ten-foot rooms common in such structures match the dimensions of the colonial-era bachelor housing in African residential estates.

In an article from April 2023, Hassan Mugambi laments that the once green, leafy suburbs of Kilimani and Kileleshwa (former European townships) are becoming concrete jungles of "vertical slums." He quotes a resident who complains that "a developer has packed an entire block comprising 900 bedsitters (single rooms), studio and one-bedroom apartments onto a one-acre piece of land" that is not supported by sewage, water, road, or other service infrastructure.[70]

The same is true of parts of the city that were never leafy suburbs. Tiny apartments in tenement buildings became the only kinds of spaces that the poor living in Nairobi could afford to live in.[71] These forms of housing are considered temporary and are typically located in areas also designated as impermanent, in the eastern part of the city. Their state of impermanence threatens the logic of permanence found in the fancier neighborhoods.

Over the last one hundred years, governments have resorted to a range of tactics to deal with the needed but unwanted populations of Nairobi: bachelor workers, natives, detribalized natives, Asians, women, the elderly, and children. Through practices such as containment, rustication, segregation, and expulsion, the people in the city were rendered temporary. Through the creation of barrack housing, native locations, and later high-rise tenements, the places where they lived were rendered temporary as well.

This situation is perhaps not so different from other places in the world where unwanted populations are relegated to ghettos, slums, and tenement cities—areas marked by disinvestment, decay, and regeneration. The anti-urbanism of Nairobi, however is based on race as well as class. It demands that we look at the way both people and places are classified as temporary. Nairobi reveals the foundations on which racialized assumptions take shape, their structural implantation, and their longevity in the shaping of daily life. Although circumstances have changed, governments have changed, and constituents have changed, the anti-urbanism built into the spaces and times of Nairobi continues to exert its force. It reverberates across all the city, making all its inhabitants potentially out of place and time, and threatens urbanity itself.

4

———

Dancing to the Sound of Nairobi

I was seated in a house in Loresho, a leafy neighborhood at the edge of Nairobi, interviewing a lady who lived in Makongeni (a Railways housing estate) at the end of the 1950s. As she recalled the dances of her youth, her eighty-year-old face lit up. She smiled and, with a twinkle in her eye, told me: "The slow waltz. The slow waltz was *my* dance."[1] She stood up and started to sing, swaying to the music. I imagined this elegant woman dancing, full of fire and grace, to a slow waltz. I saw her in the umbrella ball gowns she told me she had worn and also made for others, copied from dresses ordered from British mail-order catalogues, her skirt twirling almost straight out as she turned, a pearl necklace at her neck.

I imagine her dancing with someone she probably never knew—a man I interviewed in Karen, an upmarket suburb of Nairobi, in 2013. I see him dressed in the white tuxedo jacket he got a tailor to make the first time he traveled to England, with black trousers, smooth-soled shoes of patent leather, and socks that match his trousers exactly. He glides across the floor, improvising as the music changes, attuned to every detail of the song. His hair is parted at the side, and a bow tie adorns his neck.

I see them surrounded by similarly dressed dancers: men in black or white double-breasted suits, women in floral calf-length skirts that billow out as they turn. Some women wear shawls around their shoulders, elegant and dignified. The couples dance on the polished wooden floor in a hall with tall windows on both sides, like a church. The band plays on a stage, and drinks are served at the end of the hall. A line of chairs against the wall offers dancers a place to rest.

This dance takes place in a social hall in one of Nairobi's African residential housing estates, like Pumwani, Muthurwa, or Kaloleni. The dances are ballroom dances, European and Latin American, but they are inflected with movements and gestures revealing the dancers' ancestry in different parts of Kenya. The music is a unique Nairobi sound.

Studies of popular urban music in Africa tend to focus on migrants, emphasizing the social and cultural change associated with the rise of urban centers.[2] Many also focus, as I do in this chapter, on the transition to independence from colonial rule. They are concerned with configurations of generation, gender, respectability, and status in colonial segregated spaces and the building of new urban and national identities. Dance, music, and leisure more generally are viewed as spaces of political and cultural negotiation and change.[3] Most such studies point to the close relationship between music and politics, as well as the creation of new cosmopolitan identities. This chapter extends this scholarship by looking at the built environment where these changes occurred, in particular the ways that social halls, and the sound and movement within them, served as a challenge to anti-urbanism.

The social halls were built by the colonial administration to provide an outlet for what they perceived as the excess energy of detribalized natives. They provided exercise (such as boxing) and entertainment (films and dance) for veterans from the two world wars, and domestic training (cooking, sewing, needlework) for workers' wives, in order to produce an urban African of a certain kind. Ironically, it was through these spaces and these sounds that alternative visions of African futures and modernity also took shape. Some of the attendees at the social halls participated in the Lancaster House conferences in London that set out the terms of Kenya's independence. Others used the social halls as spaces in which to renegotiate urban sociality, restructuring employment, incorporating the global into leisure and politics, and shaping modernity on their own terms.

Nairobi became pivotal in national politics during the 1950s and '60s, as anti-urbanist policies equated the city with modernity and progress, and thus with the future. Politicians prominent in Kenya's independence movements (such as Tom Mboya, Joseph Murumbi, Argwings Kodhek, Tom Mbotella, and Mwai Kibaki, along with Pio Gama Pinto, Makan Singh, and Fitz de Souza) lived in and represented Nairobi prior to Independence and met in its social halls. And the cosmopolitan, multiethnic, urban "Nairobi Sound," the people who produced it and danced to it, the spaces it occupied, and the politics they embraced substantially influenced the transition to independence as well as the identity of the new nation of Kenya.

This chapter is about the struggle to be *watu wa kisasa*—modern city people—in the face of colonial denial.[4] In the segregated African housing estates of the 1950s and 1960s, music and dancing posed a challenge to anti-urbanism and a refashioning of the city. I examine the spaces of these leisure activities in Nairobi—and the urban identities that the activities created—in their social, economic, political, and architectural context. I describe how everyday activities can contest attempts to exclude people from enjoying the city and making it their own.

African residents of Nairobi challenged anti-urbanism by transforming the social hall from a place of pacifying activities prescribed by colonial administrators into a space for cultural production and political organizing, as well as for the integration and adaptation of international sounds, movements, and fashions. They created local urban cultures, including the Nairobi Sound, that centered the city in the national and international imagination. In the social hall, this modern urban culture took the forms of ballroom dancing, the music that people danced to, the art and styles it enabled, the advertising and industries that recognized its power, and the people who made it their own.

SPACES OF LEISURE IN A WORKING CITY

The first time I visited a social hall in Nairobi was with my father in the 1990s. We had gone to visit the neighborhood of Muthurwa, where he grew up. The Muthurwa Social Hall reminded me of a church hall with its tall windows, wooden floors, and raised stage. The building was not in the best of shape but still stood strong. As my father chatted with someone who remembered our family, I stared at the light that hit a wooden floor tile protruding from the center of the floor. In 2012, when I was working on a film project, I returned to Muthurwa Hall and also visited the halls in Pumwani, Makongeni, and Kaloleni.[5] By then, all the buildings were showing signs of wear. The land around them had been built up. Next to Muthurwa Hall stood a huge market with informal extensions. Kaloleni Hall was now situated next to a bar and restaurant. Inside the halls, ceiling panels were hanging down, floor tiles were ripped up, and some windows were broken. But all the buildings were still in use, albeit more as venues for religious meetings or voter registration than for film, music, and dance. The week I visited, Kaloleni Hall was being used for a commercial expo. When I returned in 2020, the local NGO Book Bunk had partnered with the Nairobi City County and local communities to restore branches of the McMillan Library, one of which was at Kaloleni.[6] The library had been restored beautifully, and the hall was next in line.

The idea of the social hall as a means of pacifying the working class came from 1930s Britain, where local centers were established to foster "community life" and occupy "idle" urban dwellers in the new housing estates arising out of slum-clearance schemes.[7] In settler colonies like Kenya and Rhodesia (now Zimbabwe), the fear of the idle urban resident took a racial form. The building of recreational facilities and the prescribing of recreational activities were means of controlling the native urban populations.[8]

Colonial control entailed maintaining a clear spatial and temporal division between work and leisure. As the social scientist Bodil Folke Frederiksen argues, "Work in the form it was needed by Europeans, wage labor, presupposes a certain way of computing time, of dividing a day in one's own and somebody else's time. And a certain view of space, accepting one place for work, and another for reproduction and free time."[9] The Railways, whose trains ran to precise schedules, excelled in the control of time and space. The timing of the trains and workers' shifts was marked by the *king'ora*, and the barrack housing for Railways staff regulated their home lives.

In Nairobi, the initial purpose of the social halls on African housing estates was to help resettle returning war veterans into civilian life by offering a venue for physical and social activities.[10] Between 1920 and 1960 almost every housing estate built for Africans had a social hall. One of the first and most important social halls was Memorial Hall in Pumwani, in eastern Nairobi, built by the Municipality of Nairobi Council in 1924.[11] The name Pumwani means "resting place," derived from *pumua* (Swahili for "breathe, relax").[12] It was a planned "native location" built in reaction to the 1921 rise of the East African Association and the Harry Thuku riots (see chapter 1).[13] The Muthurwa Social Hall (first known as Landhies Social Hall and later as Dallas) was built in 1923. Located in the central Railways area along Landhies Road, the hall was famous for union activity prior to Independence and later for the production of world-class boxers and footballers. In the 1930s halls were built in the housing estates of Shauri Moyo, Tobacco Village, and Bahati.

In the late 1940s, the Ziwani, Starehe, Kaloleni, and Makongeni halls were built. Kaloleni Hall, in a new, upscale government housing estate, was the largest and most elaborate. It had a grand entrance, a number of attached rooms, and a branch of the McMillan Library. At about the same time, the Railways built the Makongeni estate to house an additional five thousand workers. The housing in Makongeni still had communal kitchens, but the estate also had welfare clinics, a club, a library and reading room, a dance hall and tearoom, football grounds, and tennis courts.[14]

The huge expansion of the Railways and the civil service brought Africans— especially educated Africans—in larger and larger numbers into Nairobi. This expansion of the population was accompanied by a changing wage structure, increased industrialization, the growth of private entrepreneurship, the development of trade unions, and the creation of class-differentiated family housing.[15] The largest number of migrants came from three regions of Kenya—western Kenya, Nyanza, and Ukambani—and brought with them traditions, sounds, and rhythms that came to define the Nairobi Sound.

All the halls charged an entry fee for dances, about the same amount as going to the cinema, so they drew from a salaried audience. Usually when a couple went dancing, the man would buy the tickets. While the men waited in line for tickets, they bought the women sodas to keep them entertained. Men in Nairobi outnumbered women by four to one because of the restrictions on women living in Nairobi and the colonial expectation that workers should be bachelors or leave their wives at home in the countryside. So men without partners would dance alone.[16] Often single men would come and ask a woman to dance while her date was still in line. Although my interlocutors recalled that all men respected a woman's refusal, the gender imbalance of the city caused tensions among men, expressed in song lyrics, dance, and

FIGURE 6. Kaloleni Social Hall. Photo by author.

sometimes violence. Memorial Hall at Pumwani was notorious for fights.[17] One Nairobi resident remembers that her husband, who was a boxer, loved going there because of the possibility of a fight, while she avoided it for the same reason.[18]

Muthurwa Social Hall was very popular for both music and boxing. It was also the hall closest to the central business district and the European and Asian areas of town. The Railways recorded radio shows there, such as *Happy Hour* and *Railway Showboat*, with large live audiences. The hall also hosted many political and union meetings, and of course films. Along with ballroom dancing, the social halls hosted traditional dances (especially for weddings and funerals) and allowed people to set up their own concerts and comedy theater shows.[19]

Because Kaloleni's residents were mainly Nairobi City Council workers, it was thought of as an upscale area. Its social hall, distinguished by its architecture and size, was less heavily policed than the halls associated with Railways housing: one resident recalled that he was able to buy *chang'aa* (moonshine) in Kaloleni, but not in Makongeni.[20] It was in the Kaloleni Hall that some of the most important dance competitions were held, with participants coming from housing estates across the city. In the late 1940s and 1950s the hall also became associated not with the betterment of urban Africans according to colonial intent, but with nationalist political activism; it was colloquially known as the House of Parliament.[21]

DANCING IN NAIROBI'S SOCIAL HALLS

The social halls in African residential estates held performances of traditional dances, but when people spoke of going dancing, they meant ballroom-style dancing with live music. Ethnic organizations, other businesses, and the halls themselves hosted dances as fundraisers.[22] Pumwani, Muthurwa, and Kaloleni were the most popular dance venues, in part because of their central location. Many of the halls were close to each other because of the concentration of African residential housing. One resident who moved from Muthurwa to Kaloleni in 1945 (when Kaloleni was "brand new") remembers that it took the destruction of three football fields between Makongeni and Muthurwa to build Kaloleni.[23] Although people might cross the eastern part of the city for dances, often they went to the nearest dance hall, and, as one of my older relatives put it, "Railway people mainly stayed within the vicinity of the Railways."[24]

Pumwani had a bustling night life. Residents describe it in the 1950s as having "hotels which were open all night, . . . with music going on." They remember "attending ballroom dances, cinema going, and listening to bands hired by the municipal authority," as well as "orderly dances in the Pumwani Memorial Hall, supervised by teachers and social workers." In 1958, when Kenya's first jukebox was installed in the hall, people from all over Nairobi came to dance to its music. In 1956 and 1957, 500 films were shown in the hall, and in 1957 it hosted 110 dances and 300 meetings.[25]

The music and dance of the social halls was inspired by international influences from radio, film, and travel as well as vernacular influences from the different regions of Kenya. Both types of influence were circumscribed by colonialism. Imported music and films were restricted to those considered politically safe. This music included Caribbean sounds like son, rumba, cha-cha-cha, and calypso, and

American dance music such as the twist and rock and roll.[26] But it did not include African American music. Films were generally limited to the classic colonial genres of Westerns and musicals. Meanwhile, influences from different regions of Kenya were affected by the relative mobility of different people, due to three factors: the historic regional pull of the Railways, the location of educational facilities across Kenya, and the restrictions of the Emergency.

Kenyanized ballroom styles included the waltz, quickstep, foxtrot, merengue, cha-cha-cha, samba, rumba, and tango, along with rock and roll, twist, and calypso.[27] Different residential estates organized teams for ballroom dancing competitions, and some of the competitors went on to represent their estate and Nairobi in competitions elsewhere in the country. People could even make a living teaching ballroom dancing.[28] One Nairobi resident remembers coaching a dance group from the residential estate of Ziwani that won a competition in Kaloleni in 1956. The next year he competed himself and won a competition in Nakuru, and in 1961 he won the prize of a ram at a competition at Ofafa Memorial Hall in Kisumu.[29]

Innovation allowed for the mixing of genres and the creation of personal and local dance styles and identities. Improvisation allowed dancers to combine their heritage with this new form of dance. The ballroom coach in Ziwani explained that he never learned how to dance; rather, he said, "Dancing is part and parcel of someone who is cultured." He said his mother was an amazing dancer, and so was his elder sister, though neither of them lived in the city or danced to ballroom music. His mother was a leader in traditional dances, and his ability came from her. While still in school he spent two years in a dance troupe in the countryside. His cousin was a great player of the *orutu* (one-string violin) and a wandering entertainer who performed with an entourage of dancers made up of his younger relatives. This man made no distinction between traditional and newer forms of dance; rather, he saw the art of dance as an ability to respond to music. When I asked him if he ever danced the twist, he replied, "The twist? There was no art to it. No art at all."[30] For a dancer to demonstrate skill in improvisation, movement, and rhythm, the dance, whether traditional or modern, needed to be complex.

In her study of leisure and popular culture in early Nairobi, Frederiksen quotes Dedan Githegi, assistant African affairs officer in the 1940s, discussing why Africans did not enthusiastically take up colonial recreation activities at first. He argued that prior to being in the city, Africans went to dances to show off their dance skills, to decorate themselves, and to attract young girls. His implication was that the city did not accommodate these elements of dance.[31] Yet Africans in Nairobi integrated competition, style, and sexuality into their ballroom dancing through improvisation. Creating new steps that impressed others was part of the fun. One Nairobi resident recalls being asked by a friend—who would later become attorney general of Kenya—how to perform one of his signature steps. He replied, "Just watch. One day I will teach you. One day."[32]

Part of the dancer's skill is to move with the music, especially if the tempo changes.[33] The dancer must listen closely and have a repertoire of steps to deploy when needed. To do this, Nairobi's ballroom dancers drew on African dance traditions while also improvising new steps to add to learned ballroom steps. In dance competitions the ability to improvise could make or break the competitor.

Dancing was not an inexpensive pastime. Women dressed up in long ball gowns or shorter, less formal dresses, depending on the occasion. One Nairobi resident remembers that the skirts had gathers so that they would lift and billow out when the dancers twirled. These were called umbrella skirts. For competitive dancing, dress was as important as the steps. Even the color of a man's socks mattered. In addition, dress was a sign of class. Many people stressed that their attention to the details of style, grace, and fashion was a statement about who they were. As increasing numbers of educated Africans joined the civil service in Nairobi during the 1950s, class distinctions became increasingly important. Some residents who grew up in Railway housing said that better-paid Railway manual laborers—people like train engineers or firemen—were criticized by women when they appeared in the social halls in clothes smudged with soot or grease from the train engines.[34]

People in Nairobi absorbed many of the latest dance and dress styles from abroad through films, which helped define modern urban life.[35] Although by the late 1950s dancing to live music was in decline in other parts of the world, it was kept alive in musicals through performers like Gene Kelly and Fred Astaire.[36] With the influence of films, the growing economic autonomy of city people, and access to international style influences, came ballroom dancing on the grand scale.[37]

Social halls were also used to host ballroom dances in other parts of East Africa. By the early 1940s the African dancing clubs were organizing dances (*dansi*) in Dar es Salaam.[38] In fact, in Tanganyika, dancing in a European style (such as ballroom) to African bands was the most popular activity at social halls, as well as the halls' main source of revenue.[39] Invitation cards sent out by dance clubs designated the dress code (always Western clothing) of the occasion. The clubs rented the social halls and hired bands known as African "jazz bands," who mainly played Latin-influenced, guitar-based dance music, such as rumba, with lyrics usually sung in Swahili.[40] The historian Emily Callaci argues that through the medium of *dansi* and letters to newspapers about it, urban Tanganyikans expressed not only concerns about racial uplift in the context of racism but also "struggles over pressing matters such as social inequality, the boundaries of urban belonging, female virtue, and male access to intimacy with women."[41]

In Kenyan and Tanganyikan cities dance and music offered one means of undoing the structures of anti-urbanism that positioned Africans as people of the past. Being up on the latest films, fashion, music, and dance styles was a way of being globally aware and modern. Dance and music styles challenged the static tribal identities of the colonial imagination, allowing people to be local as well as global. They allowed tradition to influence a global style. They celebrated a global youth culture, much as popular music functions today. But this was a global youth culture of the dancers' choosing, modified by their own tastes. And neither the dance nor the songs were mimicry, for mimicry implies being out of place or time, striving to emulate a "correct" version. Rather, in African dance halls, the international styles were transformed, made current, and given flair by local interpretations.

THE NAIROBI SOUND

The music produced in Nairobi was always dance music, performed by live bands. Dance drove the production of music and vice versa, and the two art forms gave expression to the same social issues. Musicians sang about the difficulty of being urban—a theme that persisted after independence. They sang about the lack of jobs and education; the prevalence of prostitution, violence, overcrowding, poverty, and marital problems; and the difficulties of housing, love, and the pace of city life.[42] But they also sang of travel, to far-off places like America as well as within East Africa. While musicians sang of decidedly urban themes, including the foibles of the growing working class and their daily battles to forge tenable moral codes, they also sang of memories of their rural upbringing.[43]

Unlike rural musicians, who sang mainly in vernacular languages, these urban musicians sang in Swahili and sometimes in English. Swahili enabled them to reach the multilingual audiences of the city. The popular-culture researcher Joyce Nyairo argues that in these songs (and, I would add, dances), "the experience of modernity crystallizes around the key images of Western education and the struggle over new languages (Kiswahili and English), the car, bottled beer, and foreign dances."[44] As Swahili was the quintessential language of the Railways, the Railways investment in popular music on the radio also influenced the use of Swahili in songs.

The military influenced both music and dance. Veterans of the First and Second World Wars and working soldiers during the Emergency had more disposable cash than others in Nairobi. Those who had been part of military musical bands brought back their experience of entertaining troops abroad and a familiarity with Western instruments such as the guitar and the accordion.[45]

These musicians adapted the band music they had learned to local styles. Until that time local music (other than hymns or marching band music) had been stigmatized because of its association with "pagan" African religious practices. So strong was this association that in Rhodesia, the colonial government even banned specific instruments, such as the *mbira* (a string instrument).[46] However, after World War II, gramophones became popular, and so did the range of dance music records produced by the GV recording company, which influenced local musicians. The chief promoters of the new music were the army and police bands, which included rumbas and cha-cha-chas in their dance repertoires.[47] These bands played in venues such as the City Park bandstand, where they drew a large and diverse urban audience.[48] My father and his contemporaries told me of their trips to City Park as children and young adults to relax and hear the bands on weekends. One resident of Nairobi in the 1940s remembers Italian prisoners of war playing in bands at the Muthurwa Social Hall.[49]

Groups like the Sudanese Brass Band, which played in Muthurwa and other African social halls, came out of this military tradition. Some musicians who had been trained in military bands joined dance-music bands.[50] The world-famous musician Fundi Konde moved from playing flute and clarinet in a military band to singing, playing guitar, and eventually producing music. As part of the Entertainment Unit of the King's African Rifles, Konde joined East African soldiers in Ceylon (Sri Lanka), India, and Burma and played not only for African troops but for British and Indian troops as well. He had performed some 350 shows by the end of World War II. He is still remembered in parts of India. After the War, Konde acquired the first electric pickup guitar to be seen or heard in East Africa.[51] With fellow veterans Peter Colmore, Ally Sykes, and David Katuga, he formed the African Band, which toured the country, composing and performing advertising jingles and playing for the colonial broadcasting service. The band helped establish popular music in Kenya.[52]

Most people I interviewed mentioned hearing the Sudanese Brass Band play for ballroom dances in Muthurwa Social Hall. From its name we can assume the band members were among the Sudanese (Nubian) troops who served in the King's African Rifles during the war and afterward settled in Kibera. Although I could not find specific information about this often-mentioned band, Nubian band leaders, such as Mohamed Absura, were famous in Nairobi for training some of the best school marching bands, like the Starehe Boys Band, as well as marching bands for the police, the prison service, and the Salvation Army.[53]

Returning soldiers brought with them ideas of dance etiquette that were influential throughout the 1950s. One example was the manner in which a man asked a woman to dance, by bowing and offering his hand.[54] Many men I spoke with described the formality of asking a woman to dance and the crushing feeling of being rejected. One told me, "You would cross the big empty hallway to where the woman is seated. Once you get there you bow and extend your right hand, saying, 'May I have this dance?' But if she is to say no, you turn around and have to face this endlessly big room to cross back alone."[55]

The Railways had an outsized influence on music in Nairobi. A number of musicians who became famous were Railways employees, including George Mukabi, Jackton Malenya, and Daudi Kabaka.[56] In a sense, Kabaka owed his name to the Railways. His father worked at the Railways depot in Kampala, Uganda. Born on the day that the Kabaka Daudi Chwa II (the Buganda king) passed away, the baby was named after the Kabaka. Musicians with a Railways background incorporated it into their songs, including the idea of travel throughout East Africa. It is not surprising that they often performed in Muthurwa Social Hall.

The Railways also promoted popular music through their radio shows *Happy Hour* and *Railway Showboat*. These shows played at prime time and emphasized Swahili, the lingua franca of the Railways. In addition, every railway station had a wired radio that played music all day. And although workers' housing in Muthurwa lacked electric light, a wired radio was installed in every one-room house.[57] Railway workers and customers were thus closely tied to the radio, and in turn they influenced radio programming.

As the main employer in the city and the main form of travel, the Railways literally brought musicians, rhythms, styles, and sounds to Nairobi. In addition, the development of radio and recording industries in Nairobi, part of the economic boom that followed World War II, attracted musicians from elsewhere in East and Central Africa.[58] In the 1950s, finger-picking styles of guitar playing became popular across East Africa.[59] The guitarists were often accompanied by the rasp and ring of a rhythm section made up of glass Fanta (soda) bottles. This first generation of guitar and bottle musicians, who included John Mwale, Jim Lasco, David Amunga, and George Mukabi, drew heavily on Luhya rhythms and progressions associated with the *isukuti* percussion music from western Kenya.[60] Urban Luhya guitarists also borrowed the traditional Luhya *sukuma* and *omutibo* dance rhythms.[61]

These Luhya sounds in Nairobi music were nurtured and promoted by recording studios along River Road, predominantly Indian owned. The labels Capitol Music Stores (CMS) and African Gramophone Stores (AGS) had their greatest success selling Swahili songs performed by a stable of musicians. Many of their members were from western Kenya but had gone to school in Nairobi. They included people like John Nzenze, John Mwale, Jim Lasco, and Isaya Mwinamo. They produced *twisti* (a version of the twist with East African and southern African influences) but had more success with a rumba sound.[62] George Mukabi was perhaps the most famous of the finger-picking-style musicians who recorded on River Road labels, and his music incorporated the Luhya sounds into rumba.

The Nairobi Sound incorporated influences from outside Kenya as well. Konde, for instance, emphasized that his band studied and performed the latest dance hits from America.[63] In the early 1950s, the GV label distributed Latin American music, including rumba, cha-cha-cha, and samba. Kenyan rumba incorporated Cuban son and Congolese influences. Recordings by the great Congolese guitarists Jean-Bosco Mwenda and Eduard Masengo from the Katanga region of the Congo were produced in Kenya and sold all over East and Central Africa. As a result, Kenyan guitarists came to copy the Katanga style of Congolese rumba. The inspiration for *twisti* came not only from American popular music of twist and rock and roll but also southern African popular music—*kwela, sinjonjo,* and township jive.[64] In addition, people danced to the music of musicians from other regions of Africa who were resident in Nairobi, such as Mwenda and Masengo (Congo), Peter Tsotsi (Rhodesia) and Frankie and Sisters (Tanganyika).[65] In the 1960s came calypso and the influence of the American musician Harry Belafonte. Finally, there was the influence of Western music generally.

The musician and scholar John Low argues that Kenyan finger stylists "developed their own distinctive styles, easily recognizable from those of other countries."[66] Later urban bands combined rumba rhythms and two-part harmonies.[67] In addition, musicians such as Olima Anditi pushed Luo dance rhythms into acoustic guitar music, forming the beginnings of the lively Nairobi music style *benga*, which came to dominate Kenyan music after Independence. Today it is the best-known Kenyan sound. From this great melting pot of influences gradually emerged distinctively Kenyan styles that had a feeling of their own.[68]

The dance culture and Nairobi Sound of the 1950s and '60s defied anti-urbanist ideas of where and how people should be modern, what they should sound like, and how they should look. Dancers and musicians refused the city as a place of work alone and instead defined it as a place of leisure and freedom. The lyrics of their songs were social commentaries on the city. From segregated spaces in Nairobi performers reached out across the nation, Africa, and the world, and drew in ingredients and flavors to spice their unique, local, urban art forms.

TAPPING AFRICAN MODERNITY THROUGH MUSIC AND DANCE

The Nairobi Sound was popular as well as distinctive. Elite urban guitarists earned good money from performing in bars, hotels, concert venues, and dance halls; recording advertisements, and appearing in radio shows.[69] One reason for this success was the growth of a salaried urban population. Another was the emergence of programming, advertising, and propaganda aimed at a nationwide rather than regional radio audience. Because of this broader audience, the music also coincided with, and reinforced, the rise of anticolonial movements and the push for independence. The reach of the music as well as the spaces of its production—the social halls of Nairobi—helped propel national political organizing after the Emergency.

Kenya had its first regular radio broadcasts starting in 1927, intended for an audience of European settlers.[70] Radio use was heavily promoted by the colonial government. Africans in Nairobi bought radios for community centers, cafes, and bars. Frederiksen notes that radios were also "given free of charge to individual Africans thought to be influential or [who] might be hired at a reasonable price."[71] However, during the Emergency, broadcasting served counterinsurgency measures.[72]

In 1959 the Kenya Broadcasting Service came into being out of the African Broadcasting Service, with broadcasts in English on one service, Hindi and Gujarati on another, and Swahili on a third. A regional service broadcast from Nairobi in Kamba and Kikuyu, from Kisumu in Luo and Luhya, and from Mombasa in

Swahili and Arabic.[73] These services enabled recording studios to make money through sponsored programs and advertisements.[74] The radio also became a platform for promoting musicians and entertainers. The radio and recording studios began to influence both rural and urban guitarists.

If the Railways helped create a radio audience for the Nairobi Sound, the advertising industry consolidated it. After World War II, advertisers recognized that instead of marketing only to a small, wealthy European market, they could make great profits by promoting cheaper goods to the growing African market. They used music to advertise on the radio. Meanwhile, in the face of massive strikes by African employees, the Railways strove to repair their reputation through popular radio programs. They too did so by means of music played on the radio. These forces helped shape the sound of Kenya and enabled people across the country to hear, sing, and dance to songs expressing urban themes. They made rural audiences long for Nairobi, even as some of the songs longed for rural spaces left behind.

In the 1950s advertisers began to see Africans as consumers. Items such as gramophones became popular acquisitions among affluent urban residents, providing entertainment and exhibiting status in an increasingly class-conscious society.[75] In order to increase profits, however, advertisers had to build a national audience for their products. The advertising entrepreneurs Peter Colmore, Charles Worrod, and Ally Sykes were quick to grasp the opportunities of consumerism, mobilizing entertainment—both music and comedy—to sell products. In the process, they helped develop a national feeling around the music and contributed to local musicians' success in the 1960s. Their advertising jingles helped make certain products (like Aspro, a form of aspirin) into household names around East Africa. According to Sykes, "The best musicians East Africa had ever known were used to promote these products."[76] Music for radio advertising sold not only products but also songs, aspirations, ideas, and styles. Its incorporation of sonic influences from places like South Africa and the United States enhanced a sense of connection with a global urban youth culture. It helped create the Nairobi Sound.

Sykes and Colmore originally met in 1942 in a music store in Nairobi. Although Colmore was British and Sykes from Tanganyika, they were both in King's African Rifles (KAR) uniform, waiting to be transported overseas for active service, and as such exchanged greetings. Sykes was only sixteen years old. After the war Sykes came to Nairobi to take advantage of its growing economic opportunities and worked with Colmore in advertising as a public relations officer. They decided to start a band. With Sykes, a former member of the KAR Entertainment Unit, in charge, the band became very popular in Nairobi. Colmore recorded the American Top Ten hits from the Voice of America radio broadcasts, and the band played the songs soon after they were released—to white audiences in fancy Nairobi hotels and clubs.[77]

Ally Sykes was the perfect partner for Colmore. He came from a family involved in the dance-hall music scene in Dar es Salaam and had his own band, the

Merry Blackbirds.[78] He was also politically active as one of the seventeen founders of TANU (the Tanganyika African National Union), with connections across Tanganyika. He brought to the collaboration a clear understanding of the winds of change in East Africa.

In the 1940s, Sykes' father, Kleist Sykes, had started the controversial Tanganyika Islamic Jazz Club, which was part of the complicated system of ballroom dance clubs in Tanganyika known as *dansi*. Callaci argues that "through *dansi*, [Kleist] Sykes sought both to create a kind of social status based on pan-urban cosmopolitan culture, and to link Muslim identity with emerging forms of prestige."[79] Ally Sykes was well aware of the power of *dansi* and music to sell products, proclaim a modern identity, and form an audience and community. In Tanganyika, much as in Nairobi, social halls were spaces of conspicuous self-display, where young urban men and women deployed fashion, dance moves, and an elaborate slang vocabulary.[80] These displays of urban style were ways not only of claiming a cosmopolitan urban identity but also of participating in a new consumer culture.

Colmore and Sykes worked with the legendary music producer Charles Worrod. Although born in Britain, Worrod came to Kenya from South Africa, with a background in journalism, theater, and publicity, and a taste for *kwela* music. The genius of Colmore, Worrod, and Sykes was that they understood how entertainment and marketing could work together.

Colmore became a very successful media and entertainment businessman and in 1961 founded his own recording company, High Fidelity Productions, which promoted bands from across East Africa.[81] In the same year Charles Worrod bought up the assets of East African Records (Jambo Records) and launched Equator Sound Studios with the intention of providing East African music for East Africans.[82] Equator Sounds recorded some of the best-known Kenyan music of the time. The studio worked with a trained studio band, the Equator Sound Band, whose core group included the Kenyans Fadhili William, Daudi Kabaka, George Agade, and Gabriel Omolo; the Ugandan Charles Ssonko; and the Zambians Nishil Pichen and Peter Tsotsi. Many of these musicians remain household names in Kenya today. As the Equator Sound Band, they developed a cohesive style and were noted for popularizing the *twisti* beat.[83] As Worrod had worked as a promoter for the great South African *kwela* musician Spokes Mashiyane in the 1950s, the sound of the penny whistle shaped the Kenyan *twisti* beat. In the song *One for the Road* by Fadhili William, the guitar replaces the penny whistle.

Colmore could see that Independence was coming in Kenya, and along with Worrod sought to carve out a space for white producers and residents in a rapidly changing landscape. To do this they promoted songs that were national and multiracial in scope. They were also instrumental in getting the Kenya Broadcasting Corporation to hire African radio announcers.

Daudi Kabaka's song "Harambee Harambee," released in 1964, is the prime example of this combination. Originally a sailing term from coastal Kenya, *harambee* is a call to pull together. Kenya's first president, Jomo Kenyatta, used it as a rallying cry at most public gatherings, and President Daniel arap Moi continued the tradition, adding the response *nyayo*—meaning to follow in the footsteps (*nyayo*) of Kenyatta. *Harambee* has come to reference any joint action for the greater good, including fundraising and building projects. The lyrics of Kabaka's song stress unity, singing together, and pulling together to build a new state. Nevertheless, they recognize that not everyone thinks alike in Kenya. Trying to address the fear caused by the Emergency, Kabaka sings that although people predicted there would be trouble, we are not as everyone imagined. The song also speaks of the future—of an independent country full of *wananchi* (citizens) pulling together. In its last verse the song references the multiracialism of national politics just before Independence, stating that Kenyans do not discriminate, and every color is loved.

Worrod claims that he chose to produce this song to instill national pride and call everyone to pull together as one nation at Independence. He came up with the idea of basing the song on the nineteenth-century US hymn "John Brown's Body." Daudi Kabaka wrote the music, and the Equator Sound studio musicians adapted the melody to the *twisti* style using Swahili lyrics.[84] It was a clear example of the innovation and possibilities that the Nairobi Sound reflected, but also of how music reflected the dreams and aspirations as well as the fears of the moment. While selling products and music, these musicians were also selling a vision of the future.

At the same time, however, civil unrest was influencing what was played on the radio. By late 1959, the East African Railways and Harbours (EAR&H) was faced with a massive strike that led to a drop of more than 14 percent in passenger journeys—predominantly among African travelers.[85] The strikes were coordinated through the Railway African Union, which was part of the Kenyan Federation of Labor (KFL). The KFL was at the center of political organizing for independence from Britain.

Coming so soon as it did after the end of the Emergency, this civil unrest greatly concerned the colonial government, which feared a return of violence. The Railways tried to counter popular support for the striking Railways workers with propaganda. A public relations campaign provided intensive daily coverage of the strike through the press and radio. As part of this campaign, the Railways started the radio show *Railway Showboat*. The 1959 Annual Report describes the show as follows: "'Railway Showboat'—a weekly feature broadcast of interest to both staff and public—was first produced in October on the Kenya Broadcasting Service. A measure of the success achieved by this initial attempt at African radio entertainment was demonstrated by the allocation of the peak listening time to this program."[86]

The program included live broadcasts as well as studio recordings. Photos in the Railway Museum archives show some of the newly famous African artists, such as Fadhili William and his sister Esther John, performing for a live audience on stage at Muthurwa Social Hall. Fadhili and Esther sing in front of a full Latin band with congas, bongos, triple base, a brass section, and drum set. The *Railway Showboat* logo and title are displayed behind them on the wall. The location was not coincidental: Muthurwa Social Hall was the meeting place of the striking Railway workers and was regularly used for union meetings. Another photo in the archives shows Tom Mboya, the general secretary of the Kenya Federation of Labor, on stage in Muthurwa Social Hall at the Railway African Union's eighth annual conference in 1958, along with the top echelon of the union.

Railway Showboat was not the Railways' first attempt in broadcasting; *Happy Hour* was already broadcast once a week from Muthurwa. Featuring Railway workers who had formed an orchestra, it drew audiences of about five hundred people to its recording sessions.[87]

Railway Showboat, broadcast throughout the country, featured Kenyan popular music by local artists, mainly in Swahili but with a few songs in English. Because the show was aimed at a national audience, the music could not be reduced to a narrow ethnic sound. Through this program the music of artists like Fadhili William, Esther John, John Mwale, Daudi Kabaka, George Mukabi, Gabriel Omolo, and Fundi Konde spread across East Africa, amplified by the radios in every train station and brought home by the Railways workers. The music of these artists later became the music of Independence.

This body of work is still revered as a vital popular music style that could be appreciated widely both in Kenya and abroad. Rumba and *twisti* songs of this era continue to bring Kenyans of all ages and backgrounds to the dance floor.[88] Most famous in this genre is Fadhili William's 1963 hit "Malaika."[89] This is a tragic song about a man who cannot marry his love because he is too poor. Combined love and money troubles were a common theme in the music of Nairobi in the 1950s and '60s. William sang "Malaika" at the Kenyan Independence celebrations on December 12, 1963. He was joined in an encore by Miriam Makeba and Harry Belafonte, who had been invited to perform at the celebrations by Tom Mboya. Today hundreds of versions of this song can be heard all over the world. In 2019 I was walking through the streets of Paramaribo in Suriname, when over a loudspeaker I heard a Spanish version of "Malaika." It is hard to get any farther away from Kenya than that. The global popularity and longevity of the song testify to the originality and creativity of the Nairobi Sound.

In the 1950s the music people listened and danced to all over Kenya was disproportionally about Nairobi. Even rural guitarists sang about Nairobi, its money, women, education, and love—the same themes that echoed in the music played in social halls.[90] In 1993, when I was doing field work in coastal Kenya, people in the village where I was living sang songs of Nairobi to their children by moonlight—songs made famous in dance halls in the 1950s. They included songs about Nairobi neighborhoods, Nairobi dancing, Nairobi dating and love, songs about being urban that took for granted things like riding the bus, sunglasses, bottled beer, and independent women.

After Independence the Nairobi Sound became known as *zilizopendwa* (the loved ones or golden oldies). These songs exemplified a moment of hope and unity, a new state, and a cosmopolitan consciousness.[91] Yet they were also a tool used by the Railways and other authorities to soften the insistence of a radical African nationalism.

DANCING AND FREEDOM

In 1959, alarmed by the Railways strike and the potential for civil unrest in Nairobi, the British colonial government made a sweeping raid on political activities in the city. They raided the offices of Nairobi's main political party, the Nairobi People's Convention Party (NPCP). These were also the offices of the Kenyan Federation of Labor (KFL) and the newspaper *Uhuru*, produced by the NPCP. In 1959 it was illegal for parties to organize nationally, so the NPCP was using the extensive national networks of the KFL and the newspaper to reach an audience outside Nairobi. In the raid, thirty-four members of the NPCP were detained and some exiled to Lamu, on the coast, for sedition, while others were rusticated to their supposed "homes" in the countryside. All political rallies were banned by the government.[92]

One of the detainees, Tom Mboya, was held at his home in Ziwani, as was Julius Nyerere, who later became the first president of Tanzania. Mboya was a Nairobi politician who represented the "non-customary, urban developments" expressed by the dances in the social halls.[93] At the time he was the secretary general of the KFL and president of the NPCP. He was also one of the eight African members of the Legislative Council (LegCo), representing Nairobi, and secretary of the African Elected Members Organization (AEMO) of LegCo. He was twenty-nine years old.

Just two days after the raid, Mboya circumvented the ban on African political meetings by calling a song and dance meeting in the Kaloleni Social Hall. He turned the meeting into a political rally at which people sang about Jomo Kenyatta (who was then detained) and freedom, and Mboya started every political remark with "As you know, I am not allowed to make a political speech."[94] This maneuver got him on the cover of *Time* magazine in the United States.

For Mboya, a song and dance meeting was more than simply a pretext for a political rally. He is described by those who remember him from the social halls as a "lifer"—someone who lived life to the fullest. People recall him as "musical" and an "amazing dancer," their voices softening and their heads nodding in recollection. He is also recalled as a sharp dresser, "always well turned out," "smart from his head to his shoes," a man of style "in a class of his own."

The few photographs of Kaloleni that still exist include pictures of Mboya playing maracas with a band in a recording studio. There are stories of his guitar being stolen from him in Kaloleni. In 1965, Mboya helped the singer David Amunga set up the first independent music production company owned by an African, Mwangaza Music Store, as part of the process of Africanization that he initiated.[95]

In holding a political rally disguised as a dance event, Mboya adroitly used the popularity of music and dancing, the social hall space originally intended as a means of pacifying urban workers, and the communications networks of the Railways and unions to circumvent the decrees of the colonial state and to oppose colonialism. Mboya himself embodied all the aspects of social halls in the late 1950s: their dance and youth culture, their class dynamics, their music, their cosmopolitan and international outlook, and of course their politics. The rally he orchestrated demonstrates the importance of music and dance, and the social halls, to the negotiation of independence in Kenya and the envisioning of what could come next.

As I was writing this chapter, I spoke to my cousin about it, trying to get his take on dance in Nairobi. He asked what kind of music I was interested in. When I mentioned *twisti*, his body dissolved into liquid motion, imitating the style and feel of the 1950s and humming along with the music as he moved. I wondered then how to describe this style. It was twist with a twist. It was nostalgia for a time before we were born. And it was a memory held bodily rather than consciously, absorbed through years of watching our elders dance.

Decades after these tunes were released, Kenyans are still listening and dancing to the *zilizopendwa* hits. Indeed, *zilizopendwa* remains the most popular choral style in music and church festivals.[96] For many years "Harambee Harambee" was played before the broadcast of the news on the Voice of Kenya radio, and it became a fixture of everyday life in Kenya until the 1990s.[97] I remember hearing it every time we turned on the radio for the news as my family sat around the dinner table. I also remember slightly different lyrics around nation building. Where the original lyrics included *tuimbe pamoja* ("let's sing together"), I remember *tuijenge taifa* ("let's build the nation"). But I wonder if that was my mind filling in the concerns of the time.

The Nairobi sound and dance of the late 1950s and 1960s were unique products of the circumstances of rising salaried African urban employees, the independence movement, and trade union action. They encapsulated the dreams and hopes of a better tomorrow while reflecting the trials and tribulations of the urban present. Yet the space of music and dance remained a negotiated and contested space that others, in particular advertisers and the Railways, sought to co-opt. Through the overlap of recreation, politics, labor, and advertising in the social hall, music and dance mingled with city and national politics, cementing Nairobi's cosmopolitan modernity.

Africans transformed the social halls in residential estates from spaces for the domestication and control of African labor into spaces of protest, innovation, and creation. They thus came to be a way of taking back the city, of staking a permanent claim to its space. These radical uses of social halls in Nairobi were a challenge to anti-urbanism. The dancers and other users made these spaces their own, creating sounds and steps that were uniquely Nairobi.

5

Remnant of a Green City in the Sun

When I took schoolchildren on a tour of Nairobi's City Park in 2017, they begged me to take them into what they called the "deep forest." They expected caves and waterfalls and adventure. They ran from the sunlit central gardens down to the paths that lead to the forest, making it hard for the teachers and guides to keep up.

Their excitement was tangible. They were enthralled to see owls by daylight and climb the lianas. They marveled at how far they could see under the dense canopy of the tall indigenous trees whose shade inhibits undergrowth. They were thrilled to see butterflies and safari ants and spiders' webs and to wade through the tall grass under the groves of jacaranda trees near the river. They raced through the yellow-barked acacias in the sunken gardens and past the buttress roots of the mugumo fig trees along the riverbanks. They jumped the many small streams and piled onto the bridges to watch the river run beneath them.

The children's enthusiasm made me remember my own hours of play in City Park and the endless possibilities of nature. My sister and I waded through the river and made rafts that we floated downstream. We visited every part of the forest and spent many weekends under the less-than-watchful supervision of my mother, who was busy birdwatching.

For many long term-residents, City Park, situated in the very center of Nairobi, holds beautiful childhood memories of nature and adventure, particularly recollections of the deep forest that contrasts with the concrete jungle of the city itself. According to the guidebook *City Park: The Green Heart of Nairobi*, "Despite its isolation and modest size, City Park—and its precious remnant tract of dry upland forest most especially—supports an uncommonly diverse flora and fauna."[1]

Remnant is a fitting term. The indigenous forest at City Park, along with Oloolua Forest, Ngong Road Forest, Karura Forest, and the forested slopes in the

87

FIGURE 7. City Park with bougainvillea trees. Photo by author.

Nairobi National Park, gives some idea of the dry upland forest that covered much of the Nairobi area before the Railways and colonial settlement took down the trees.[2] City Park is a remaining piece of this forest belt that formed a dividing line between the agricultural highlands and the pastoralist plains. Although fragmentary, a remnant also has continuity, a connection to something larger in the past and also to the future. A living monument, it stands as a witness to something that is lost but also as the possibility of something found. In other words, it is a surviving trace.

Many surviving traces can be found in City Park. In 2009, scientists from the National Museums of Kenya and a local advocacy group, Friends of City Park, undertook a biodiversity survey that identified more than 1,000 species of plants and animals in the park. The 560 plant species identified included 100 species of trees. About 110 of these plant species are of high conservation value, rare or threatened because their natural habitat elsewhere is dwindling. These plants too, are remnants—natural reminders of abundance now reduced by a shrinking habitat and an expanding city.

This rich and diverse plant life supports a variety of birds and wild animals, from Sykes and vervet monkeys to spectacular forest birds, colorful butterflies and other insects, reptiles, and amphibians.[3] City Park even used to have a resident leopard. Like the rare plants, this leopard was a remnant of once-abundant populations in a once-extensive forest. Perceived as a threat to humans, however, it was removed fifteen years ago—to the joy of the monkeys, who have, as a result, hugely increased in numbers.

This forest remnant at City Park provides an opportunity for an increasingly urban public to interact with unique natural habitats that represent the original ecosystem of Nairobi. But it is also something more.

In *Nairobi in the Making*, Constance Smith describes Nairobi as a landscape saturated with "recalcitrant structures that refuse to disappear."[4] These, too, are remnants that simply won't go away, in spite of new developments, shifts in ecological diversity, and political and economic shifts like decolonization, disinvestment, and structural adjustment. Like Nairobi, City Park holds remnants of a past we can't ignore or overlook. The park itself is a remnant of decreasing public green spaces and parks with free access; it holds the deep-forest remnants of the area's original biodiversity; its manicured gardens are remnants of both a colonial past and a skilled, permanent staff (much of it lost to structural adjustment). The forest and the gardens spark childhood memories and serve as inspiration for social and environmental movements. Such remnants, reminders, and remains sustain the park's future possibilities, but they also signal its fragility.

In these respects and others, City Park can be seen as a microcosm of Nairobi itself. The anthropologist Michel-Rolph Trouillot suggests that traces are products of the historical process.[5] Although the terms *microcosm* and *remnant* may appear contradictory, if we take seriously Trouillot's suggestion, Nairobi's remnants indicate not just what has gone missing but also what is still present—traces that stand as living and changing witness to the past and what the city once was, as well as a complex, contradictory, and troublesome remainder in the present. It thus remains a malleable structure with which to build imagined futures.

Looking at City Park as both a remnant and a microcosm of Nairobi, this chapter considers everyday efforts to establish permanence (cultural, biological, and political) and the people who curate and narrate that permanence. These processes illustrate how regular people and their everyday existence can contest the anti-urbanism of city planners, administrators, capital, and private corporations.

REMNANTS OF A COLONIAL URBAN PARK

In the space that became the city of Nairobi, near the small village of Pangani, was a triangular forest bound on two sides by small rivers. This forest is said to have been gifted to the colonial government by a Kikuyu clan. The circumstances of this gifting have generally remained unspecified, as this story has been passed down through generations. The third side of the triangle was cleared and settled in 1903 by Europeans to form what became the neighborhood of

Parklands. The ninety-hectare triangular forest became known first as the Nairobi Forest Reserve and later as the Municipal Forest. In the 1920s, gardens were carved out of the forest, a maze designed, a bandstand built, a bowling green laid out, a hockey pitch leveled. The forest was declared a public park with the name City Park.

This park, one of the few locations with no race restrictions in a segregated city, helped build Nairobi's reputation as the "Green City in the Sun." Over time, other parts of the forest were felled to make space for cemeteries, sports grounds, and residential development. All around the forest grew up a new city with new neighborhoods—Ngara, Highridge, and Muthaiga—and the park's role evolved with the expanding urban landscape.

City Park's landscaped gardens, which were carefully designed by City Park Superintendent Peter Greensmith from 1947, were intended to maximize beauty, using flowering plants suited to the climate of the area. Realizing this vision required extensive and meticulous maintenance and a good stock of plants in the nursery. At the center of the garden is a now-silent bandstand that once drew hundreds of visitors to mingle and listen to the music. Paths through the indigenous forest surrounding the gardens are lined by flowering trees. Off to one side, on the edge of the forest, is the now-overgrown maze, commonly referred to as *mtego wa panya* (the mousetrap) in Swahili. The maze was made of kei-apple hedges just tall enough to obscure the view of any potential exits to a person inside, with the thorns of the kei apple preventing anyone from cheating by pushing through the hedges.

The children's joy at the deep forest at City Park is an interesting response in a park otherwise designed to tame nature and population—a project replicated by colonial governments across the British Empire in city parks from Tanganyika to India, Malaya, and New Zealand.[6] In October, the white jacaranda trees that bloom at the center of City Park are highlighted against the magnificent magenta of the bougainvillea, both species of South American origin. Together with the light purple of the normal jacaranda and the pink of the local Cape chestnut, these plants all testify to Britain's reach across the world and acquisition of species from far-off lands.

As studies of nationalism have shown, colonial tools have often been redeployed in national projects after Independence.[7] Today, City Park is designated a national monument under the jurisdiction of the National Museums of Kenya, in the Ministry of Culture and Heritage. It is managed by the Kenya Forest Service and the Nairobi City County Government. Still, if we think of the park only as remnant of colonial forms of power, how can we celebrate and reclaim the children's enthusiasm for the "deep forest" and the green spaces within the city? Can we think of such parks as existing beyond their colonial designs to become part of a postcolonial (if fraught) present and future? What can they tell us about the city of Nairobi? City Park has taken on new meanings and purposes for every generation—meanings that reflect an urban sensibility and make the park more than the remnants of an anti-urban colonial past.

MICROCOSM OF A GARDEN CITY

A few years ago, a colleague at a conference in Nairobi said to me, "We have gone from 'the Green City in the Sun' to a cartoon city." Puzzled, I asked her to explain. She pointed out that cities in cartoons are composed entirely of straight lines and sharp angles, high-rise buildings with crowded streets and sidewalks. They have no trees, gardens, or greenery.

Yet tourist brochures, government documents, novels about Nairobi, presidential addresses, and environmentalist complaints about changes in the city continue to invoke the label of the Green City in the Sun.[8] Few who use it, however, think about the tensions between city planning and organic growth, or the various conflicts and concerns of commercial and government entities over land, public health, administrative expense, and racial segregation that produced Nairobi's plentiful open spaces, tree-lined boulevards, landscaped roundabouts, and gardens.[9]

From the beginning, the Railways tried to forestall price gouging by land speculators by buying up as much land as possible in Nairobi.[10] The company ended up with way more land than it could use, some of which today forms greenbelts along the railway tracks in Upper Hill and other parts of the city. At the same time, colonial officials were using open space to segregate Europeans from African and Asian residents, supposedly in the interests of public health. Colonial administrators thought African children were a reservoir for malaria and associated bubonic plague with the living conditions of Asians.[11] Accordingly, the colonial government sought to limit the number and mobility of children—and thus families—in the city and restrict where workers could live (see chapter 3).

The increasing number of Africans in Nairobi were crowded into "native locations"—areas of temporary housing that were once swamps in the low-lying part of Nairobi. In contrast, European houses in the hills were designed with ample gardens, with space between their houses and their domestic staff quarters to prevent the spread of malaria.

In his book on urban agriculture in Nairobi, Donald Freeman identifies roads and riverbanks as formative elements of Nairobi's open spaces.[12] Nairobi's roads were designed to be wide enough for a wagon pulled by a full span of oxen to turn (a width that accommodates multiple lanes of modern traffic). Roads in the hilly part of Nairobi were built with green verges and ditches to control surface water runoff during the rainy season, and riparian areas had buffer zones for flooding and malaria control. Of course, these roads served only certain sections of town. This layout remains a visible feature of Nairobi's affluent suburbs, whereas the lowlands are characterized by crowded streets without trees or greenery.

Nairobi city planners eventually picked up on the idea of the garden city, originated by Ebenezer Howard in Britain at the end of the nineteenth century, just as urban planning became an international practice. It was an experiment intended to create compact, efficient, and healthy cities through tightly controlled layouts, with satellite housing areas planned around industrial and business regions and separated by greenbelts.[13] Garden cities were promoted as an antidote to tenement housing and overcrowding in industrial British cities as well as an effort to preserve nature and greenery. However, the implementation of the design led to protests. From early on garden cities were seen as attempts at class segregation, as their low housing density did not address the needs of the poor. In addition, the expansion of urban communities and industry into rural areas was often seen as land grabbing.[14] Nevertheless, the concept was exported around the world.[15]

Garden cities in Africa differed substantially from those in Britain. The architect and urban historian Liora Bigon argues that "the implementation of Garden City ideas in Europe before World War II usually meant suburban self-contained development and a community or co-operative developer—under private or public–private partnership. In colonial Africa, on the contrary, at the very most the implementation before the 1930s meant simply a low-density residential form under government control with parks or other kinds of greenery."[16]

In industrial Europe and America, garden cities allowed wealthy residents to escape the density and diversity of the city while concentrating poorer residents in urban areas.[17] In colonial garden cities, leafy, low-density housing was usually reserved for white colonial employees and other expatriates, while the rest of the city was crowded and devoid of green space. This pattern of "dual cities"—cities with racially segregated areas marked by distinctly different architecture, layout, and services—is typical of colonial urban planning. [18] In Nairobi, the implementation of the garden city concept included segregated land use; the creation of distinct neighborhoods; tree-lined boulevards with grass medians and landscaped roundabouts; broad riparian verges; and, of course, parkland and forests.[19] The Nairobi master plan of 1948, intended to govern Nairobi's transition from a municipality into a "colonial capital," also set out density limits for European residential areas and maintained limits on the number of Africans in the city, although it did acknowledge the possibility of a few permanent African workers and their families living in Nairobi.[20] These anti-urbanist interventions attempted to create a garden city at the equator, a green city in the sun.

City Park was central to this vision. The landscaping of the boulevards, and roundabouts, as well as the gardens surrounding public buildings such as Parliament, were designed by Peter Greensmith, and the plants were supplied by the City Park nurseries. The Green City in the Sun was a label that reflected Nairobi's status as a model garden city in the tropics. Its closest rival, Singapore, became (to residents' chagrin) the second royal chartered city after Nairobi.

The garden city vision for Nairobi did not generally extend to the areas of Asian and African settlement. Nevertheless, Aurora Martin and Pauline Bezemer argue that between 1929 and 1948, Nairobi moved from creating African residential estates based on barrack-style housing for single male laborers to a garden city model.[21] It was first applied in the 1930s to the neighborhood of Shauri Moyo, whose design placed "schools and shops around 'quadrangles' for the first time, which consist of circular and rectangular roads that enclose small green spaces and are slightly set back from the main road." It was seen as a way to quell social unrest regarding housing and address Nairobi's urgent housing needs.[22] Shauri Moyo's "garden" plan was distinctly more limited than that of Parklands. The plans for Ziwani and Starehe (1942–46) and later Kaloleni (1943–48)—with its ample lawns, hedges, and trees, and the idea of long-term residence implied in nuclear family housing—embraced garden city concepts and reinforced the idea that Africans would settle in town for their *working* lives (but not forever).[23]

Even today a clear disparity remains between densely populated parts of Nairobi (for example, Eastlands) and what the press calls "the leafy suburbs" (such as Muthaiga, Karen, and Kilimani), with their trees, gardens, and parks. This distinction, a visceral remnant of colonialism, today segregates residents by class rather than solely by race.

For African residents, the unsegregated public green spaces produced the strongest memories of the garden-city aspect of Nairobi. In his memoirs, former Moody Awori (vice president of Kenya from 2003 to 2008) reminisces about Nairobi in the late colonial and early postcolonial period: "I remember the Jacaranda trees on part of Uhuru Highway flowering from November to January and Kenyatta Avenue with majestic palm trees and the bougainvillea rich in white, red, and yellow colors. I remember City Park, well laid down and looked after, where we took our children on Sunday afternoon to hear the Police Band and where the children played in *Mtego wa Panya* grass square with many rows with seemingly, no entrance nor exit and with no litter. And Nairobi Dam with well-organized Sailing Club—a lost paradise."[24] Access to green space for Asian residents was gradually increased as organizations such as the Sikh Union, the Aga Khan Sports Club, the Patel Club, and the Goan Gymkhana requested space for sports fields. All these facilities are situated near City Park (in Parklands, Ngara, and Pangani), and some were set on land leased from City Park.

After Independence, much of the segregated colonial garden-city design survived, including the gardens around Parliament. Then as now, City Park was a meeting place for Nairobi residents, denizens of both the garden city and the less green and spacious neighborhoods.

CHILDHOOD MEMORIES

As a child growing up in Nairobi in the 1940s and 1950s, my father, Hilary Ng'weno, would regularly walk across town to visit City Park. This unsegregated green space in a segregated city held a special attraction for my father, who grew up in the Railways neighborhood of Muthurwa. With a band of other children from Muthurwa, Pumwani, Shauri Moyo, and Kaloleni, he would visit the park on a Sunday to hear the police or army marching bands play in the bandstand. The children would then head for the maze, one of their favorite spots. The maze attracted Kenyans of all walks of life—Africans, Asians, Europeans, the young, the old, families and couples. The children, being regulars at City Park, had figured out how to get to the middle of the maze and how to get out again. They loved to see adults get lost in it. How clever they felt. City Park was their escape into nature. Heading home at the end of the day they would pick *zambarau* (Java plum) and loquats from the trees at Pangani, exotic trees planted long ago by Indian Kenyans.

One of my father's contemporaries, AH, whom I worked with in Friends of City Park, used to come to City Park from a different direction: from Ngara, at that time a predominantly Asian residential area. He smiles as he remembers walking in the park in bare feet. Now a respectable elder, with children who studied and live abroad, he was then often called a *chokora*—a street urchin, a wild urban child. This word, he told me, comes from Gujarati and became part of Nairobi's vernacular sometime in his youth.

He, too, remembers the bands, the maze, and the forest. He tells me that the maze was called *bhul bhulamari*—"to get lost and found"—in Gujarati.[25] Coming from Ngara, he would enter the park from what was then aptly called Forest Road (renamed Wangari Maathai Road in 2016). To him City Park was nature. It was beautiful. It was music on Sundays and picnics. The community always congregated there. He has pictures of his children playing in the park—just as my family has pictures of my sister and me there.

BKK, a retired scientist who volunteers at Friends of City Park, remembers visits to the park as opportunities for exploration and play, but also as an integral part of family life.

> My granny lived across the road on Forest Road, where there was a little lane to the left of [what is] now Simba Union (then Sikh Union), the foundation stone of which was laid by my grandfather, Hakam Singh, who was one of the LegCo [Legislative Council] members. As kids one of the most pleasurable experiences, which was so precious that it recurred in my dreams for years after my childhood, was to be packed off with our ayahs and a picnic, whereupon us kids proceeded to have a most magical few hours in the park. My memory is of running down the little downward sloping lane to the sunken garden, rolling down beautifully manicured meadows, mostly of running everywhere. We always went into the maze, which was an exhilarating, albeit scary, experience. Catching the bands if we were there for weekends was also a lot of fun. And then back to Granny's, which was a treat in itself. She lived in the posh part of Forest Road, whereas we lived off Juja Road.[26]

For my father, AH, and BKK, childhood memories of colonial Nairobi are enhanced by the sense of freedom they found in City Park. All three were drawn to the park by the maze, the bandstand, and the forest. Such memories and feelings are shared by people from across the British Commonwealth. When William

Cunningham Bissel interviewed Fatuma Amina Idris, a Zanzibari revolutionary, he noted, "The eyes of this revolutionary positively lit up when she recalled the public spaces of her youth during the colonial period—Victoria Gardens with its ayahs and children in prams, where she went to play with her closest female friends (*mashoga*); the weekly concerts by the Sultan's Police Band in Forodhani Bandstand or in the park between the sea and the English Club."[27]

While these childhood memories can be dismissed as colonial nostalgia, such a reading loses the complexity of what it means to be a child in a city, the importance of public green spaces to urban life, and place-making-practices that go beyond colonial intent. These memories testify not only to the limited entertainment and recreation possibilities for African and Asian children in colonial Nairobi but also to the significance of the integrated space of City Park.

The city planners could fathom neither African urban inhabitants nor Asian permanent inhabitants. Representing both these categories and three different communities, what my father and his two contemporaries have in common is their understanding of Nairobi as their permanent urban home and City Park as an essential site of their memories of home. As AH told me, "City Park is a central part of Nairobi. I am a Nairobi man. I am not going anywhere. I have a plot in Kariokor Cemetery, established in 1902 or so. This is my place."

Like BKK, whose dreams of City Park refused to go away, AH centers his identity as a Nairobi man through City Park: he is not leaving, even after death. Although parks served to reinforce colonial ideas about the division between work and leisure, City Park also became an escape from the confines of the colonial city. It became a space of freedom from which even those who were not meant to be in the city could take ownership of it and create a sense of belonging.

THE CARE OF REMNANTS

Memories of place also anchored those who worked at City Park, the people who literally made these spaces. The maze, the bandstand, and the forest were created and maintained through the painstaking work and care of gardeners, wardens, and planners. Gardening at City Park required a delicate balance between the management of the indigenous forest and the propagation and cultivation of native and exotic species in the manicured gardens. The park's designer, Peter Greensmith, went on to design the Parliament gardens, the roundabouts in central Nairobi, and many hotel gardens across Kenya. At City Park, Greensmith developed unique varieties of plants—bougainvillea and hibiscus in particular—that today populate gardens as far away as Bengaluru, India.

In 2015, I had the exceptional opportunity to join a walk through City Park with its retired master gardener to identify rare plants as part of Friends of City Park's preservation efforts. As he walked through the park, the master gardener exclaimed, "Aiy ya yaiiieeee! Wow!" and shook his head in wonder. As he looked at

FIGURE 8. City Park bandstand and white jacaranda. Photo by author.

a patch of robust forest, or a rare plant, or a corner of garden particularly well laid out, he would say, "This is wonderful! Eh, and this is beautiful! This is amazing!" His enthusiasm was infectious. He was delighted to be back at City Park, delighted to see his garden again, delighted to see that all the wonders he had worked to create were flourishing.

The master gardener had worked with Greensmith not only at City Park but also at the plant nursery Greensmith created in Lang'ata, now part of the International Union for the Conservation of Nature. He explained to us why certain plants were unique, where they came from, and why they were placed in specific locations. He told us that Kenya's second vice president, Joseph Murumbi (who is buried at City Park), gave the first president, Jomo Kenyatta, one of two rare yellow Nandi flame trees (known abroad as African tulip trees) propagated at City Park. It still grows today at State House, the president's official residence.[28] The past came alive in his eyes as he walked through the gardens of his working life, each plant sparking a new memory of the production of beauty.

The gardener's delight was surprising, as many of us instead were seeing the neglected state of the park. Before the structural-adjustment changes to government spending in the 1990s, City Park had a workforce of 250 people.[29] By 2011, there were no personnel, facilities, or resources allocated specifically to the management of City Park. Until 2020, when the park was taken over by the Kenya Forest Service and the county government was taken over by the Nairobi Metropolitan Services, City Park was simply one of the open spaces under the care of the City County Parks section.

The decline in personnel and finances affected all aspects of City Park's maintenance, resulting in the construction of illegal structures, encroachment by neighboring buildings, unauthorized clearing of trees, dumping of garbage, and safety problems. In addition, the park came to rely on casual labor rather than permanent, skilled employees. Some senior employees were replaced by inexperienced, though more highly educated, staff. A remnant permanent staff of eight to twelve people struggled to maintain the central garden and had no resources to attend at all to the deep forest.

For one of the few remaining permanent employees, her job was tightly bound up with her identity and her sense of self-worth. She reminisced about the park as a workplace that had nurtured and recognized her knowledge, but also as a place that her work had helped to create. "The park had flowers that we used to take to State House. I do not know if those flowers can be found anymore because their structures fell a long time ago. . . . We were proud of our work. . . . In this park we had seven nurseries, but now there are only two remaining."[30]

City Park is not alone in its decline. Documenting the nature of and challenges facing green spaces in Africa in 2014, the urban and regional planner Collins Adjei Mensah noted that from Addis Ababa to Abidjan to Kumasi, the entities in charge of parks and gardens had been crippled with shortages of labor, expertise, and funding.[31]

The problems of City Park, with a few permanent, skilled employees struggling to preserve the facade of the park by maintaining the center gardens at the expense of the deep peripheral forest, are also representative of those of the city. By 2022, Nairobi administrators—whether the Nairobi City County Government or its new parallel administration, the Nairobi Metropolitan Services—were struggling to keep areas beyond Nairobi's central business district serviced, clean, and maintained. Amid job loss, underemployment, and frustrating work, there is little space for delight.

THE "DEEP FOREST" IN A CONCRETE CITY

Forest covers most of City Park, supporting an array of plant and animal life. The deep forest provides shade from the equatorial sun. It is a dry forest with widely spaced trees whose dense canopy keeps it clear of undergrowth. The soil is brown and rich in organic matter. The forest is framed by the exquisitely delicate foliage of the croton trees, punctuated by the giant diospyros, the erect pillarwood, the elegant albizia, and the tall markhamia, with its bright yellow flowers. The beautiful pink flowers of the Cape chestnuts and the creamy white flowers of the crabia contrast with the dark green of the forest foliage. The deep forest also hosts potent trees like the medicinal warburgia (*muthiga* in Kikuyu, after which the nearby neighborhood of Muthaiga is named), and two species of acokanthera or arrow poison trees. The park is perhaps most famous for its many fig (Ficus) species, including the strangler fig (*mugumo* in Kikuyu) that grows on other trees and buildings. These trees are interlaced with over seventy-five species of lianas.[32]

The abundance and diversity of plants and animals in Nairobi was and is particularly important to those born and growing up in the city. Some African and Asian residents were able to enjoy these benefits of the garden city as they moved into once-restricted neighborhoods of the city after Independence. Green spaces also became more important as the city's population burgeoned. Open land belonging to the Railways, farmland, and rangeland were built over with houses and then with high-rise apartment buildings. Today, the residents of these poorer, densely populated areas of the city, with few trees or gardens, are the main users of City Park.[33] For them, the park offers an escape, a place of rest, peace, natural beauty, solitude and solace, a refuge, and a place for replenishment of the soul.

This particular understanding of nature derives from growing up as an urban person. Remembering the 1940s, my father said: "As a child, I loved to come to City Park to see the monkeys and squirrels. It was my escape into nature. As a child born in the city with no rural background, I remember the sounds of birds as the soundtrack of the park, providing atmosphere and novelty for us children as we explored."[34]

His sentiments were echoed by a writer about fifty years his junior, a contestant in an essay competition on Nairobi green spaces held by Friends of City Park. She states:

> There's nothing that pleases my soul better than having a rest beneath a tree . . . not just any tree, but where there are a variety of them; after all, variety is the spice of life. I find it more exciting having a meal alone or with a friend with entertaining music

from birds' chirps, cool air and ravens hanging around for remains than sitting in a hotel with deafening music, hot and nose-irritating air and ragamuffins hanging around to snatch your food away ruthlessly. Most people resign to settle beneath the trees to escape the scorching rays of the sun or even after "tarmacking" for long and having nothing to spare for Caesar. Trees are significant to me. Whenever I feel frustrated and depressed, I find my peace in the sweet scent of the flowers and leaves. They calm my blood and my heart in a way that only nature can comprehend.[35]

For people raised in an urban setting, nature means the music of birds and the scent of flowers and leaves. They do not reminisce about an agrarian landscape or a tough agricultural working childhood but instead invoke the uniqueness of nature and its importance in a city that is becoming increasingly difficult to live in. The essayist points to City Park as a refuge from the difficulties of urban life, loud music, polluted air, insecurity, glaring sunlight, poverty, and endless hours fruitlessly looking for work.

One of Friends of City Park's employees told me in a 2021 interview that for him, City Park is an oasis in the middle of chaos. "There is a beauty that you can't get anywhere else, a mixture of history, flowers, trees, paths—a feeling you can't re-create in your own garden."[36] Or, as another participant in the essay competition put it, "Having lived in the urban polluted jungle that is Nairobi for all my life, having a nice lush green field to rest [in] is quite a luxury." City Park is a place to access nature in a city quickly becoming less and less green.

But is escape really possible?

Not only does development shrink the green spaces in the city, but it changes them as well. City Park is bounded on one side by the Kibagare River, where I played as a child. With its source in Loresho, at Nairobi's highest elevation, the Kibagare River is fed not only by rainwater but also by surface runoff and water from storm drains. On its way through the city it collects rubbish and refuse—raw sewage and plastic waste in the form of synthetic clothes, plastic bags, and, to a lesser extent, plastic bottles. Both the sewage and the plastic waste are signs of the changes the city has undergone as a result of growing prosperity, development, and global connectivity, along with the decline of municipal services and increasing urban density.

A 2017 study of the Kibagare River, commissioned by Friends of City Park as part of a cleanup initiative, revealed that the river had high levels of organic matter, fecal coliform bacteria, and nitrogen from sewage contamination. The sewage was entering the river from broken sewer pipes and through storm drains. In addition, the water was contaminated by solid waste from several dump sites upstream from City Park.[37]

The broken sewer lines result not just from poor maintenance but also from the increasing pressure on the wastewater infrastructure caused by the rapid construction of high-rise buildings in Parklands, Westlands, Brookside, and Muthaiga. These lines were built for a much smaller urban population, and their capacity was not expanded along with the new developments. The plastic waste is also largely a result of this intensive construction. By far the most common objects clogging city rivers are plastic cement bags (along with plastic milk bags). The bags that held the tons of cement used to build the high-rise apartments upstream now fill the river at City Park. They hang off bridges, branches, and rocks after the rains. They block narrow river channels, causing floods.

Cement bags were not always plastic. They used to be made of paper from the local Webuye Paper Mills. In the 1990s, when structural adjustment and competition killed off the paper mills, the cement industry switched to plastic bags.[38]

Unlike the cement bags, clothes may not seem like garbage. But the clothes in the river are evidence of Nairobi's participation in the throwaway economy so prevalent the world over. These clothes are remainders of the global secondhand clothing trade. Used and discarded clothing from other continents is sent in bulk to places like Kenya, where it is sold at a fraction of its original price, enabling residents of Nairobi to participate in fast fashion—and the waste it creates.

Most of this secondhand clothing is made of nylon or polyester, as synthetics keep their color and shape better than natural fabric and last longer. The same qualities render these fabrics nonbiodegradable. Not only are more clothes being thrown into the river, but once they are there, they never go away.

Clearly, the rivers at City Park are hardly playgrounds for children today. The pungent detritus of the city that collects in the rivers clashes with the tranquility and beauty of the rest of the park. Like the threatened deep forest, and the neglected gardens, these remnants call upon visitors to do something.

BUILDING OVER THE GREEN CITY IN THE SUN

Developers in Nairobi are cognizant that Nairobi is becoming less and less green. Greenery, and parks in particular, are recognized as a luxury that must be capitalized on. New developments have names like Park View, Park Place, Park Side, View Park, and so on. No matter how far they may be from an actual park, the association suggests luxury, desirability and, most importantly, monetary value. Real estate in Nairobi that is actually near any of the city's remaining green spaces—City Park, the Arboretum, Uhuru Gardens, Uhuru Park, Central Park, Nairobi Museum grounds, golf courses, the Giraffe Center, Ngong Road Forest, Karura Forest, and Oloolua Forest—commands premium prices.

The loss of green space is not unique to Nairobi. Collins Adjei Mensah points out that in Kumasi, Ghana, "once the Garden City of West Africa," green spaces now constitute only 10.7 percent of the total land area, and the same is true in many African cities.[39] In the 1980s and 1990s, many government institutions privatized their holdings as part of the structural adjustment process. States redirected their power away from managing social goods such as parks and toward ensuring that these assets could produce private profitability for the state and private companies.[40]

From the 1980s to the 2000s, Kenyan politicians exploited their control over public land to buy favors and votes, or to amass resources for themselves and their parties. Many green spaces in Nairobi have been affected, as is evidenced by Nobel laureate Wangari Maathai's struggle against the destruction and privatization of three green spaces in Nairobi: Karura Forest, Jeevanjee Gardens, and Uhuru Park.[41] In the 1990s, City Park's land was subdivided into private plots despite its status as a public park.

The World Health Organization recommends that a healthy city have a minimum of nine square meters of green space per city resident and that all residents live within a fifteen-minute walk of green spaces.[42] In 2007, Nairobi had only five square meters of public green space per resident, including all parks and forests (but excluding Nairobi National Park).[43] Counting only Nairobi's public parks, without the separately managed forests, the area of public green space was only 211 hectares (about 520 acres), or 0.7 square meters per person, in 2007.[44] It has been declining ever since. Parks that were planned to serve a population of 250,000 people in 1948 today serve 4.3 million.

One of the founders of Friends of City Park is unwilling to give up on the garden city ideal. She sees City Park as an essential component of sane urban living in the city where she was brought up, a place of wide boulevards and treelined streets. She argues that the new planners and developers of Nairobi seem to have "no concept of natural landmarks. Like, do they not understand that as they remove the acacias [trees] on Mombasa Road, they are removing an important part of what makes Nairobi what it is for those who call the city home? There are certain things that I look to on the horizon and I know I am home."[45] As the Green City in the Sun has lost its roadside trees, as walls have replaced kei-apple hedges, and as habitats that were once wildlife friendly have been paved or built over, green space in Nairobi is akin to a birthright that is being stripped for parts.

BUILDING BLOCKS OF EQUITY

A few years ago, I was sitting with a environmentalist in his twenties, talking about the difficult work of conservation. I was complaining about the entrance fees to green spaces like the Nairobi Arboretum and Karura Forest (both the principle and the amount). He replied that fees are needed because "people only value things they pay for." I was struck by his phrase, which I have heard repeated over and over again since the beginning of structural adjustment, and which has been used by officials and politicians to justify these entrance fees for green spaces.[46] Usually the speaker is a politician justifying increased costs: first for entry to national parks, then for general government services. The phrasing reflects a turn to a neoliberal form of government reliant on fees, rather than taxes, for revenue. The collection of fees is seen as morally superior to taxation, which is regarded as a corrupt process.

Starting in 2010, with the charges for entering Karura Forest, Nairobi's green spaces, especially forests, have become increasingly inaccessible to the poor. When a fifty-shilling entry fee was instituted for the arboretum, protests were held at Freedom Corner in Uhuru Park.[47] The protests, however, were unable to sway the Kenya Forest Service. I was living across a small valley from the arboretum when the fee went into effect. Usually in the morning you could hear children playing in the park, visitors praying, and large numbers of people walking to work under the shade of the trees. In the eerie silence that followed the introduction of the fees, it seemed that life itself had been sucked out of the park.

City Park is one of a very few parks (along with Uhuru Park, Central Park, Jeevanjee Gardens, and Kamukunji Grounds) that are still free to the public in Nairobi. In this respect, too, the park is a remnant—a reminder of a city government that once collected taxes rather than fees to support public services and amenities.

Fees, by definition, are a regressive means of revenue collection, as the poor pay a larger portion of their income for the same services as the wealthy. In addition, they can be imposed without any democratic form of decision making or scrutiny. Yet despite extensive literature to the contrary, officials, politicians, donor agencies, and NGO staff parrot the neoliberal adage that people value only the things they pay for.[48] They argue that fees are the only way to keep the parks safe.

Since its founding, City Park has welcomed Nairobians of all walks of life, of different races, genders, and ages. Entertainment held there, such as bandstand concerts, were free and open to all. As many Europeans left Nairobi, however, and those who remained moved farther out of town (along with other wealthy residents), public entertainment ceased. The maintenance and security of the park declined. With these changes, the profile of the park's users also changed. Residents of adjacent neighborhoods used the park less, and those from more distant, poorer neighborhoods used it more. Because of these shifts, compounded by the underfunding and understaffing that began with structural adjustment, City Park has become more and more neglected by the state.

In the United States, as the urban geographer Scott Larson has observed, white flight and suburbanization saw a similar "erosion of support for the creation and maintenance of urban parks and other public spaces" as the users changed.[49] Later, the neoliberal regeneration of parks was aimed at economic development and reinvigorating downtown districts. This regeneration reconfigured the uses and users of the parks through security features, such as benches that discouraged sleeping as a way to deter use by the poor and the homeless. Larson notes that proponents of regeneration in the United States also turned to new mechanisms for funding their projects—including concessions, public-private partnerships, and other forms of profit seeking. He describes the High Line in New York City, a park developed on an elevated railway line, as "the hallmark of a broader urban redevelopment movement in which city governments increasingly view high-design, 'world-class' parks as driving mechanisms for economic development, 'tools' geared as much toward attracting tourists and catalyzing real estate values as creating use amenities for local residents."[50]

Regeneration efforts for City park are following similar patterns. For instance, a proposal by the Ministry of Transportation, Infrastructure, Housing and Urban Development, which was part of the World Bank–funded Nairobi Metropolitan Services Improvement Project (NaMSIP), included fees, concessions, fencing, and limited entrances. Such efforts are mainly justified by ideas about safety and a general fear of the poor. Notably, they consider the principal stakeholders to be the (middle-class) community immediately surrounding the park, rather than the wider city population and the poor people who are currently its main users. The NaMSIP proposal was ultimately modified based on feedback from Friends of City Park.

In 2013, the Aga Khan Trust for Culture (AKTC) also offered a regeneration proposal based on a public-private partnership. It too included concessions, fencing, limited entrances, and fees. AKTC is part of the Aga Khan Development Network, which includes a number of business, development, and philanthropic Ismaili institutions in Kenya. From the perspective of many of these institutions, City Park is a source of value. It is overlooked by Aga Khan Academy, Aga Khan Hospital, and Aga Khan Primary School, as well as by a number of housing and business offices owned by the Aga Khan community. The regeneration of the park along the lines they proposed, attracting mainly middle-class users, would directly benefit the nearby businesses and institutions. And of course it would significantly increase the value of the surrounding real estate.

Keeping City Park free and public has been a primary concern of Friends of City Park, which operated under the aegis of Nature Kenya (a national conservation organization) until 2022. One of the founding members of Friends of City Park was introduced to birdwatching through the Wildlife Clubs of Kenya at her school. In 1993, she started going on Nature Kenya's Wednesday morning bird walks through the park. When she decided to form a "friends" organization for the park, my parents soon joined. The park's potential was as central a concern to her as its preservation. "I grew up with a garden and knowing what gardens could be like. I grew up seeing City Park and what it could be. It could be so incredible."[51]

On December 14, 1996, Friends of City Park rallied public support for the park's long-term preservation by taking out a full-page ad in the *Daily Nation*, exposing the extent of the encroachment and land grabbing at City Park. They pointed out that the park had been irregularly and illegally subdivided and that the subdivided land had been privately allocated. Although the ad did not elaborate the details, most of those allocations were to politicians.[52] Friends of City Park continued their advocacy by engaging strategic partners—notably the City Council of Nairobi, the National Museums of Kenya, and the public.[53]

After a ten-year struggle, Friends of City Park commissioned a land survey to establish baseline information about the park's boundaries. As a result, an area of sixty hectares (spanning most of the park) was declared a national monument under the Government of Kenya's National Museums and Heritage Act. Nevertheless, some important sections, such as the maze, lay outside the protected area. It was not until 2016 that the maze was finally declared part of the City Park National Monument.

The saga has continued. In 2010, with the creation of the National Land Commission (NLC) under Kenya's new constitution, legal measures were enacted that could be put in service of protecting the park. The NLC was tasked with investigating and dealing with illegal and irregular land acquisitions, and its first concern was the illegal allocation of public land. In 2014 it revoked fourteen private title deeds for plots of land within the sixty hectares of City Park. Yet as of 2020, when the Kenya Forest Service took over the management of the park, these title deeds had not been surrendered.

Friends of City Park has worked both alongside and against multiple government agencies, NGOs, and donor agencies (local and international) on projects to protect City Park. As a result, the organization was threatened with a lawsuit for "standing in the way of development."[54] Indeed, Friends of City Park is itself a defiant remnant that reminds people of the history and public nature of the park.

Remnants in City Park serve as building blocks for new futures. After the 2017 river survey, Friends of City Park worked with government agencies, private stakeholders, a consulting firm, and the Nairobi Metropolitan Services Improvement Project—Integrated Urban Water Management (NaMSIP-IUWM) on an initiative to rebuild the sewer line on Limuru Road. [55] Today the organization is working on a master plan for the park derived from the concerns, aspirations, and issues raised by stakeholders, including the river cleanup.

FIGHTING FOR A CITY PARK FUTURE

On a bright October day in 2012, Friends of City Park held a treasure hunt for children from surrounding primary schools. Each group of children was given a map, a starting clue, and a supervising adult to make sure they did not fall in the river. They were then let loose to find other clues hidden around the park. Afterward, one teacher said that her students were proud because they had demonstrated they could read a map. That was not my initial impression: once let loose, the children, without a glance at the map, started to run in all directions, their assigned adult struggling to keep up. But soon they became more systematic in following clues and finding their way around the park. Hours later, they returned, tired, hungry, proud, and delighted, their assigned adult totally exhausted.

The treasure hunt was designed to educate the children about the nature and history of the park. This history runs deep for Nairobi's long-term residents. At a 2016 stakeholders' forum, the elderly philanthropist Manu Chandaria spoke emotionally about his childhood memories of City Park and of the need to preserve history by preserving the park. Many members of Friends of City Park—and even government workers charged with changing the park—had similar treasured memories.

More than recollections or nostalgia for a past, childhood memories of the park form an emotive and powerful impetus to act on behalf of the children we once were, as well as for the children yet to come. These memories thus connect the past with the future. Even as a band of Eastlands children and a *chokora* grow up, move into the middle class, and disperse to different areas of Nairobi, City Park is a reminder of home. Unlike migrants to the city, the home these Nairobians left behind is the city where they still live.

As City Park struggles for survival, childhood memories reappear as testimonies to efforts to make Nairobi, and Kenya more generally, home. During my years of participation, most members of Friends of City Park were middle-class people, long-term residents of the "leafy" neighborhoods. Few others could afford the time to participate. These members were thus predisposed to feel an affinity for the concept of a garden city. But a number, like my father, had also moved from Railways estates and other less affluent neighborhoods. For them, City Park symbolized the connection between past, present, and future of a divided city.

Today, there are many proposals for renovating the park—and the city. The obstinate remnants, users, and memories of City Park remind us that we now have the opportunity to rethink and rewrite the segregationist ideas behind the garden city, as well as the narrative of neoliberal "regeneration" built on top of it. In "A Park Called Freedom," Lutivini Majanja considers Uhuru (Freedom) Park, a Nairobi park developed after Independence. He asks us to look not just at the monuments to Kenya's independence struggle but also at the ordinary spaces where people relax. He asks us to look at all the users—not just the protesters or celebrators, but also the homeless and those washing their clothes in the ditches. He asks us to see beyond the park to recognize the city that is reflected in those users and uses. Finally, he makes an impassioned plea "to make Uhuru Park a place where all of us, in our different bodies, Nairobi residents and Nairobi's visitors, are free"—in other words, to live up to the ideal of the name through an inclusive, holistic view of the park.[56]

We can think of Nairobi's surviving green spaces, including City Park, as remnants and reminders of the parks that have disappeared and the gardens dug up for high-rise buildings and parking lots, and of government based on taxation rather than fees. But they are also remnants of childhood memories, of beauty, leisure, care, and advocacy, of adventure, peace, and rest. They link generations, the living and the dead. They challenge anti-urbanism, ushering in new identities and new dreams.

These spaces are also reminders of the segregationist planning that situated all the parks in one part of the city and the postcolonial longevity of this spatial layout. The shrinking of City Park's greenery, its enclosures, the land grabbing, and the pollution of its waters reflect practices occurring throughout the city.

Yet as a microcosm of Nairobi, City Park also allows us to consider dreams of how the park and the city can be. This space of dreams is not just imaginary: it is produced through the work of caring gardeners, its daily use by visitors, its preservation and conservation by advocates, and the regeneration of nature within it by the plants and animals, the sun, and the rain.

Elements of City Park are remnants of what they once were. The forest is not the same forest as before Nairobi came to be. The garden is not the garden of the master gardener's memories. The river is no longer safe to play in. Yet these remnants can inspire powerful new visions of the future.

Remnants are not static, but they can be recalcitrant—not only in the sense of calcifying, ossifying, sticking out, and getting stuck, but also in the sense of displaying stubbornness, resistance, defiance, and contempt in the face of anti-urbanism, in the sense of taking permanence for granted. In March 2020, City Park came under the purview of the Ministry of Environment and was taken over by the Kenya Forest Service. Tasked with making legacy projects for President Uhuru Kenyatta, these agencies, along with the Kenya Forest Research Institute and the National Museums of Kenya, seek to transform City Park into a "world class" botanical garden, an urban agriculture demonstration site, a research location, and a space for tourism.

Community activism and advocacy on behalf of City Park has mirrored the stubborn nature of the park itself. Recalcitrance can be mobilized as defiance; defiance can be solidified into building blocks. This combination of dynamism and contumacy produces intergenerational urban connections that can fashion ideas of past, present and future. City Park both enables and blocks the future by not letting people forget.

6

———

Remains of an Unrealized Yesterday

The equatorial high-altitude light filtered through the leaves of the tall croton trees, casting shimmering shadows across the abstract statues in the garden
on the edge of City Park Cemetery. Just behind a large granite head tilted toward
the sun, a bougainvillea with deep purple flowers obscured two graves. The primary schoolchildren rushed to read the inscriptions, standing on the flat granite
slabs and peering at the words. Their teachers turned to me, their volunteer park
guide for the day, in worry. Was it okay that the kids were standing on the graves?
I shrugged.

The children turned to ask who was buried here. I asked them, "Who do you
think?" They replied, "The king and the queen!" I laughed. "What king and queen?"
I asked. "We don't have those here. Look more closely." The children peered at the
words and replied, "Sheila and Joseph Murumbi." I asked them who these two
people were, but they were unable to answer. They were simply mesmerized by the
quiet of the place, the importance of the site evident despite the graves' simplicity.
They expressed their reverence through their wide-eyed interest.

I told them stories—long-forgotten stories of their country and the people who
shaped it. I told them stories of a man who loved African art and collected mas-
terpieces, some now surrounding the graves in the memorial garden at City Park,
others taking up the entire ground floor of the National Archives. I told them the
story that the retired City Park gardener had told me about how this man also
loved plants, decorated his garden with plants from City Park, and gave our first
president, Jomo Kenyatta, a rare yellow Nandi flame tree, which still stands in the
garden at State House.

I could have told them other stories as well—stories of segregation, wars, independence, and assassinations, of futures forestalled and dreams unrealized. But I did not.

FIGURE 9. Joseph and Sheila Murumbi's graves in City Park. Photo by author.

I didn't know how to. Yet these stories surrounded us as we stood at the two graves. They whispered through the flowering trees and resonated off the lichen-covered tombstones. Like the remains, these stories rested in place, waiting to be found.

The children told me stories of the few times they had been to a cemetery— mostly to visit the graves of grandparents. I was reminded that when I posted a picture of City Park on the Nostalgic East Africa Facebook page, someone had asked me to visit the grave of her ancestor, now that she lived abroad. The last time she had been in Nairobi she had felt City Park was unsafe to enter.

Later, after we had walked through a good portion of the park, the school group gathered for drinks and snacks at the restaurant. The Sykes and vervet monkeys eyed our food, watched in turn by adults keeping them at bay with sticks. I asked the children to name the most memorable thing about their trip to City Park. Many shouted, "The owl!" Others, "The deep forest!" A number of children said, "The cemetery." I asked who was buried there, and they called out in unison, "Murumbi!"

The restaurant manager watched them, wide-eyed. Afterwards she came up to me with her hand over her heart and tears in her eyes, saying, "They remember Murumbi." In truth, the children were way too young to "remember" Joseph Murumbi, who died in June 1990, too young to know that Murumbi helped negotiate Kenya's independence at the Lancaster House conferences in London in the early 1960s. Nor were they, or even their parents, born when Murumbi became Kenya's first foreign minister in 1964 or its second vice president in 1966, or when he resigned a few months later, disillusioned by the assassination of the activist Pio Gama Pinto. They do not remember that he asked to be buried in City Park to be near his friend Pinto, even in death.

Why would these children's remembrance hold such poignance for this woman? Half of Kenya's population was born after Murumbi's death, and the rest of us seem to have forgotten him. What memories and stories are being called up from the ground at City Park? What futures do these stories allow and recognize—and what pasts?

Officially there are two cemeteries in City Park, City Park Cemetery and Forest Road Cemetery. The cemeteries make up one-third of the green spaces of the park. Yet most visitors do not notice the cemeteries unless they take a shortcut through the grounds from Muranga Road in Pangani through to Limuru Road, starting either at the Mathare River or the corner with Wangari Maathai Way. This chapter looks at the park from a different perspective, shifting away from its environmental and social significance to emphasize the political history it contains.

Cemeteries and graves can help us understand the implications of death for life in Nairobi. The City Park cemeteries, holding an assortment of national heroes, Commonwealth war veterans, victims of the Emergency era, and an assassinated freedom fighter, evoke a complicated past and various possible futures. The remnants, remains, and reminders in the cemeteries illuminate social, political, and cultural aspects of Kenya's history and the nature of belonging in Nairobi.

A grave is not only a ritualized place to inter a dead body but also a place to tell a story about—to commemorate—a life. A cemetery is a collection of such rituals and stories. In the context of anti-urbanism, the historian Sarah

Balakrishnan argues that cemeteries can be understood as "repositories of archival evidence for tenancy and residency," providing histories of urban permanence.[1] Graves can establish longevity and belonging through ancestors—what scholars might term *ancestrality*. At City Park, graves and cemeteries challenge anti-urbanism by enabling claims to longevity and location through "ancestors" who rest there.

Urban cemeteries in colonial Africa, including those at City Park, were typically segregated, often by both race and ethnicity. The decisions about who should and who should not be buried in cemeteries make them carefully curated, highly political as well as social and cultural spaces. In looking at graves and inscriptions, I also consider those whose are not, or not yet, buried or commemorated and the politics they reference.

The cemeteries at City Park are sites of memory on scales from the familial to the national to the imperial. Scholarly work on burials and commemoration in Africa has often focused on presidents or famous politicians, highlighting how burials and forms of commemoration such as statues are tied to ethnic and national visions.[2] It has examined the ways individuals cultivated a constituency, usually through kinship affiliations (familial, ethnic or national), that has enabled their influence to persist long after death.[3] These events can show us how heroes, memories, and historical understandings are constructed and sustained.[4] The anthropologist and political scientist Wale Adebanwi observes that death and burials provide "resources for creating meaning and legitimacy in moments of tension" and thus enabling political dreams.[5]

Residues, remnants, and remains calcify, solidify, and become structures that are, in the words of Michel-Rolph Trouillot, "too solid to be unmarked, too conspicuous to be candid." Indeed, "they embody the ambiguities of history."[6] As archives of dreams as well as of belonging, the graves at City Park offer a critique of anti-urbanism. They touch on the overlapping contexts of the mundane, familial, national, imperial, regional, transcolonial, and transoceanic while calling up issues of land ownership, belonging, migration, removals, rural-urban relations, civic citizenship, the forgotten, and the city of Nairobi itself.

Perhaps what moved the restaurant manager to tears was less the recollection of Joseph Murumbi himself than the memory of what he stood for, the events he participated in, and the dreams of the time. Such a recollection evokes thoughts of possibilities realized and yet to be realized. Remembering Murumbi through the children allows for possibilities that cannot be realized by individuals alone and the contemplation of futures that did not take shape. It allows for generational continuity.

The graves at City Park allow people to remember a future that did not happen while forgetting a past that did. The remnants, remains, and remainders they hold, and the dreams attached to them, leave traces that disturb colonial and national narratives, through overlapping and entangled processes of remembrance and forgetting.

SEGREGATION IN THE CITY CEMETERIES

On October 20, 2016, amid the profusion of natural beauty that makes the season such a special time in Nairobi, people came in the dead of night to place official beacons in City Park. The beacons demarcated a very large plot of land for excision, the first step in privatization and titling. The plot was rumored to be the site for a new mansion for the governor of Nairobi. The public was alerted to this clandestine action by the sight of felled trees. There was a swift response from the community, thanks to the Friends of City Park and the press (*The Star*). They pointed out that the timing was particularly ironic given that the beacons were placed on Mashujaa Day—National Heroes Day. The uproar forced the eventual removal of the beacons, and this section of City Park was saved.

Of the two cemeteries in the park, City Park Cemetery is more often visited. It lies near the main entrance to the park, just beyond the nursery and a parking lot with a little red Coca-Cola kiosk. It is set back from the pedestrian path behind a patch of tall croton trees and a kei-apple hedge, now obscured by piles of road construction debris. The entry to the cemetery is marked by an archway of orange bougainvillea and a small wooden chapel whose walls have fallen off, exposing the altar. The cemetery is divided into four sections by a path running down the center, crossed by a kei-apple hedge.

If you take the long walk through the gardens of City Park and then through the forest, crossing the Kibagare River, you arrive at the other cemetery, the Forest Road Cemetery. This cemetery runs along Wangari Maathai Way (once known as Forest Road). The first graves you see there are neat, straight, military graves with identical white tombstones, set in a manicured green lawn bounded by a low, carefully trimmed hedge. This is the Commonwealth war graves plot, holding the remains of seventy-three soldiers of World War II and five of World War I, beautifully maintained by the Commonwealth War Graves Commission.[7] This careful interment and remembrance of military veterans stands in stark contrast to the treatment of Africans who died in Nairobi but by law could not be buried in the city.

Depending how you define a hero, there are a number of heroes buried at City Park. Beyond the war heroes and the national heroes Pinto and Murumbi, there is Archibald Shaw, a British Christian missionary among the Dinka people in Sudan, also known by his Dinka title, Macuor. These graves of nationally and internationally known figures represent efforts to commemorate specific individuals, groups, and histories. They lie near the simple graves of people who are remembered only by their families. These efforts to remember cut across colonial

FIGURE 10. Commonwealth wargraves, City Park Forest Road Cemetery. Photo by author.

and postcolonial history. They reflect the segregated nature of life and death in Nairobi during the colonial era, a fissure that bleeds into the present.

Apart from Murumbi, none of those buried at City Park are racially African, and besides those in the Goan part of the cemetery, none are Asian. In colonial Nairobi, there were separate cemeteries for those deemed "non-European" (or nonwhite) and "non-native." These included the Nubian Muslim Cemetery at Kibera and the Asian Muslim cemeteries located in Kariokor: the Ahmadiyya Muslim Cemetery, the Aga Khan Shia Imami Khoja Ismaili Cemetery, the Dawoodi Bohora Cemetery, and the Saaj Shia Cemetery.[8] The Hindu crematorium is also located in Kariokor.

Within the cemeteries are two ethnic sections: a Goan section in the City Park Cemetery and a section for Jewish graves in the Forest Road Cemetery. These sections reflect the conflicts inherent in British colonial definitions of whiteness and Europeanness. Jews were generally seen as European but not Christian. Goans (legally citizens of Portugal) were seen as Asian but Christian.[9]

Africans who died in Nairobi were expected to leave and to be buried "at home"—presumed to be a rural, tribally defined place, preferably on a native reserve. Colonial governments throughout Africa feared that interment in the city would attach local populations to urban spaces.[10] Thus until Independence and the expansion of the city limits to include Lang'ata Cemetery in 1963, there was only one public cemetery open to Christian African civilians within the city limits—the Detribalized Native Cemetery in South C, on the southern edge of the city. The lack of burial spaces for the majority of Nairobi's residents was a reflection and reinforcement of the anti-urbanism that designated Africans as rural rather than urban.

Another colonial law provided a perverse incentive for African families to abide by this policy. The Crown Lands Act enabled the colonial government to appropriate all "abandoned" and vacant rural land. To avoid losing their land, urban Africans started using graves and burials to secure land in the countryside. One of the main social institutions in urban settings was the village association, whose main function was to raise funds to return bodies to the countryside for burial.

The City Park cemeteries are a remnant of these anti-urbanist policies and practices and a reminder of who was supposed to belong and remain in Nairobi. But the cemeteries at City Park tell other stories as well, stories that complicate the anti-urbanist narrative.

REMEMBRANCE

If you visit the City Park Cemetery you will most likely notice that some of the plots are carefully maintained, swept and cleaned every day, while others lie in disrepair. Most of the well-maintained graves are cared for by the Commonwealth War Graves Commission, like the military graves at the Forest Road Cemetery. The commission states that the City Park Cemetery "contains one Commonwealth burial of the Second World War. The commission also cares for 80 nonwar burials in the cemetery."[11]

In 1917, in lieu of repatriating fallen soldiers, the British set up the Imperial War Graves Commission (later renamed the Commonwealth War Graves Commission) to commemorate soldiers buried elsewhere. The commission, made up of members from Australia, Canada, India, New Zealand, South Africa, and the United Kingdom, is tasked with caring for the graves and memorials to the 1,700,000 men and women of the Commonwealth forces who died in the two world wars.[12] It is responsible for cemeteries and memorials at twenty-three thousand locations in 153 countries. Six of these sites are in Nairobi.[13]

The Commission had a mandate to treat all soldiers equally in death. A 1918 report for the commission stated, "All, whatever their military rank or position in civil life, should have equal treatment in their graves. . . . No less honor should be paid to the last resting places of Indian and other non-Christian members of the Empire than to those of our British soldiers."[14] Each soldier's name was to be engraved on a headstone over an identified grave, or on a memorial to the missing. This mandate was extended to apply to the dead of World War II.

The Commonwealth war graves at City Park hold the remains of British (European) soldiers. The other Commonwealth war graves around Nairobi include some African graves, but in no way do they account for the number of East African soldiers and members of the Carrier Corps (the conscripted labor force that carried supplies for soldiers) lost during the two world wars. So where are these other war heroes laid to rest?

In November 2019 Channel 4 in Britain aired the documentary *The Unremembered: Britain's Forgotten War Heroes*, narrated by David Lammy, a Black British member of parliament. *The Unremembered* explored how the Imperial War Graves Commission treated African war dead, particularly in Kenya, after World War I. It gave the lie to the commission's claim of treating all war veterans equally in death and showed that a vast number of those who served in the East African Carrier Corps remain unnamed and uncommemorated.

Although the commission at first reacted defensively to the documentary, it eventually commissioned a study on the issue. The study concluded that "between 45,000 and 54,000 casualties (predominantly Indian, East African, West African, Egyptian and Somali personnel) were commemorated unequally."[15] Some were commemorated collectively rather than individually, and the names of some of the missing were listed in registers rather than on stone memorials.

The study also found that a further 116,000–350,000 East African and Egyptian casualties were not commemorated by name or possibly not commemorated at all. "Contemporary attitudes towards non-European faiths and differing funerary rites, and an individual's or group's perceived 'state of civilization', influenced their commemorative treatment in death." The report goes on to say that "whilst more than 4,200 KAR (members of the King's African Rifles) are known to have died during the conflict, only 401 are commemorated by name—more than half of whom are British officers and non-commissioned officers."[16]

The report acknowledges that although some Africans volunteered to serve Britain during World War I, an equally high number may have been forcibly conscripted or coerced into enlisting by political, physical, and economic threats.[17] My previous research chronicles how mandatory conscription contributed to changing kinship patterns among Digo communities in coastal Kenya.[18] Unequally treated in life, these forcibly conscripted soldiers were forgotten in death. Most Kenyans have no idea what the Carrier Corps did.

Thus, while the war graves at City Park represent an effort in remembrance, they are also an active form of forgetting. They explicitly commemorate the British, but not the Africans, who fell serving the British Empire. Built on the colonial structures of segregation, memorials to the dead of the two world wars perpetuate the inequality they knew in life. These forms of commemoration celebrate some as heroes and dismiss others as cannon fodder. The carefully maintained graves of the war veterans at City Park are haunted by the hundreds of thousands who go unremembered.

NATIONAL HERO AND ART COLLECTOR: JOSEPH MURUMBI

City Park also holds the graves of those involved in another war—the war for independence. The most significant freedom fighter in City Park's cemeteries is one whom few commemorate or remember: Pio Gama Pinto. He was buried at City Park at the request of his good friends Joseph Murumbi, a fellow politician, and Fitz de Souza, a politician and lawyer.[19] Murumbi himself asked to be buried in City Park to be close to his friend, Pinto, in death. When the time came, however, City Park Cemetery was full. Murumbi and his wife, Sheila, are buried just outside the cemetery, as close as possible to Pinto's grave.

Surrounding the graves is a small sculpture garden. Shaded by crotons, Cape chestnuts, and jacarandas, it holds some of the modern African art that Murumbi was famous for collecting. You could visit the sculpture garden without ever noticing the two graves that lie nearby, their black granite slabs blending into the shadows under the purple bougainvillea.

Today, few Kenyans know who Murumbi was, yet he is commemorated in no less than four different locations across Nairobi: at City Park, the National Archives, the Old Provincial Commissioner's Office and African Heritage House. All these commemorations highlight Murumbi's legacy as a collector and patron of the arts and barely touch on his political contribution. Alan Donovan, Murumbi's friend and fellow art collector, became the chair of the Murumbi Trust, and it was he, and the trust, who designed and built the memorial sculpture garden.

Murumbi was born Joseph Anthony Zuzurate in 1911 in Nairobi, the child of a Goan father and a Maasai mother. He went to study in Goa when he was seven. On his return to Kenya in 1931, his father—who had recently lost his house and money—asked him to buy land and settle among his mother's people.[20] However colonial restrictions prevented him from buying rural land, as he was classified by the British as Asian and therefore allowed to purchase only urban property. In order to buy the land, Zuzurate renounced his Asian status and became Maasai. He took his maternal grandfather's name, Murumbi.

In 1952, after meeting Pio Gama Pinto, an activist, journalist and fellow Goan Kenyan, Murumbi entered politics and joined the Kenya African Union (KAU), the primary African political organization of the time. Pinto and Murumbi became fast friends. When the leaders of the KAU were detained during the Emergency (1952–58), Murumbi became its secretary general. Pinto and Murumbi used the press, in particular newspapers in India, to publicize British brutality in Kenya. Murumbi participated in the Lancaster House conferences to negotiate Kenya's

FIGURE 11. Joseph Murumbi Peace Memorial Sculpture Garden. Photo by author.

independence and was instrumental in drafting the nation's first constitution. After Independence, he served as Kenya's first minister of state and foreign minister and then as its second vice president.

After Pinto's assassination in 1965, Murumbi became disillusioned with politics and dedicated himself to art. As the premier collector of African art in the region, he established national policies for heritage preservation regarding art and artifacts. In 1972, along with his wife, Sheila, and Donovan, he established Africa's first pan-African art gallery, called African Heritage, which became a showcase for African culture and art.[21]

Murumbi was especially interested in pioneering East African artists. For instance, he commissioned Francis Nnaggenda's colossal work *Mother and Child*, which today stands in front of the National Museum of Kenya. The sculpture garden at City Park contains works in this modern East African style, including pieces by Nnaggenda, Elkana Ongesa, John Odochameny, and Expedito Mwebe. The National Archives, which Murumbi was instrumental in setting up, also houses part of his art collection, along with his extensive stamp collection.[22] Murumbi also became a collector of plants, including unique varieties propagated in the nurseries of City Park.

The location of his grave outside the cemetery enabled the creation of the sculpture garden to memorialize both Murumbi and his idea of African art. However, this memorialization obscures his role as a politician. Murumbi intended his City Park burial place to signpost that of his friend Pinto. However, his commemoration as an art collector allowed for new stories to be told that downplay the proximity of Pinto's gravesite and quiet the alternative visions of tomorrow that it suggests.

FORGETTING PIO GAMA PINTO

Although Pio Gama Pinto's grave is less than fifteen meters from Murumbi's gravesite and garden, it is not easy to find in the overgrown cemetery. A keen observer might spot the small wooden signpost in the tall grass that bears only his name. The grave's marble headstone once bore an embossed photo of his handsome face. About ten years ago, the photo was stolen. While otherwise indistinct in style from the surrounding graves in the Goan part of the City Park Cemetery, Pinto's grave stands out because of the political nature of his epitaph:

> Pio Gama Pinto
> Born 31.3.1927.
> Assassinated 24.2.1965
> Socialist and Freedom Fighter
> Political Detainee 1954–1959
> Member of Parliament 1963–1965
> If he has been extinguished yet there arise a thousand beacons from the spark he bore.

Born in Nairobi, Pinto, like Murumbi, was sent to school in India when he was eight years old. Eleven years later, he joined the Indian Air Force for a short while and then worked at the Post and Telegraphs Company in Bombay (Mumbai), where he participated in a general strike and got his first experience of mass action

FIGURE 12. Sign to Pio Gama Pinto's grave. Photo by author.

FIGURE 13. Pio Gama Pinto's grave. Photo by author.

and organization. It was in India that he became a journalist and political activist opposing the Portuguese colonial government in Goa. He was a founding member of the Goa National Congress, which sought to liberate Goa from colonial rule.

Avoiding arrest in India, he returned to Kenya in 1949 and became involved in resistance against British colonial rule, mobilizing his connections with Indian newspapers for support. He became active in the Mau Mau, supplying arms, cash, and medical supplies while helping to strengthen resistance organizations.[23] He campaigned against the British excision of Kipsigis and Kamba land through the courts and through British contacts in Parliament.[24] After his clandestine support of the Mau Mau was discovered, he was detained by the British on Manda Island, and later in Kabarnet in the Rift Valley, from 1954 to 1959.

Pinto extended his fight to end Portuguese colonialism to Mozambique, Angola, and Portuguese Guinea (now Guinea-Bissau). He assisted nationalist and political refugees from other parts of Africa, especially Tanganyika. In addition, he started a Konkani (Goan-language) paper in Nairobi and formed the East African Goan League to raise awareness of the social and political realities in Goa. Along with the Kenyan politicians Tom Mboya and Mwinga Chokwe, he offered to organize an international volunteer brigade to liberate Goa. The Indian prime minister, Jawaharlal Nehru, used military force to take over Goa in 1961.[25]

After Kenyan Independence, Pinto became a powerful strategist and aide to Jomo Kenyatta and later became a member of parliament. He was a powerful voice for land redistribution, seeking to establish rent-controlled urban areas to protect tenants. He also worked to establish free health and education services and to minimize wealth disparities.[26]

By 1965, Pinto had come into serious conflict with Kenyatta and the political elite regarding the accumulation and distribution of land bought from Europeans as part of the Independence deal. Pinto suspected Kenyatta of appropriating the land as personal property or distributing it to cronies while huge numbers of people remained poor and landless. [27] He was a strong believer that Uhuru, or Independence, meant *uhuru* (freedom) for all. In his words: "The sacrifices of Kenya's freedom fighters must be honored by the effective implementation of . . . a democratic, African, socialist state in which people have the rights, in the words of the KANU [ruling party] election manifesto, 'to be free from economic exploitation and social inequality.'"[28]

Armed with a list of farms and land stolen from citizens by the government, Pinto sought to organize a vote of no confidence in the president. His friend Fitz de Souza, a lawyer and at one time deputy speaker in Kenya's parliament, recounts coming into a room where Kenyatta and Pinto were arguing over the issue. De Souza took Pinto aside, warning him, "In the eyes of most Africans . . . you are just a Muhindi [Indian], you are perfectly dispensable, but he is not. . . . There will be two shots fired at you and no one will remember you in a year's time."[29] Pinto left Nairobi for Mombasa and planned to leave for Mozambique. However, he was convinced by Murumbi—who could not believe that Kenyatta was a threat—to return to Nairobi.

On February 24, 1965, Pio Gama Pinto was assassinated in his driveway. Kisulu Mutua, who was arrested and jailed for the murder, received a presidential pardon in 2001 after thirty-six years in prison, on the grounds that torture had been used to gain a confession. This left the controversy over Pinto's assassination wide open. The report of the Truth, Justice and Reconciliation Committee of 2013 found that Pinto's assassination "was motivated by ideological differences that were at the heart of the global Cold War but also mirrored in domestic Kenyan politics." It also found that there was sufficient circumstantial evidence to conclude the government was involved in his killing.[30] Pinto was mourned everywhere, and many leaders of African countries, as well as ordinary citizens contributed to the fund set up by Murumbi to educate Pinto's children and resettle the family in Canada.[31] Nevertheless, the historian Godriver Wanga-Odhiambo argues that the governments of both Kenyatta and Daniel arap Moi tried their best to erase Pinto's legacy by preventing efforts to commemorate him, including the proposal by the Nairobi City Council after his assassination to rename Grogan Road as Pio Gama Pinto Road.[32]

Unsurprisingly, Pinto is a complicated national hero. He fought not only for Kenya's independence but also for that of Goa, Mozambique, Portuguese Guinea, and Angola. He was assassinated for remaining true to the ideals of the independence struggle, including the rights to land and freedom. As a socialist, he clashed with the predatory new elite, who were backed by the United States. Pinto thus became a hero that the nation wants to remember but needs to forget so as not to explode under the pressure of its internal contradictions. His obscure grave at City Park is emblematic of those contradictions. Yet it is a trace that cannot easily be erased—a remnant of the politics of Independence and dreams of a different tomorrow.

REMEMBERING ALTERNATIVE FUTURES

Pinto's neglected gravesite stands in contrast to his commemoration on a stamp in a 2008 stamp series titled "Heroes of Kenya."[33] In 2010, Kenya abolished the public holidays Kenyatta Day and Moi Day (named after its first two presidents) and replaced them with Mashujaa (National Heroes) Day, allowing, at least in theory, for the remembrance of different kinds of heroes. Demanded by opposition parties and activists in order to diversify a politics long centered on the presidency, the new space of the "national hero" serves as an empty vessel to be filled through active remembrance of multiple communities.[34]

Acts of commemoration and acts of forgetting are both powerful political tools. In Zimbabwe, the National Heroes Acre cemetery and a narrative of war sacrifice solidified President Robert Mugabe's power.[35] By contrast, Jomo Kenyatta concentrated his power as president by silencing the narratives of war sacrifice and Mau

Mau. The journalist and author Ken Walibora Waliaula argues that the establishment of Kenyatta Day centered Kenyatta as "the one through whom known and unknown other 'heroes' would have to be remembered in the nation's collective memory." National Heroes Day represents an attempt to loosen Kenyatta's tight hold on the narrative of the national hero.

In Kenya, burial traditions that allow for forgetting stand in contrast to European-style cemeteries and efforts of commemoration.[36] Nevertheless, because of the importance of burials to nationalism, until 2006 (over forty years after Independence) there was only one mausoleum built by the government: that of Jomo Kenyatta, built in the heart (or perhaps the head) of Nairobi, next to Parliament and City Hall. It is small by European or American standards but an imposing structure nonetheless, heralded by a lane of flags and protected by a fence. Its location in urban Nairobi, rather than Kenyatta's rural birthplace of Gatundu, identifies Kenyatta with the entire nation and with modernity rather than tradition.

Martin J. Murray argues that new national identities are forged out of struggles over "recovery and suppression of past memories." Crafting a specific triumphalist narrative requires suppressing other stories. National history and identity are thus shaped as much by forgetting as by remembering.[37] The telling of national history in Kenya, as a postcolonial country, centers on conflicts over land and freedom. History is used to validate the legitimacy of claims to territory as well as to legitimize the meaning of participation in struggles for the state. Pinto's assassination was tied to both these issues.

At City Park, the national narrative is called into question by the traces of other histories in the same space. The commemoration of Pio Gama Pinto at City Park is complicated by the traces of racial segregation, a product of colonialism and anti-urbanism, that enabled his burial there yet continued to exclude Murumbi.

It is not a straightforward story.

At City Park Cemetery, most visitors don't venture beyond the hedge at the far end of the cemetery. But if they did, they would see a small house that has had extensions added as the years passed. The residents often sit by the graves, playing with their children and washing their laundry. The family is present to guard the water pump. Beyond the house and the space where the children play are several well-tended graves, including common graves with multiple headstones commemorating British military pilots who died between 1952 and 1956.

These graves are among the eighty "non-war burials" tended by the Commonwealth War Graves Commission.[38] The dates on the graves (1952–56), and their occupation as military pilots, indicate an altogether different war—the war against the Mau Mau during the State of Emergency (1952–58). Theirs was a form of service to empire whose commemoration does not sit easily within a national monument in a postcolonial state.

When David M. Anderson and Paul J. Lane write about the difficulty for Kenya of dealing with the "heroic bones" of Kikuyu fighters who joined the Mau Mau,

FIGURE 14. Mass graves, of British military pilots, City Park Cemetery. Photo by author.

along with the "non-heroic bones" of Kikuyu soldiers who fought for the British, they pose the question: how do we deal with heroes and antiheroes in the post-Independence situation?[39] How, indeed, do we accommodate them in the same geographic space at City Park? The authors characterize these issues as a "wicked problem"—one that is resistant to resolution and can be considered from multiple perspectives. The graves at City Park that hold British dead recalling the Emergency, the war graves that recall the unremembered, Murumbi's grave that recalls Pinto, and, in particular, Pio Pinto's grave that recalls a future that did not happen all pose wicked problems of unfinished history.

As Kenya approached its fiftieth anniversary and many of the Independence generation started to pass away, concern was expressed about the lack of historical knowledge of these times. There was public outcry at the deplorable conditions under which former freedom fighters and nationalists lived and died. With the devolution promised by the 2010 constitution, which transferred many powers to local government, there was also renewed interest in local spaces and how they were connected to the rest of the nation. These concerns brought changes in the memorialization and containment of the narrative of Independence and its heroes.

The material and visual culture historian Anne E. Coombes states that "between 2006–2007 there was a spate of mausolea erected (with promises of future mausolea) with government funding."[40] Mausoleums were erected for Bildad Kaggia and Paul Ngei, who were detained during the Emergency, and for Kisoi Munyao, who hoisted the Kenya flag at the top of Mount Kenya at Independence. In addition, existing mausoleums were refurbished, including those of Tom Mboya (assassinated in 1969) on Rusinga Island in Lake Victoria and the Nandi leader Koitalel arap Samoei in the Nandi hills, both of which had been constructed without any help from the government. But nothing changed at Pinto's grave.

Unlike the others suddenly remembered fifty years after Independence, Pinto was not from a large or politically powerful ethnic group that needed appeasement. Nor had he mobilized an ethnic or racial community while alive.[41] While intimately connected to Kenyatta's success, he had challenged it as well. And he paid for that challenge with his life.

It is ironic that Pinto, an anticolonialist, socialist, and nationalist, is buried not far from the graves of those he fought against, in a segregated section of a segregated cemetery.[42] Originally, he was to be buried in the relatively new public cemetery at Lang'ata, which remains Nairobi's main cemetery. However, Joseph Murumbi and Fitz de Souza decided he should be buried at City Park instead, in a family plot next to his father.[43]

The Goan Kenyan lawyer Fitz de Souza defended Kenyatta at the Kapenguria trials during the Emergency and, like Murumbi, participated in the Lancaster House conferences. He was a member of parliament and served as deputy speaker of the House until 1970. Why would these nationalists choose to bury Pinto at City Park rather than Lang'ata? I was sadly not able to ask De Souza about this choice before his memory faded, and he does not refer to it in his memoirs.

Perhaps De Souza understood the politics of race better than Pinto. Burying Pinto at City Park put him in the center of Nairobi, in an accessible public space. Placing his grave in the Goan section of the cemetery symbolically centered Goans, and Asians more generally, in Kenyan history. It identified them as founders of the nation, as freedom fighters establishing the legitimacy of the state. Pinto's epitaph calls on Kenya to recognize his history as Kenya's history—socialist and freedom fighter, political detainee, member of parliament. But it also identifies him as a martyr—assassinated. His grave claimed a home in the city for Goans and, by extension, Asian Kenyans; and his deeds claimed a place for them in Kenya as well. After all, there is no greater political sacrifice than death.

The placement of Pinto's grave was a criticism of the African nationalism that sidelined Asian Kenyans after Independence. It highlighted his identification with Kenya as a freedom fighter. Proclaiming him to be a socialist was a protest against the new government structures that maintained profound inequalities of land and wealth. The statement that he was assassinated was a bellow against the silencing of protest. And it was also a remembrance of the future that might have been.

Looked at yet another way, Pinto's burial in at City Park can be seen as establishing an ancestral claim to land.[44] After Independence, burials continued to serve as a way of laying claim to "ancestral lands" in rural areas. It also became a way of claiming permanence in urban areas (see chapter 8). Claiming land through ancestors establishes a presence across generations. The moral weight of ancestors and their existence in a realm prior to and beyond the state legitimizes the land claims. As an Asian Kenyan Pinto was unable, unlike Murumbi, to own land anywhere but in urban spaces. Burying him at City Park, in a family plot next to his father, makes an ancestral claim to the city of Nairobi and Asian Kenyans' place in the city.

FUTURES BUILT ON REMEMBRANCE

When the schoolchildren read the Pio Gama Pinto's epitaph, they turned to me and asked, "What does *assassinated* mean?"

I replied, "To be killed."

"Who killed him?" they asked.

I was at a loss for words. How could I answer these children, when the president of Kenya at the time was Jomo Kenyatta's son Uhuru, named for the very freedom and independence Pinto fought for and about? I mumbled something about the government, and the children lost interest and moved on. The traces of that complicated history lingered and followed me throughout the day.

Others, too, have found their way to Pinto's grave. In 2019, a poster appeared at City Park inviting people to a presentation titled "Pio Gama Pinto: Reflections in his Struggles for Socialism and Liberation." It was to be held at Pinto's grave. The poster bore a smiling Independence-era photograph of Pinto.

The presentation was hosted by the Dandora Community Justice Centre, in partnership with Ukombozi Library. Dandora, a low-income and high-density neighborhood of Nairobi, is located a considerable distance from City Park. The Community Justice Centre is one of several grassroots organizations that have arisen to fight police violence, extrajudicial executions, and the criminalization of poverty in Kenya.[45] According to the United Nations Office of the High Commissioner for Human Rights, Kenya's first social justice center was started in 2015 in Mathare. Today there are over one hundred of these centers.[46] Coordinated through the Social Justice Working Group, they work with the Police Reforms Working Group and the Missing Voices Project to document and remember the executed and the disappeared in Kenya, to collect data to hold the police and government accountable, and to support the families of those killed.[47]

Ukombozi Library (Liberation Library), the partner organization hosting the presentation, aims to make progressive leftist literature and books on the practice of liberation available to activists and Kenyan youth. It was set up in downtown Nairobi in 2017 by underground activists and the Progressive African Library and Information Activists' group (PALIAct).[48]

Ukombozi Library also promotes books published by Vita Books, including a biography of Pinto by Shiraz Durrani, a librarian and activist. In the early 1980s, he wrote an article in *The Standard* newspaper in which he called Pinto a national hero and accused the government of killing him. The article resulted in two visits by the Special Branch of the police, after which Durrani fled to Britain as a political refugee. In 2018 Durrani published the book *Pio Gama Pinto: Kenya's Unsung Martyr, 1927–1965.*

The 2019 remembrance sponsored by the Dandora Community Justice Center was followed by a number of activities commemorating Pinto, organized by the Mathare Community Justice Center's Organic Intellectuals Network. They included visits to Pinto's grave, a Pinto study group, and a seven-part podcast on Pinto in Sheng (Nairobi creole) called *Until Everyone Is Free.*[49]

But why is Pinto's grave a focal point for activism? The grave was an anomaly among the other commemorations that mobilize ethnic or racial constituents in struggles for political power.[50] His commemoration as a nonethnic, nonracial, urban ancestor allowed his uptake in class struggles. His story resonates with inhabitants of Dandora and Mathare who are familiar with anti-urbanist violence. His grave provides a public site of mourning for all others killed or disappeared at the hands of the government. It forges a connection between the socialist liberation movements and those seeking justice for state-sponsored violence. Mzalendo Wanjira, a member of the Organic Intellectuals Network, wonders, "What would the present Kenya look like had Pinto's ideas and dreams for Kenya materialized?"[51]

Pinto's grave offers an opportunity for considering not only forestalled pasts but also alternative futures for individuals and communities. Gathanga Ngung'u, another member of the Organic Intellectuals Network, insists that "life must be lived forward; nonetheless, it is the past the informs the decisions we make for the future."[52] Unlike the restaurant manager mourning Murumbi, and Murumbi mourning Pinto, and Pinto mourning the broken promises of Independence, the community justice centers of Dandora and Mathare are grounded in the present and are looking forward to frame a new, just future.

TRACES THAT DO NOT LET US FORGET

A long time ago, my aunt told me that she was building herself a house in the countryside, as she felt her children would not do it for her, and she would have nowhere to be buried. The obsession with where and how to be buried is particular to western Kenya. People there used to be buried in their houses, which were then allowed to decay along with the body or were taken down after a year.[53] My aunt's house was a round, one-room structure made of mud and wood, set in a compound with many similar structures. The anthropologist Constance Smith makes the argument that as long as these houses remained, so did the memories of the deceased.[54] However, with time, both the house and the body would become dust, and this process of decay would allow people to forget. These burials were a form of transient remembrance that allowed people to move on, to build a new house for another person.[55]

Now that most houses are durable structures of stone and cement, this tradition has changed. People are buried on family properties in elaborate cement graves. The graves mark the ownership of land (either as a family or as a clan). As family compounds become more and more crowded with graves in densely populated western Kenya, the cement slabs are used for drying crops. According to Smith, these changes have halted the organic process of forgetting.[56]

Cemeteries are not just resting places for the dead; they are sites for processes of remembrance, commemoration and memorialization by the living. This is especially true of the graves and cemeteries at City Park. Graves offer archival evidence that helps materialize connections between the past and the future. They enable recognition and claims of ancestry in ways that cremations, for instance, cannot. Public cemeteries, unlike private family burial sites, allow any visitor to contemplate those who are buried there and to participate in personal and communal acts of making meaning from their deaths. Pinto can symbolize Asians in Kenya; at the same time he can represent all victims of assassination. This fungibility creates the possibility of shared symbolic ancestry for disparate groups and individuals.

In the cemeteries at City Park, the overlapping and entangled acts of remembrance and forgetting produce a cacophony of narratives in the silent space of the graves. First and Second World War soldiers remembered and forgotten. Empire remembered and forgotten. A segregated world remembered and forgotten. Wars for Independence remembered and forgotten. Nationalists remembered and forgotten. Freedom and land remembered and forgotten. Dreams of a home and belonging remembered and forgotten. Dreams of a new tomorrow remembered and forgotten.

The cemeteries at City Park are regularly visited, if not by descendants of those buried, at least by ornithologists, naturalists, historians, picnickers, casual visitors to the park, and now by activists. These cemeteries, in their various states of upkeep and neglect, and the people that visit them, provide remnants of histories that trouble actions in the present.

As City Park struggles for existence against encroachment and destruction amid the increasing privatization and rapid development of the city, its buried remains bear witness to efforts to challenge anti-urbanism and to make Nairobi home. The traces and narratives it holds, whether colonial, nationalist, socialist, artistic, Jewish, or Goan, complicate Kenyan narratives of nationalism and race. Those who visit the graves may have no personal ties to those at rest there. Rather, they may be moved by childhood memories of freedom and recreation, and political dreams of freedom and equality, to adopt these particular stories as their own and use them as a basis for forming new communities and new ways of belonging to the city.

City Park demonstrates the legacy and instability of anti-urbanism. Tasked with making legacy projects for President Uhuru Kenyatta, the Ministry of Environment, the Kenya Forest Service, the Kenya Forest Research Institute, and the National Museums of Kenya are seeking to transform City Park into a "world class" botanical garden, an urban agriculture demonstration site, a research location, and a space for tourism, among other things. One idea that emerged as part of this process was that the relatives of those buried at City Park would come back to visit their ancestors. In the process, they would bring revenue. Although the idea tries to monetize remnants and remains, it will also have to reckon with the remains of history that this process will disinter.

7

Place of Sweet Water

Nairobi was named after the water that runs through and beneath it,
and it became what it is today because of this water.
The important thing about the water was its sweetness.
A water without alkali, a drinkable, cool water.
Nairobi—place of sweet/cool water.
Place of water.

Once, in the middle of April, during the long rains, in the not-so-distant past—say 150 years or so ago—a drop of rain fell on a tall albizia tree growing in the red soils in the cool highland forest that later became the city of Nairobi. The droplet united with the dew that had accumulated in the cold of the night, when the clouds sleep on the hills. The moisture rolled off the leaves and down the thick trunk of the albizia onto the undergrowth, dripping down into the red soil between fern stems. As more drops formed, some of the water sank into the ground and gradually flowed downhill, and some formed a trickle on the surface.

These trickles of water came and went with the rains and the years. The moisture above the ground made what we have come to know as a wetland. As the trickles collected, they carved a track through the red soil and became a stream. And the stream thought it could go places, and it began to run downhill at a faster and faster pace, collecting more trickles and raindrops along the way.

This stream began at Loresho, around what became the grounds of KARO (Kenya Agricultural Research Organization). It turned north to flow behind what became Patch (Nairobi School) and into the neighborhood of Kyuna. Then it straightened its course, heading southeast. The red soil of its banks was held in place by the roots of huge mugumo fig trees and towering crotons. The air slowly warmed as it headed downhill to Spring Valley. Here the stream was reunited with its underground half, which had sunk into the red hill soils and now came welling up as springs. Whole once more, the stream cut itself a deep path. More streams ran to join it, excited to start their journey to the sea.

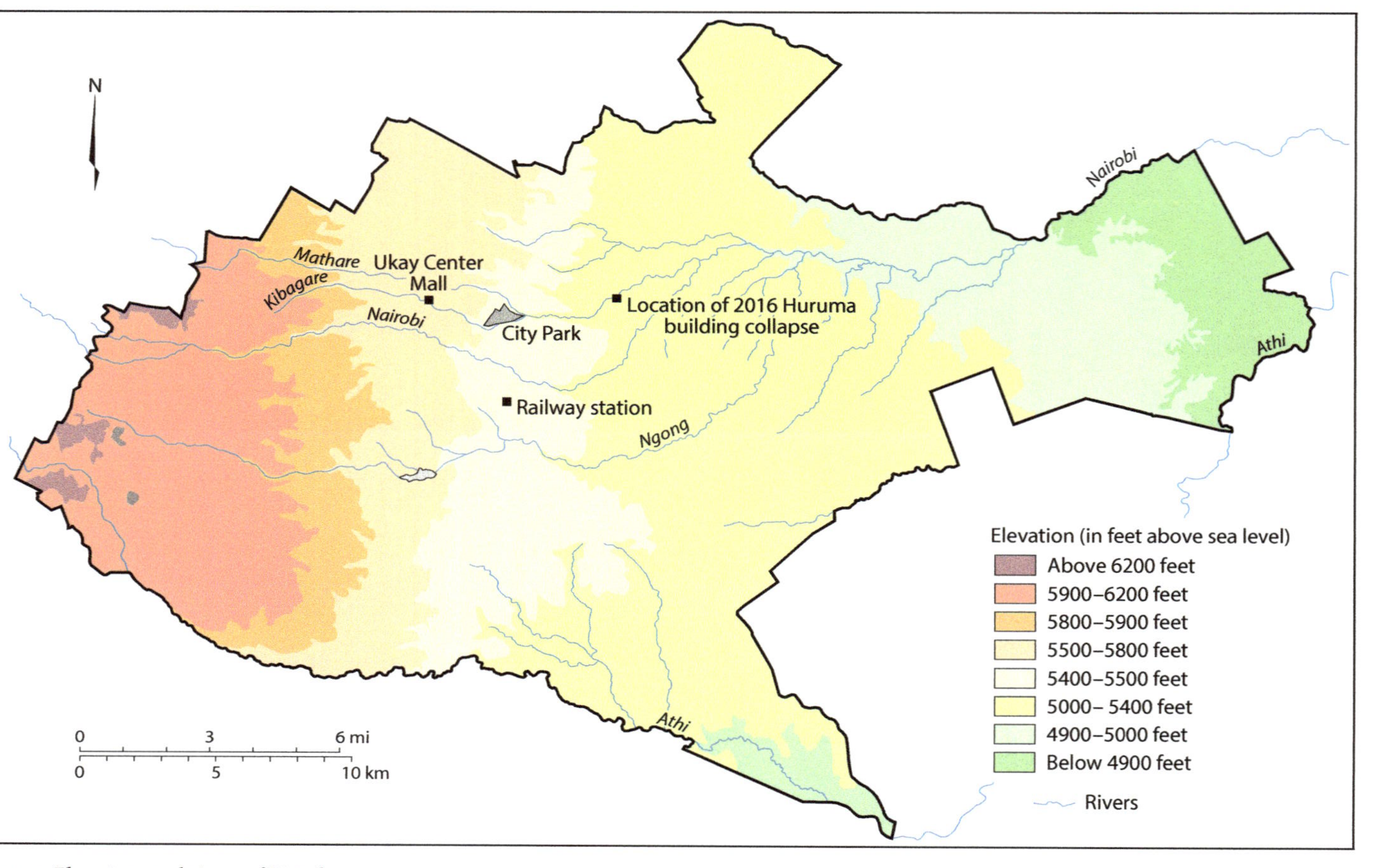

MAP 3. Elevations and rivers of Nairobi.

FIGURE 15. Kibagare River and fig tree. Photo by author.

The stream, overcome with the joy of movement and now even more powerful, overflowed its banks inside today's City Park, fertilizing and flooding the carefully planned wetland plants below the maze. In recognition of its power and generosity, the stream was given a name: the Kibagare River. Excited at its recognition, the river joined a formidable neighbor, which had also just recently become a river.

The neighboring river began in much the same way. However, this river had its source in the rural highlands northwest of Nairobi, almost at Kikuyu. Leaving Kiambu, it flowed down and entered Nairobi north of Loresho. Separated by a ridge, the two streams unknowingly raced each other. The second river grew bold in Nairobi, rushing past Spring Valley and Parklands, painting a swath of green among the tall buildings that now line its banks. Its course almost passed through City Park but then veered away at the last minute, as if to avoid spoiling the glory of the Kibagare, which luxuriated in the tall trees and gardens of the park.

As the Kibagare River leaves the greenery of City Park, its clear waters blend with the red swell of its neighbor, tinted by the rich highland soil, and the two become the Mathare River. The Mathare River rushes downward into regions where the weather is warmer and the land drier. The river makes a distinct green path through a maze of concrete high-rises as it rushes past Pangani and Mathare toward the flat lands of Huruma, Kariobangi, and Grogan, tracing the contours of ancient swamps in the black clay soils of the plains, and past the dump at Dandora.

At Dandora Phase 4 housing estate, the Mathare joins the Nairobi River. Happy at this family reunion, full of laughter, the waters meander through the flat land until they find another sibling, the Ngong River, at New Njiru Town. Just past the Dandora sewage pools, the city spits the river out onto flat plains of black cotton soils shaded with yellow-barked acacia and thorn trees. Outside Nairobi, it joins forces with the even more powerful Mbagathi (Athi) River, which flows through a different part of Nairobi.

A forest raindrop descends 1,500 feet within Nairobi alone, and then another 5,000 feet downhill to the Indian Ocean.

This chapter is about the Kibagare/Mathare River, its fraught journey through the city, and the social, environmental, and human interactions that result in hydrological change. These changes in the distribution and movement of water through and beneath Nairobi are illustrated by the collapse of a residential building in Huruma in 2016 and the demolition of a mall in Parklands in 2018. One structure was taken out by the river, the other by the state; one situated in the lowlands, the other on higher ground; one located in a poor neighborhood, the other in a wealthy one; one built on black soil, the other on red; one new, the other about thirty years old; one taken down during the rainy season, the other during the dry; one owned by a Kenyan developer of African descent, the other by a Kenyan developer of Asian descent; one residential, the other commercial; one causing the loss of fifty-two lives, the other the destruction of millions of shillings' worth of goods. Both buildings were simultaneously permitted and condemned.

Although people speculated about the "real" reasons for the demolition of the mall, this chapter does not seek to solve that mystery. Rather, it explores what changed in the river to precipitate both the collapse and the demolition, and what the consequences of these changes might be for how we think of Nairobi and plan for its future. What role has anti-urbanism played in these changes? This chapter draws on observations of the river over many years, people's impressions of the effects of infrastructure projects, newspaper reports of building collapse and demolitions, place names, and analysis of the geology and topography of the city to examine the human imprint on the Kibagare River, and water more generally, in Nairobi. How is this city of sweet and cool water understood, managed, and planned for? How must this conception change to bring about a more equitable and just future?

Collapse, demolition, and the riparian environment define modern Nairobi. All these factors are inflected by the effects of climate change. This chapter asks how taking the perspective of the *longue durée* might allow us to imagine a new politics of and for the city, and for other cities in the context of rapid urbanization and climate change.

Hydrology and topography place Nairobi at great risk from the effects of climate change. This risk is produced and exacerbated by infrastructure development, building, growing overall wealth, and, in particular, by a city layout driven by anti-urbanism.

A RIPARIAN PROBLEM

When a six-story apartment building in Huruma collapsed in April 2016, killing fifty-two people, Kenya was in the midst of its long rainy season, which typically lasts from March through May. The Associated Press reported that rescue teams were delayed by hours-long traffic jams caused by flooded roads.[1] The building had already been condemned by the government. President Uhuru Kenyatta ordered the arrest of its owners and demanded a survey of other structures in the area to find out whether they were also at risk of collapsing.[2] In local and international media, the collapse of the building was blamed on three factors, in order: heavy rainfall, shoddy construction, and lack of enforcement of building regulations.

A chorus of politicians registered their outrage at the collapse with calls to fight against corruption in housing construction. News reports argued that some property developers took "advantage of a high demand for housing in Nairobi" and bypassed building regulations "to cut costs and maximize profits." The rooms were quickly occupied at a rent equivalent to $35 a month. Jacob Kiruma, a local resident who once lived in an adjacent building, was reported as saying, "The collapsed building was built in less than five months." In addition, he pointed out, "The buildings were constructed too close to a river."[3] The collapsed building was, according to a local member of parliament, "built less than 5m [15 feet] from a river, when it should have been at least 30m away."[4] The area legislator Stephen Kariuki blamed the county government for failing to follow through with the demolition of condemned buildings.[5]

Although the collapse of this building had the highest death toll, it was not the first or the last in the poorer parts of Nairobi. In August 2016 a six-story building collapsed in Kariobangi South, not far from Huruma. In April 2017 and December 2019, deadly collapses of six- and seven-story buildings occurred in Eastlands.[6] In 2016, *The Nation* published a list of previous high-rise building collapses, including a four-story building in Zimmerman in 2016, another in Roysambu in April 2015, a six-story building in Huruma in January 2015, a five-story building in Kaloleni in December 2014, a building under construction in Mlolongo in June 2012, a six-story building in June 2011, and a five-story building under construction in the CBD in January 2006.[7] All but the last were in the low-lying areas of Nairobi, and all collapsed during or just after the rainy season (either the March–May long rains or the October–December short rains). Rain, the urgent demand for affordable housing, the unstable black cotton soils of the lowland plains, and corruption form a deadly combination.

Building collapse had become so common that in 2015 Kenya's president had ordered an audit of all the country's buildings to see if they were up to code.[8] In Nairobi the audit focused on the lowland parts of Nairobi that were becoming a

FIGURE 16. Demolitions in a riparian area near the Nairobi Arboretum. Photo by author.

concrete jungle of high-rise buildings: Eastlands (Umoja, Kariobangi, Huruma), Dagoretti, Kasarani, Zimmerman, Kahawa West, Roysambu, Githurai 44 and 45, Garden Estate, and Thome.[9] Kilimani, an affluent neighborhood in the hills, was also included because of a wall collapse that resulted in fatalities.[10]

The audit was carried out by the National Construction Authority, which had been set up in 2011 to address the recent phenomenon of collapsing high-rise buildings. It reported that of the buildings surveyed, only 42 percent were fit for habitation. The report recommended the demolition of buildings constructed on major watersheds. A government official, Moses Nyakiongora, was quoted as saying that construction within five meters of the highest flood level of a river was considered an encroachment into riparian reserves.[11]

The word *riparian* made a violent entry into the vocabulary of many Nairobians in August 2018, when wealthier parts of the city were stunned by the unannounced demolition of several well-known, long-standing buildings. These included a Shell petrol station at the corner of Arboretum Drive and Ring Road Kileleshwa, which had been there since the 1970s and which housed a Java House Café (known as Java Arboretum); a mall (the Ukay Center) on the Kibagare River in Parklands, colloquially known as Nakumatt Ukay; South End Mall on Lang'ata Road; and the gardens, swimming pools, and backyards of a number of houses in Kileleshwa. The official reason for the demolitions was that the buildings were sited on riparian land

and that the owners had either ignored or infringed building regulations regarding proximity to rivers. Some four thousand buildings were designated as illegal.

After the first dramatic demolitions, none of the remaining illegal buildings were brought down. These included a building owned by the governor of Nairobi, Mike Sonko, who had declared that he would take it down himself.[12] Nor were adjacent structures demolished. There was speculation aplenty as to the real reason for these demolitions, running the gauntlet from hits on political opponents to the nonpayment of bribes, attacks on Asian Kenyans, and the politics of devolution. Nobody took seriously the argument about riparian protection—at least in 2018. By 2024, however, *riparian* had become an accepted reason for structures to be demolished or claimed by the state.

The public reaction was not only to the suddenness of the demolitions (owners and tenants were given no notice to vacate) but also to the official rationale. Demolishing buildings in the name of protecting the environment was unprecedented in Nairobi. Residents found themselves wondering about the *real* reason for *these* demolitions.

RIVER OR STREAM?

I was in a taxi coming from the airport when the driver said, "Do you know Nakumatt Ukay has been demolished? It is on a river." Which it really is—okay, was. The building was literally on top of the river.

According to the newspapers, Kental Enterprises Ltd., the owners of the Ukay Center, having received notice that the building was scheduled for demolition, went to court in August 2018 to obtain a restraining order against what they termed an illegal demolition.[13] They sued the National Environment Management Authority (NEMA), the Nairobi City Government (NCG), the Water Resource Management Authority (WRMA), the National Youth Service (NYS), and the attorney general of Kenya. They argued that the Nairobi City Council (NCC, which had since become the NCG) had approved their building plans in 1994, and if the NCC had authorized them to build, then subsequent laws changing the definition of a riparian section "offend[ed] their property rights."[14] But the court declined to hear the case. On August 10 bulldozers started demolishing the building.

Since the court case was never heard, there is no public record of the arguments in the case. However, one of the owners, Pejul Shah, was quoted in a newspaper article as saying, "There is no river whatsoever under the building, what there is, is a stream which is at the back of the building."[15] Kental Enterprises sued the Kenyan government in 2019 for compensation of Ksh 2.3 billion (US $23 million), claiming that the demolition was compulsory acquisition.[16] This case has yet to be decided, so again there is no public record of the arguments.

Now let me first say, I don't know whether the owners of the Ukay Center actually made the argument in court about the building not being on a river but on a stream; whether Kenyan law truly makes any distinction between rivers and streams (I could find none); or whether streams fall under the category of *riparian* in legal terms or in building codes. But here are the pressing questions as they relate to urban planning in a city like Nairobi, which is built on hills separated by river valleys: Was the watercourse a river or a stream when the Ukay Center was built over it? And has the nature of the watercourse changed, and if so, why?

BUILDING IN A WATER CITY

Nairobi became the principal stop on the railway across Kenya, and eventually the capital city of the country, because of its water. It was the first site of freshwater after the endless plains, with their alkaline lakes, stretching inland from the Indian Ocean. The surrounding forests also provided wood to fuel the steam engines. The railway line, and the center of the modern city, runs along the dividing line between the hills and the plains. Half the area of the current city is highlands, accommodating about 28 percent of the population, and the other half is lowlands, home to the remaining 72 percent.[17] The elevation drops almost 1,000 feet (300 meters) between the highlands of Kikuyu and Karen and the lowland of the Athi River plains (starting at Wilson Airport or at Huruma in Eastlands) and another 500 feet (160 meters) to the city's sewage pools at Dandora .[18] As a teenager, I used to leave my home in Upper Hill for Kianda High School near Kangemi, 400 feet higher up. I left a warm, dry, sunny place to arrive twenty minutes later (in those days) in a cold, misty, overcast place. I never learned to bring a sweater. I spent my four years of high school sniffling in the cold.

It is this elevation difference that makes water such a problem for the city. Although none of the rivers in Nairobi are big rivers, when the rains come and the rivers rise, water flows quickly and forcefully downhill. It brings with it the consequences and debris of upstream development in wealthy neighborhoods downstream to affect the poor.

Flowing down from the hills and separated by ridges like fingers on a hand until they meet in the plains, Nairobi's rivers shaped the city's layout and are reflected in the names of its roads and neighborhoods: Valley Arcade, Valley Road, Spring Valley, Mathare Valley, Mukuru kwa Reuben, Mukuru kwa Njenga, Brookside Drive, Dam Estate, River Road, Riverside Drive, Ziwani, Ngara, Ridgeways, High Ridge, Thigiri Ridge, Loresho Ridge, Red Hill, Upper Hill, and so on.[19] This configuration is a leading cause of the city's traffic problems. Most of Nairobi's major roads follow watercourses.[20] Bridges have made it possible to cross some of the river valleys, but many journeys to different parts of town require travelers to take one road to the center and another, sometimes almost parallel, road out again.

The valleys and ridges in Nairobi also determine the life chances of its residents. Today, as in colonial times, wealthier residents generally live on higher ground and the less wealthy and the poor on lower ground. Most of the lower plains of

Nairobi are now dominated by tenement buildings over six stories high. These new development projects rest on the same anti-urbanist foundations that structured the colonial city and designated much of the urban population as out of place, temporary, and in the way of development.

The flow and control of water have been integral to this pattern of development. The European fear of malaria led to the relegation of African residents to the swampy lowlands and the generous spacing between houses in the hills. Riparian areas were left undeveloped, providing space for the amenities of the envisioned garden city and leading to the riparian land allocations and sales of the 1990s. The colonial administrators mandated a minimum of twelve-foot (four-meter) wayleaves (areas of no construction) along all rivers, streams, and drainage lines to allow for spraying and clearing of vegetation to control malaria. Swamps and low-lying areas were drained and canalized.[21] The current city was built on top of this old malaria-control blueprint.

Perhaps because of their confused origin, current riparian laws are confusing and difficult to enforce.[22] In addition, new concerns such as flooding, degradation of the riparian environment, and building collapse emerged with the rapid growth in the population density of the city from the 1990s.

Much of the land where tenements are built was originally public land alienated for industrial development, which later became the object of significant real estate speculation.[23] Such property transfers of public land have consistently resulted in disputes over ownership. They also reflect a longstanding practice of using land to pay off government debts, promote industry, reward loyalty, gain resources, and win elections. During the 1990s it was also used by the government to solve liquidity problems due to high inflation, devaluation of the currency, and reduction in international lending to Kenya.

In 1980, Kenya was one of the first countries to sign a structural-adjustment loan agreement with the World Bank, which required the country to restructure its government, economy, trade, and finance. During the 1990s, with the end of the Cold War, development aid from both superpowers to Africa declined. The percentage of Kenyans living in poverty increased from 35 percent in the 1970s to 50 percent by the end of the 1990s. In 1993 the Kenyan shilling was devalued (losing about half its value against the US dollar) and then floated on the open market, which increased its volatility. Unable to borrow money from the World Bank and IMF during the 1990s, the government borrowed internally at double-digit interest rates. Kenya's economic growth decreased from over 7 percent in the 1970s to 2.2 percent during the 1990s. This economic situation was exacerbated by a severe drought.[24] Inflation hit its highest level ever in 1993, reaching 46 percent and putting Kenya into a fiscal crisis that the government solved through issuing treasury bonds and doubling interest rates.[25] In the late 1990s few individuals or institutions, other than religious organizations and banks, had money for building in Nairobi.

In these desperate circumstances, the government used land as currency, allocating much public, vacant, and unused land in Nairobi for development. The effects of these allocations were compounded by corruption: some public lands mandated for other uses, like City Park, were subdivided and allocated at that time. Land in the eastern parts of Nairobi was allocated or sold to the relatives and friends of officials in the Lands Office, who were by and large Kikuyu.[26] This land distribution, combined with the preferential transfer of former European landholdings—just after Independence—especially the farms incorporated as part of the expanded city to the north and east—to Kikuyu landlords, resulted in an ethnic concentration of landlords in the city.[27] Thus the unlawful and irregular acquisition of land during the 1990s and early 2000s was built on and in turn reinforced older political patronage.[28] Because of this corruption, allotment letters were hard to turn into title deeds. Allotment letters and sales agreements came to replace title deeds as informal proof of ownership. In addition, because of the vague legal status of areas on the eastern side of Nairobi, including Huruma, and their incorporation into the city in 1963 (which expanded the city's area fifteen-fold), there were no formal planning or zoning guidelines for these areas.[29]

Many of the 1990s allocations and buildings exist with both the approval and disapproval of the state, making them legal and illegal at the same time. The allocation of public, utility, and riparian land alongside old buffer zones, Railways land, and other government land has added to the regulatory confusion and tenure conflicts. The legality of these allocations is being increasingly challenged today. When accused of having acquired the land illegally, the "owners" argue they have the papers to prove ownership. At the core of the problem is the issue of who had the authority to allocate public land in the first place.

These areas comprise many of the open spaces on the city's periphery that were not subject to zoning and planning during colonial days. With the neoliberal turn and private development of the 2000s, they became what the urban scholar Marie Huchzermeyer describes as tenement cities, "dominated by private landlordism in the form of dense, monotonous, multi-story districts." She argues that the multi-story building trend in Nairobi has created one of the densest tenement districts in urban history.[30]

On that fateful April in 2016, residents of one of those tenement buildings in Huruma were alerted to a problem with the building when the windows cracked and broke. Many began to move out the next day. However, others had no money to move and nowhere to go.[31] Some were able to borrow money from their bosses with hopes of moving the next day. By evening, however, the building had collapsed, killing fifty-two of those who remained.

Huruma is a relatively new neighborhood consisting of tightly packed high-rise buildings, with no open spaces or trees. According to the 2019 national census it has a population density of 107,805 residents per square kilometer (about 430 per acre).[32] Its buildings are poorly ventilated and poorly lit, generally have no piped water, and lack drainage. In comparison, the older neighborhoods of Nairobi West and South B, which also have recent high-rise developments, were found to be fairly well built, with above-average accessibility and drainage.[33] Most estates in these other areas have open space where children can play. This is absolutely lacking in Huruma, which imitates the colonial barracks housing of ten-by-ten-foot rooms on a vertical scale. No wonder people, and especially children, from Huruma flock to public parks, such as City Park.

No government since Independence has been able to keep up with the ever-increasing demand for housing in Nairobi. The 1970s saw the construction of low- and mid-income housing projects, such as Madaraka Estate, consisting of four-story buildings with two- or three-bedroom apartments. Residents were tenants of the Nairobi City Council. There were also efforts to increase house ownership through site-and-service projects such as the development of Dandora in the 1970s, funded by the World Bank. Low-income individuals were allotted land that had a wet core (piped water and sewage connections), and they were expected to build a house while making loan repayments.[34] Many of those allotted land through such initiatives, finding themselves unable to meet the payments in addition to paying rent elsewhere while their houses were being built, sold their allotments. In the 1980s, Mathare North and Kayole Estate were built as site-and-service projects, again funded by the World Bank. These developments had plans for rental buildings up to four stories high in the style of the estates owned by the Nairobi City Council. Nevertheless, in 1999 the rental units were ten-by-ten-foot rooms. In 1999 in Nairobi 66.6 percent of households occupied single rooms.[35]

In one respect, these developments had antecedents in 1920s colonial Nairobi, in the building of the first "African location" of Pumwani. Yet they also epitomized neoliberal approaches being implemented in other parts of the world.[36] Indeed, the global trend toward housing privatization represented "the reorganization of state power away from managing social goods to ensuring the private profitability of those assets."[37] Even with the efforts of the government to provide housing and encourage home ownership in Nairobi, 84.7 percent of households in 2004 were renting, and 70.7 percent of these households rented from private landlords—either companies or individuals. In Mathare Valley, where Huruma is located, land-buying companies started to build "room-units" as early as the 1970s, doubling the population.[38]

By the 1990s, there was considerable pressure on owners to develop any vacant land for fear of losing it, as well as pressure to develop vacant land regardless of ownership.[39] In addition, the Lands Office was failing to maintain records and enforce the building code. Not only did the buildings constructed in the 1990s exceed the four-story limit, but their footprints also exceeded the mandated limit of 50 percent plot coverage to fill the whole plot. Both of these violations caused difficulties in service provision. In addition, most structures were built using non-professionals (except for electricians). Donor-mandated cutbacks to government as part of structural adjustment meant a sharp decline in building inspections and enforcement of building codes.

Whole sections of Nairobi were thus shaped by anti-urbanism and corruption as the city expanded. Anti-urbanism had determined where there was "empty" space for building in Nairobi and also concentrated both housing demand and poverty in specific parts of the city. Corruption determined who had access to land and the kinds of structures that were built.

WHERE LAND BECOMES WATER
AND SPEED HAS CONSEQUENCES

Nairobi has grown constantly, with large migrations from rural areas to the city and an increasing number of people born in the city. Most residents of Huruma are recent migrants, while most of the residents of Parklands or Westlands (where the Ukay Center was located) are long-term residents. In both places, however, patronage and tenant mobilization have been used to advance political interests, militate against demolitions, and validate fragile tenancy. Indeed, the demand for housing makes land brokerage common to both high- and low-income development in Nairobi. The main difference is the level of political patronage involved.

Until hit by COVID in 2020, Nairobi's booming high-end real-estate sector was famous as a destination for global capital.[40] This growth was accompanied by an even greater demand for low-income housing, which led to shoddy construction. The Sunbeam supermarket collapsed in 1996, and other collapses occurred in the Ushirika Estate and Tena Estate (1998) and the Industrial Area (2000).[41] According to the property and real estate development company Willstone Homes, by 2021 eighty-seven buildings had collapsed in Nairobi, resulting in over 180 documented deaths[42]

The 2016 Huruma building collapse was unique in the number of people who lost their lives but not in other respects. Most multistory buildings in Kenya have not been constructed to international standards.[43] Many of the buildings in Huruma exceed the height regulations by two stories or more. They are constructed with subpar materials (including an unstable mixture of sand and cement), with foundations too weak for the weight of the building, with too little time allowed for the cement to cure and harden, and circumventing regulations and regulators in an effort to squeeze out every last penny of profit. Constance Smith describes this form of "gray development" as "a semi-licit assemblage of circumvented planning laws, pliable oversight, off-the-books negotiations, opaque documentation, an opportunistic construction industry using poor-quality materials."[44]

In 2015 a government audit of buildings in Eastern Nairobi found that only 30 percent of the buildings audited were compliant with respect to regulatory approval, plot coverage, accessibility, and ownership.[45] In Huruma, fewer than

5 percent of the buildings were compliant, and most had questionable structural integrity. In addition, poor drainage in the area creates a high risk of collapse. These problems have persisted. A 2017 audit conducted by the Buildings Inspectorate at the Ministry of Lands, Housing and Urban Development flagged 388 Nairobi houses as very dangerous and another 323 as unsafe. In 2018, most of the condemned buildings were still standing.[46] With four hundred construction projects a month to oversee, the fifteen government inspectors were overwhelmed. Moreover, they faced the threat of assault by developers and their workers when they visited building sites.[47]

Buildings that are hastily constructed without the oversight of professionals end up with subpar foundations, resulting in sinking and settling, especially if heavy rains destabilize the ground around them.[48] Most building collapses in Nairobi have occurred during the rainy season, in the plains area or where groundwater is present. The Sunbeam supermarket collapsed after rainwater had accumulated on a canopy that fell on people walking below.[49] A building that collapsed in Kaloleni in 2014 had a foundation unsuitable for the marshy ground on which it was built, which made the building shift.[50] Similarly, water had filled the foundations of a building that collapsed in Mlolongo in 2012.[51] Here, too, the wrong type of foundation was used.

The plains area of Nairobi is characterized by black cotton soil, whose capacity to absorb and release moisture (due to its high clay content) can change the soil volume by up to 30 percent.[52] It loses its strength completely in wet conditions, a phenomenon known as liquefaction.[53] Such soils pose a challenge for engineers everywhere in the world, and more so in tropical countries because wide daily and seasonal temperature ranges and distinct dry and wet seasons cause dramatic fluctuations in their moisture content.[54]

As Tim Ingold and Cristian Simonetti point out, solid ground is not a given, as we tend to believe: it must be engineered. Specifically, "Foundation builders require a knowledge of the ground that is both local and intimate" and must wrestle solidity from a turbulent, semifluid mass.[55] For buildings on black cotton soil, the foundation can account for up to half the cost of the building.[56] Creating a stable foundation may require removal of the black cotton soil to a depth of 1–1.5 meters. In addition, black cotton soil should not come into direct contact with the foundation masonry; reinforced concrete in the foundation must be of a certain density and strength to protect the supporting steel from water damage; construction should be done in the dry season; and the foundation should be deeper than cracks in the soil, which may extend several meters down.[57] The size of the building should be limited. If the black cotton soil is deeper than six to nine meters, it should be treated as water and a raft foundation designed to deal with it.[58]

Engineering techniques like encasing stone column foundations can mitigate the problems of building on black cotton soil. In stone column foundations, some of the soil is replaced with columns of crushed gravel. This increases the load the foundation can bear, decreases the risk of liquefaction, and enhances drainage. However, the stone column's capacity to bear a load depends on lateral confinement by the soil that surrounds it. Black cotton soil provides poor lateral confinement. To prevent the column from bulging and the soil moving into the spaces between the stones, the column must be encased in permeable synthetic fabrics known as geotextiles.[59]

Another strategy is to use a mat or pile foundation. A pile foundation has deep pilings to transfer the weight of the building to a hard rock stratum below ground level. A mat foundation is a concrete slab that extends across the entire area of the a building. However, mat foundations are unsuitable for areas where the groundwater level is above the load-bearing surface of the soil because of the risk of scouring and liquefaction.[60] Scouring is the lateral erosion of the soil by water, as when a river eats away at its bank as it turns a corner.

All these techniques for building safely in black cotton soil involve additional expertise and expense. Yet in Nairobi the areas where these approaches are needed are also the poorest areas of the city, whose residents have few resources to build housing or monitor its construction for safety. They are also the areas with the poorest services and weakest regulatory oversight. And, most importantly for this chapter, they lie in a floodplain. As Ingold and Simonetti point out, "The poor, lacking the resources to reclaim or consolidate their lands, are invariably at greatest risk, for the distribution of access to reliably solid ground maps closely onto global inequalities of wealth and power."[61]

Most residential building collapses in Nairobi have occurred at night, when the load that the foundation must bear is increased by the weight of all the occupants—and by the additional weight of the water residents carry into the building from outside taps. Combined with hydrological movement, this increased load can cause liquefaction of the ground around the foundation or the bulging, tilting, and slipping of the foundation.

A CHANGE IN THE WEATHER

On the day of the building collapse in Huruma, it had been raining for two days. The rain gauge at the Muthaiga Club (upstream from Huruma on the Mathare River) registered the daily rainfall on April 28 and 29 as 99 millimeters (3.9 inches) and 80 millimeters (3.2 inches) respectively. Indeed, on April 28 Nairobi received one-third of its average April rainfall in just three hours, causing flash floods and leaving the city's traffic in chaos. The Nairobi and Ngong Rivers overflowed, uprooting trees and damaging buildings and vehicles.[62] More rain on April 29 caused flooding, deaths, and multiple building collapses.

According to the landscape architect Sunday Julius Abuje and colleagues, the climate of Nairobi is becoming wetter. Between 1984 and 2016, Nairobi's average rainfall increased by 50 percent. My own study of recorded rainfall at the Muthaiga Club shows that the average rainfall in the decade 2005–2014 was 30 percent higher than in any previous decade since 1945. The rain during April, in particular, and the combined rain in April and May was also higher for those years than in any previous decade. Moreover, surface runoff has nearly quadrupled because of the 162 percent increase in the built-up area of Nairobi since 2002, particularly the high-rise infill development in Kileleshwa, Upper Hill, and Kilimani.[63] Such development reduces green space, increases the area of impermeable surfaces, and reduces stormwater percolation, thus increasing runoff. Similarly, the hydrologist George Okoye Krhoda and geographer Alice Monene Kwambuka document a 50 percent increase in built-up areas along the Ngong River between 1976 and 2013.[64] Abuje and colleagues calculate that the overwhelmed drainage infrastructure and disappearance of wetlands results in "about [a] 43 percent chance of flooding every two years."[65]

A RIVER OF PLASTIC

In 2016 and 2018 the increased rainfall and resulting runoff combined with other new features of Nairobi to increase the speed and power of the waters flowing through it.

The Ukay Center was constructed in 1994, during a decade that saw the end of the Cold War, a global economic slowdown, and structural adjustment. In Kenya, an insolvent government was using land as currency to pay off debts as well as to obtain political favors. In addition, 1994 saw a political crisis after the first multiparty elections, in conjunction with the massive devaluation of the shilling and a severe economic downturn. Thus, when the mall was built, few complained, except about its lack of beauty. Its environmental impact on the Kibagare River went unremarked. In fact, in Terry Hirst's 1994 book the *Struggle for Nairobi*, the Kibagare River appears on maps only as a small tributary of the Mathare River, not significant enough to merit a name of its own.[66]

Around 2007, however, people started to wonder how the mall owners ever got permission to build over a river. The road past Nakumatt Ukay began to flood in the rainy season, with culverts overflowing and water damaging the road surface. Around 2013 the road downstream from the mall became impassable during the rainy season. Everyone was complaining.[67] It became glaringly obvious that the mall was built on a river.

The government was blamed for the flooding and for failing to maintain the drainage system, which had become blocked by garbage.[68] Plastic bottles, bags, and synthetic clothing were piling up in the river and blocking the culvert under the road and the grills on the river under the mall. The plastic pollution grew along with the city's wealth. Advertisers and restaurant owners promoted the sale of bottled water, with the implication that tap water was not safe to

FIGURE 17. Construction garbage in a Nairobi river. Photo by author.

drink, and the bottles were discarded. The bags were a form of advertising and were ubiquitous.

Today, now that single-use plastic shopping bags have been banned, the main items clogging the river are cement bags and clothing. Rhino Cement bags, in particular, are ubiquitous in Nairobi's rivers. And with the introduction of secondhand clothing markets, Nairobi has been inundated with plastic clothing. It is cheap. It is long-lasting. And it ends up in the river.

REGENERATING A RIVER AND A CITY

The demolitions of 2018 took place under the aegis of the Nairobi City Regeneration Programme (NCRP) and were ordered by President Uhuru Kenyatta. As explained by the publication *Business Today*, the NCRP "seeks to rehabilitate Nairobi River and its network of tributaries by identifying and sustainably addressing sources of river pollution, reclaiming riparian land and initiating landscape management activities which include tree planting."[69]

The NCRP was not the first government initiative to address river quality in Nairobi. The Nairobi River Basin Rehabilitation and Restoration Programme (NRBP), which operated from 1999 through 2008, was an initiative spearheaded by the United Nations Environment Programme (UNEP) in a joint undertaking with the Government of Kenya, UN-Habitat, the United Nations Development Programme (UNDP), the private sector, and civil society.[70] The project was implemented by the minister for the environment and natural resources, John Michuki. The NRBP focused on measuring water quality and building government technical capacity. According to the sociologist John O. Kakonge, it failed because it did not sufficiently involve residents of riparian areas, had unclear and highly technical data, and lacked enforcement authority.[71] The NRBP was followed by the Ministry of Water and Irrigation's 2016 master plan for the rehabilitation and restoration of the Nairobi River Basin. This initiative was more people-centered, aiming to change the behavior of those living and working along the river. It also aimed to establish "green zones" of self-governing communities working toward a less polluted environment.[72]

One of the main stumbling blocks for both projects was the intended eviction of people living along the river. The national and county governments were unable to move people who were living in the riparian areas and had nowhere else to go.[73] The little land available for relocation was of low quality, without services, and far from employment areas.[74] Another stumbling block was corruption, including the actions of politicians who exploited the initiatives to gain votes and amass land for themselves.[75]

Nonetheless, the pollution-reduction focus of these two initiatives was enhanced by the Rivers Sewerage Improvement Program, which increased the area of the city with wastewater services from 40 percent to 48 percent between 2012 and 2017, and the Athi Water Works Development Agency sewer development, which built a new main sewer line along the Kibagare River.[76] The first phase of the NCRP continued to focus on waste entering rivers in low-income, high-density residential areas. The second phase, which began in 2021, included the Nairobi River Life Project.

According to Urban Pathways (the UN-Habitat initiative supporting the project), the Nairobi River Life Project was "a joint flagship initiative of the Nairobi Metropolitan Services (NMS) and UN-Habitat aimed at reclaiming Nairobi River as a shared public asset. . . . [Urban Pathways] will provide the technical expertise to restore the river system and prioritize the riverfront development."[77] Urban Pathways waste-management projects are supposed to be community focused but with the capacity to scale up. This initiative was undertaken in agreement with the Nairobi Metropolitan Service (NMS), which was a temporary, parallel governing body for Nairobi, created in a moment of political crisis under Governor Mike Sonko.

Wangui Kimari and Jessica Parish describe the Nairobi River Basin Program as an example of a local "sustainability fix," funded internationally, that is concerned with remedying pollution associated with intentionally underdeveloped, neglected, and degraded spaces and communities. It thus perpetuates a singular rehabilitation narrative that identifies the main problem as waste, rather than neglect of the community by the government.[78] Narratives identifying people or places as the problem in need of solution are typical of regeneration projects. Tom Slater argues that "to target for 'regeneration' a place and its people is to imply that they must be *degenerate*, and 'revitalizing' a place suggests that it is full of *devitalized* individuals, or people *not vital* to a city."[79]

Echoing similar concerns regarding a city in Brazil, Robert Coates argues that narratives attributing problems to a single cause, such as pollution, heavy rain, or climate, exclude urban growth as a factor by refusing to recognize its significance to those "who are frequently displaced in processes of uneven and hazardous urbanization."[80] Coates argues that all development projects tend to take an event, instance, or occurrence and place it into a wider narrative arc to give it significance. These narratives frame the way we look at problems.

These writers are demanding that we look at and narrate problems and disasters differently. I look at them through a framework that I call *the perfect storm*. This is the moment when everything that could go wrong goes wrong at the same time, making the cumulative effect much greater than the probable separate consequences of the individual events.

A PERFECT STORM

Although the two events seem unconnected, the 2018 demolition of the Ukay Center helps us understand the collapse in Huruma in 2016 as a perfect storm by showing what had been happening to the river and the adjoining land. It also shows that the causes lay upstream, both geographically and metaphorically. It points not only to lax or corrupt government but also to the anti-urbanist historical structuring of wealth and privilege that is still piling up in the river, blocking its pathway, and suppressing its energy.

FIGURE 18. Kibagare River in flood. Photo by author.

The river was a stream in 1994 when the Ukay Center was built. It seems to have become a river somewhere around 2007. Thus, the narrative of the Ukay Center could run like this: Once upon a time a mall was built (with all sorts of suspect permissions) over a wetland stream. Because of the construction of houses, malls, offices, temples, and roads upstream that changed the volume and speed of its water, the stream became a river. So perhaps if I had been a judge on the Ukay Center court case (now defunct), and if there were a legal distinction between stream and river for riparian areas—which I suspect there is not—I would side with the owners of the Ukay Center. They built on a stream, and through little fault of their own, it became a river.

Applying the same logic to the collapse of the Huruma building, I might narrate it as follows: Once upon a time a building was built (with all sorts of suspect permissions and construction materials) on solid ground. Because of the demand for and lack of housing, the concentration of poverty, corruption within the Land Office, decades of government neglect, the lack of services, the fact that the only vacant land was on black cotton soil, a buildup of wealth and construction upstream, and a change in the weather and the river, the ground beneath the building became liquid, and the building collapsed. The owners were partly, but not solely, to blame.

With the demolition of the Ukay Center and other buildings in the name of riparian protection, middle-class and upscale residents of Nairobi tried to discover the real reason behind the decisions. Conspiracy theories of many kinds were advanced. But the demolitions reflected no sudden outburst of concern for the environment; rather, the changing environment created an increasingly urgent need to act. These demolitions reflect the performative style of the governor of Nairobi at the time (Mike Sonko) and perhaps the national government of the time. They also reflect the placement of the river in a narrative of neoliberal city development (regeneration) in the promotion of what Coates calls "hazardous urbanization."

But perhaps the questions of whether or not the mall should have been there, whether the river was a stream, and whether the building collapse resulted from rain or from corruption, are not the ones that need answering. Instead we might ask, How can we use the story of this changed river to think about the future of this city of water? What new politics of and for the city are possible in this context of rapid urbanization and climate change?

These questions require us to investigate geographies of marginalization that map onto city hydrology, intensified and magnified by concrete dreams of development, as well as lifestyle and consumption habits that alter geology, hydrology, and climate. We must address this amassing of dangers that give rise to a perfect storm.

Development policy for Nairobi needs to take hydrology as a founding principle. But it must also look for the larger causes of instability and floods, whether race, politics, trade, poverty, or transportation.

The Colombian city of Cali is built, like Nairobi, with half of the city in the hills and half on flat land, with a river running through it that is fed by tributaries flowing from steep mountains. Being on the Equator like Nairobi, it has two rainy seasons when the rains swell the rivers. Also, as in Nairobi, the newest and poorest part of the city is in the river floodplain. Thus, although flooding is frequent, only the poorer segments of the population are regularly affected.

Another city remarkably similar to Nairobi is Karachi in Pakistan, which has two rivers with highly variable seasonal flow and a rapidly growing population. The architect and urban planner Arif Hasan identifies several factors that have worsened the city's flood problems: the stormwater drains that run through Karachi, the lack of sustainable and affordable housing, pollution, solid waste, and poor design and construction of large buildings. More recently these issues have been exacerbated by massive real estate development in the hills north of the city that has destroyed natural drainage and collection areas. Thus, "When it rains, areas immediately south of this region . . . are completely submerged by floodwaters from the hills." The government of Sindh (the province where Karachi is located) tried to mitigate the flooding by rehabilitating the sewage treatment facility and rebuilding the city's main sewage lines in the 1980s. However, the new and old sewage systems did not connect.[81] In Karachi as in Nairobi, most proposed solutions involved the relocation of substantial numbers of people and the endangering of another large number of poor people living near a changed river.

What these cities have in common—along with other colonial garden cities, like Kumasi in Ghana—is their mixed topography of hills and flat plains; the concentration of low-income, unregulated housing near rivers; the lack of sustainable social housing policies and affordable housing for the poor; development in wealthy hilly areas; different types of soils across the city; increasing density and more high-rise buildings; and rivers with highly variable rates of flow. These characteristics make these cities particularly vulnerable to the effects of climate change. And yet it is less the effects of climate change than the anti-urbanist infrastructure, its arrangement, and wealth disparities, along with the lack of preventative planning, that cause the poor downstream to pay for development upstream with their homes and lives.

8

No Place like Home

Elizabeth steps out of her car, ignoring the barking dog bounding toward her. She reaches out a hand to pet the enormous beast, who instantly falls in love with her. Inside the house, she sits with my parents' dog at her feet, explaining to my mother that she is a socioeconomist, and she works for the engineering company that will be building a new road across the railway tracks to Upper Hill. She has come to inform us that yet again, our house is in the way.

Again. Still. Once more. This is a different new road from the road I describe at the beginning of this book. The new new road is taking shape five years after that first new road was supposed to go through the house. In anticipation of the impending destruction, my parents ceased all house and yard improvements. In the intervening years, the kei-apple hedge has grown through the power lines and become too dangerous to cut. Homeowners have formed a united front to avoid being forced to surrender land without compensation.[1]

A month before Elizabeth's February 2017 visit, bulldozers had appeared at the end of Masaba Road, which runs next to my parents' place, to start construction on the old new road. And here we are again. Still. Once more. And here we will continue to be until we modernize, develop, surrender, or disappear.

Elizabeth also tells us of a plan to build a link road through our neighborhood from another part of town. I ask about the connection to the road that is finally under construction, and she says this one is different. But the aim is the same: to reduce traffic congestion for those traveling from outside our neighborhood and city.

A few weeks later, I spend five hours in a public meeting about the new new road, organized by the Kenya Urban Roads Authority (KURA). Again. Still. Once more. By now I have been to phase 1 meetings, phase 2 meetings, Masaba Road meetings, Nairobi Master Plan meetings, and meetings all over the city. This latest one is a resettlement study—the first I have heard of in the five years of this process. When the old new road was proposed, no one talked of resettlement. Nobody from the government even came to talk to us. Rather, we learned about the project from our neighbors.

This time, residents at the meeting are more cynical and more demanding. Once again all our neighbors are there, but this time there are also others, because the proposal for link roads and raised highways affects all of Nairobi's hilly, middle-class neighborhoods. The old residential part of town is being turned commercial. Again.

Most people leave the meeting disillusioned by the process, by their lack of power, by the planners' deafness and disdain toward their issues. They resolve to take up the issues in different ways, since these official meetings are proving so unproductive. They rely heavily on the Upper Hill Residents Association, but they also form more local alliances with their immediate neighbors.

Here is what we think we know:

Legally, property taken by the state must be either surrendered or purchased by eminent domain.

Legally, if not surrendered, a property cannot be demolished.

Legally, road reserve boundaries do not change without being gazetted (officially announced) and undergoing accompanying processes of surrender or eminent domain.

Legally, an X marked on the side of a culvert does not constitute notice of demolition.

Legally, notice of demolition must be delivered in writing to both tenants and landowners.

But these legalities were not part of the experience in our neighborhood or in most other parts of Nairobi. Thus, we form pacts to deal with the onslaught of change on our part of the road. The Upper Hill Residents Association now facilitates conversations with KURA. We send all sorts of letters to KURA, to the Ministry of Lands, the City of Nairobi, and the contractors on the job. We inform them all that we are not surrendering our land.

New roads. New new roads. Roads for the future. Waiting. Rushing. Delays. Five years. Five hours. Cynical. Jaded. Frustrated. Bulldozed.

In order for the new roads, high-rise buildings, and infrastructures of the modern city to go up, something must come down. Decisions about what should go are fraught with tensions and frustrations on all sides. The tensions are framed by different understandings of place in the city, and how places and the people related to them are imagined in the future of Nairobi.

No matter how fast the pace of change, modernity is never quite achieved, traffic congestion never quite eliminated. It is an endless cycle. Demolition and development must be repeated on structures that are newly relegated to the past. Time and space are rearticulated in the production of infrastructure.

Whose future is being imagined?

This chapter engages questions of development, demolition, and competing futures by looking at the precarity of making Nairobi home. The anti-urbanist concept that no one is from the city renders urban residents out of place and therefore subject to displacement. The political, geographic, social, and conceptual implications of anti-urbanism are illustrated by the scale of the destruction required to build the modern city of neoliberal dreams. The demolitions in Nairobi in 2020 illustrate the long history of demolition as a form of urban governance.

Development, as a particular construct of modernity—the idea of progress fueled by capitalism—depends on anti-urbanism. It holds the promise of new urban possibilities—usually for people other than the current residents. Demolition, as the mechanism though which development is achieved, is the supreme tool of anti-urbanism. If urban populations are imagined as only temporary, then they cannot be rendered homeless in the city. In addition to rendering people and buildings out of place, demolitions and the threat of demolitions disrupt time, creating a state of uncertainty and waiting, with extremely high stakes.

By displacing people in space and time, anti-urbanism opens up opportunities for political land brokerage that tie home, land, and development to politicians and election cycles and untether them from formal legal land relations and policies. The contested space of demolitions is a site of struggles over class, citizenship, corruption, state capture, and judicial or executive power. These struggles are often hidden, silenced, or erased in discussions of development. At heart, these are struggles about how to be urban and how to govern urbanity, but they are also struggles over the process of decolonization and the production of acceptable futures.

LOCKDOWN, CONTAINMENT, AND DEMOLITION

In early 2020 Nairobi was locked down to prevent the spread of coronavirus. In addition, on April 6 the Ministry of Health mandated that movement in and out of the cities of Nairobi and Mombasa would be curtailed until July 2020. These containment zones were established in an effort to protect the countryside from the illness, which had been brought to the cities through foreign air traffic.

Amid the chaos of the pandemic, including job and food insecurity, social isolation, and the new containment measures, the Nairobi City Water and Sewerage Company (a government-owned company within the Water Ministry) saw fit to evict five thousand people from Kariobangi North on May 4 as part of a plan to build a "modern wastewater recycling plant" on the land.[2] Properties were demolished and residents left homeless. The area was guarded by heavily armed police to prevent any residents from returning.[3]

The timing of the demolitions produced an unusual uproar from other citizens as well as politicians. By May 8 the demolitions had been halted. But the damage had been done: within two days, the sewage company had demolished homes and buildings, including six schools. Most of the houses, and their residents, had been there since 2008.[4] Nevertheless, they woke up to "find their homes being brought down without any prior notice."[5] One resident, Titus Ndambuki, said that the district commissioner had told them to start looking for alternative places to live, but that notice had come only three days prior to the demolition.[6] And even if one subscribed to the anti-urbanist idea that every urban Kenyan's true home is in the countryside, nobody could leave Nairobi.

Sharon Maombo, in *The Star*, quoted Tobin Simba, newly homeless, who said he feared for his children's well-being in the middle of the COVID-19 pandemic, and he had nowhere to go.[7] The local government ward representative, Julius Maina Njoka, stated that "most of these people are elderly and other with young families. With the curfew directive and schools closed, chances are that the virus will spread like wildfire."[8] Ndambuki echoed this concern, observing: "We never imagined that the government can leave its people homeless during these tough Covid-19 times."[9]

Demolition and displacement. Again. Still. Once more.

Some of the first demolitions in Nairobi occurred during another public health emergency: the outbreak of the plague in 1902, when the entire Indian Bazaar was burned down by the colonial government. As Godwin Murunga points out, European segregation efforts based on a myth of "inherently unhygienic races" were readily visible elsewhere, too. In Cape Town in South Africa and Dakar in Senegal, "plague epidemics provided justification for separation and, ultimately, residential segregation of people on the basis of race."[10] Indeed, across the world in the early twentieth century, public health, sanitation, and town planning were used as rationales to create the "ideal" urban population of cities through racial segregation, displacement, dispossession, and whitening.[11] Such practices were enacted through demolition.

The destruction of the Indian Bazaar set the tone, the legal precedent, and the regulatory structures for subsequent demolitions and displacements in colonial Nairobi. In 1922, 1923, and 1926, Africans were displaced from Kaburini, Mji wa Mombasa, Mji wa Maskini, Racecourse Road, Canal Road, and Kileleshwa, all supposedly for sanitation reasons.[12] These settlements, originally transit camps on caravan routes, became the original African settlements of Nairobi, home to relatively well-off African Muslim populations.[13] Public health and sanitation concerns helped legitimize an anti-urbanist policy framework restricting their residents' competition with Europeans and instituting racial segregation.

Demolitions and displacements enabled the British colonial government to crowd Indian and African populations into the marshy lowlands of Nairobi with few services. The epidemics of malaria in 1913, 1922, 1926, 1935, and 1940 were used as justifications for establishing a buffer zone between the marshlands and European settlements by pushing Africans further and further into "the swamp" and the outskirts of town.[14] Overcrowding, a product of the colonial distribution of land and resources as well as colonial restrictions on settlement, was considered unsanitary and an excuse for demolition.

One way anti-urbanism operates is to extend the negative associations of a place to the people who live there, and vice versa. Officials understood the swamp of Nairobi as unsanitary because it was a reservoir for malaria. But Murunga argues that by 1907 the swamp was seen not as an unhygienic site but as a site with unhygienic people.[15] Since then, demolition sites have been taken for granted as dirty and unhealthy, and their residents as out of place, by colonial and postcolonial governments as well as the general public.

Nairobi was founded on a planned lack of service to the majority of its population, as exemplified in the "native locations" and the Indian Bazaar. Today the problem of neglect continues. The recent decline in the provision of services is described in the memoirs of the former vice president, Moody Awori. He writes that when he lived in Eastleigh in 1958, it was "beautiful, with well-lined streets of shops downstairs and affordable flats on top floors." Today, however, "even on the best of days, the streets are in a mess with garbage strewn all over. In the rainy season, Eastleigh is a quagmire."[16]

The urban sociologist Tom Slater argues that in the neoliberal state, disinvestment, neglect, and depreciation are deliberate policies that facilitate acquisition of property for regeneration and redevelopment. Derelict areas "do not simply 'appear' as part of some naturally occurring neighborhood 'decay'; they are actively produced by clearing out existing residents via all manner of tactics and legal instruments such as landlord harassment, massive rent increases, redlining, arson, the withdrawal of public services, and eminent domain/compulsory purchase orders."[17]

Typified in practices like cutting services to Railways housing in Muthurwa in 2010 (discussed in chapter 2), vague tenancy documents, dodgy land brokerage, and the general stigma associated with Eastlands, presumptions about health in anti-urbanist thinking have shaped the way Nairobi operates. In 2020, the implications of this thinking were apparent for all to see.

By April 4, 2020, two weeks after the first case of COVID-19 was recorded in Kenya, the establishment of a curfew as a prevention measure had already created uproar, in part because it made no allowance for the fact that people, especially the poor, have to travel considerable distances to and from work. The curfew had been enforced by the police in extremely violent ways.[18] People out after curfew were beaten with canes and arrested. Three people had been killed and many injured. At the time, more people had been killed by the police than by the virus.

Kenyans are great users of Twitter and came out in full force blasting the government. The minister of health, who was otherwise very popular, responded with the kind of logic characteristic of repressive regimes: the police should not use excessive force, but if people did not want to be whipped or hit, they shouldn't be on the street. He too was blasted on Twitter. Nairobi's governor, Mike Sonko, declared that the police would not be arresting anyone, since the courts were not operating. However, the closed courts did manage to find time to declare the police brutality illegal. Kenya's president later apologized "for the excesses that may have happened."[19]

In that moment of crisis, Kenya, like many postcolonial states—including India, Pakistan, Botswana, South Africa, and Zimbabwe—fell back on the coercive tools of the colonial state. They were illustrated by pictures of police wielding sticks and whips to enforce pandemic curfews and lockdowns. For a year Nairobians lived in constant fear of being caught out after curfew. Employers had to rearrange schedules so that employees could leave work in time to get home before curfew. Meetings were held only in the mornings.

Containment and curfew were extensions of the anti-urbanist practice of defining urban residents as out of place—and out of time in more ways than one. Out of time to get home. Out after curfew time. Out of time to leave the city. Being out of time was already part and parcel of the urban structure of Nairobi. The most obvious manifestation of being out of place and out of time is being too late to stop the demolition of your dwelling.

In Nairobi, as in many cities across the world, demolitions remove homes, and their occupants, that are seen as standing in the way of development, and thus in the way of modernity and the future. This thinking casts both homes and occupants as part of the past.

RUSHING, WAITING, REPEATING

At a public meeting in 2017, we were informed that the new new road project was running late. It should have been completed that March. As of March 2025, it still had not been started. Again. Still. Once more.

The old new road project had run late as well. Why the delays? One KURA representative blamed property owners. Tired of dealing with the public, he told us that the projects had been delayed because people refused to surrender land. When asked why KURA was building a four-lane road on land that has only six houses, the planner replied, "We are not building that road for you and your six houses. You will be gone, and the houses will be replaced by high-rise buildings. This road is for the future."

Again. Still. Once more. Planning for a future that excludes the very people being asked to surrender their land for free. No wonder they refused.

I asked why KURA didn't change the design of the road to accommodate the resistant residents. Couldn't the road be designed to fit the space available? I cast the problem as one of demographics. Many residents were elderly and retired.

If they were displaced without compensation, they would have no means to relocate. The KURA representative dismissed my suggestion with disdain and said they were not changing the plans. We were at an impasse.

At the same meeting, I wrote in my notes that the deputy county commissioner (DCC) felt called upon to lecture us: "'Roads are important. The main agenda is to decongest roads. It is high time KURA is undertaking this. Yes, there are some pains and some gains. We need a level of accommodation and resilience. Although some are disadvantaged here, now I can move faster to my destination.' (I think here he was talking as one of the audience)."

He asked the public to be resilient, as he recognized that the changes would be painful. But as Slater argues, "Urban resilience serves as a screen that deflects analytic and political attention away from the structural and institutional conditions that are forcing urban dwellers to be resilient in the first place."[20] The DCC continued, "It is an issue of modernization. Roundabouts and T-junctions require overpasses. Although traffic jams are not as they were before, it means less time in traffic. Wider roads. The government's objective is to make lives of Kenyans more convenient. You are being asked to have a give-and-take culture. We [that would be us in the audience] need to cede ground. Especially for that which does not belong to you. Give it back to the government." Then he cajoled us: "Conflict resolution. We the government are here. Don't feel helpless. If a contractor is not cooperative we can try to find a middle ground. I [again he was referring to us in the audience] might be hurt, but it will assist the larger public to benefit."

Still. Once more.

These conversations are about being out of place and time, as framed by the politicians and bureaucrats who told us residents that we should sacrifice our homes and equity for the benefit of car-owning commuters; for a neoliberal, unjust, and unequal modernity; and for a future that we were not meant to be a part of. None of our local government representatives stood up for their constituents that day. None of them questioned the plan or even asked for it to be made more humane. (They did, however, support finding a way for KURA to make the contractors comply with law and contract.)

In that meeting, the local government representatives reflected an old Kenya—one in which government commands, where the people are presumed to be stupid, ignorant, and in need of education about how to be modern. The consultants emphasized a new Kenya, where citizens have constitutional rights, where designs and plans matter, where concerns must be listened to. KURA sat half in the old Kenya and half in the new.

Officials at the meeting told us there was no time. The consultants emphasized that they would normally have shown us the final plans, but time had run out on their contract. Time for what, exactly? Five years earlier, we had been also

FIGURE 19. Bulldozer in Upper Hill. Photo by author.

been told there was no time. Then, there had been no time for an environmental and social impact assessment (ESIA). Then and now, the urgency of these projects had lasted until election season, and then they had languished. Again. Still. Once more.

One month prior to our new new road meeting in 2017, we had woken up to the sight of bulldozers taking out the boundary of our property for the old new road. Three gray-haired residents stood in front of the bulldozers waving copies of letters documenting their refusal to surrender their land. The scene devolved into a shouting match. The engineer arrived—a female engineer this time. She was a revelation. Although she couldn't change the overall plan, she listened to and worked with residents. She was the first engineer to articulate that the new roads were going to benefit *us*—the citizens and residents of Nairobi and this neighborhood. She, too, shouted at the contractors: "What are you doing? These are your clients! You must obey them!"

It was a novel idea, that *we* were the clients, that our voices had authority. Reluctantly the contractor called off the bulldozers. We sent out more letters of protest and demand. Again. Still. Once more. Then nothing happened. We were left to repair the damage at our own expense. Then we waited—until the next time, until the next rush job, the next corrupt contractor, the next election cycle, the next plan, and the next new road design. We heard nothing further. The rush job was left unfinished.

THE PROBLEM OF PUBLIC LAND

The legal option of surrendering land, even if it entails no compensation, at least contains the potential for refusal. Surrender, however, is an option accorded only to residents in certain parts of the city who hold secure title deeds to their land. Those who were evicted from Kariobangi for the construction of the wastewater plant had no such choice.

The plant was a component of the Nairobi Integrated Urban Development Master Plan, funded through a Ksh 20 billion (US $200 million) loan from the African Development Bank (ADB) and the Agence Française de Développement (AFD).[21] The project aimed to boost Nairobi's capacity to treat wastewater by over 55 percent, a considerable and much-needed increase given that, in 2020, the city's capacity for water treatment was at only 40 percent of what was needed.[22]

From the point of view of the Nairobi City Water and Sewerage Company, the demolitions were reclaiming public land that had been illegally taken. The company argued that land fraud had left nowhere for the expansion of sanitation facilities. Indeed, the Ministry of Water and Sanitation claimed that land intended for sewage facilities such as drying beds, trickling filters, and wastewater overflow areas had been "grabbed."[23] From this perspective, the current inhabitants had no legal claim to the land, and direct demolition was an appropriate course of action. On the ground, however, things were not so simple.

Allotment of land is a process by which government land is transferred to ownership by private individuals or companies. It originated with the 1902 Crown Lands Ordinance (revised in 1915) that deemed all "unoccupied" land as the property of the Crown.[24] While some of these lands became "native trust lands" under the Native Lands Trust Ordinance of 1938, any native lands that became vacant reverted to the Crown. Although communities had already begun challenging the legality of this process by the 1920s, this ordinance is the foundation of the private and public property system in Kenya.[25] That is to say, the property regime is based on a structure in which multiple claims already exist.

After Independence, Crown lands became the property of the government, which allocated land parcels to settle land claims in rural areas, to promote business and industry, and to reward and gain political loyalty. In Kariobangi and Ruiru, residents had letters from the government allotting the land to them, and they were waiting for title deeds to be processed. As one resident, Ndambuki, stated: "We have the letters and we have been paying rent for the past 12 years. How can the government claim that we are here illegally?"[26] In Kariobangi North, some of this allotted land had already been allocated for public use before it was allotted to individuals and land-buying companies. Thus, both the sewage company and the residents had documented claims to the same piece of land (as happened with plots of land within City Park).

Again. Still. Once more.

Demolitions in Nairobi have generally occurred on public or government lands that have been allocated to others in legally fuzzy and contestable ways. Land possession in certain areas of Nairobi has been tolerated as "legal" according to the whims of those in power. Demolitions usually take place when the government or private developer has finally raised the funds to build on the land and encounters long-term residents with allotment papers or title deeds to land that has been lying vacant for years.

Demolitions for redevelopment can fall under the general category of gentrification. According to Slater, "Gentrification commonly occurs in urban areas where prior disinvestment in the urban infrastructure creates opportunities for profitable redevelopment, where the needs and concerns of business and policy elites are met at the expense of urban residents affected by work instability, unemployment and stigmatization."[27] This was definitely true of Nairobi from the 1980s onward, when government lands in Nairobi were privatized as part of structural adjustment and neoliberal government.

Gentrification can include removal of unplanned or unauthorized housing or occupations (like street vending), houses on a road reserve (public land set aside for roads), houses too close to riparian areas, and houses in private land disputes. In 1970 and 1971, multiple evictions in low-income areas left forty-eight thousand people homeless.[28] In 1974 in Kibera, unauthorized housing and non-Nubian settlements were demolished.[29] In 1984 street vendors were removed to the outskirts of the city.[30] Operation Bulldozer, carried out between 1990 and 1992, resulted in numerous demolitions: in Muoroto over forty-five thousand people lost their homes.[31] Between 2000 and 2005 about three thousand houses were demolished on the grounds that they were built on road reserve. In 2006 at least twenty thousand people in Mukuru and Malaa village were evicted from "private" land by means that included a deliberate fire. Some residents had lived there for over fifty years.

In 2004 the Advisory Group on Forced Evictions at UN-Habitat publicized the potential eviction of 30,000 people from Nairobi public utility wayleaves, and in 2007 Habitat International Coalition publicized the threatened eviction of 354,000 people along the line of the railway and the new Southern By-Pass from Waiyaki Way through Kibera to City Cotton.[32] These evictions were partially suspended. In 2013 296 houses were threatened with demolition in Runda, an upscale neighborhood of Nairobi, because they were allegedly built on road reserve. The wealthy inhabitants of Runda, who held title deeds to their land, halted the demolition after a long court battle. In the same year, three thousand residents of Deep Sea and City Cotton lost their houses to the construction of a link road connecting with Thika Highway.[33] In 2018, in addition to the riparian demolitions discussed in chapter 7, 30,000 people in Kibera were displaced to construct the Southern

By-Pass, and 10,000 people in Kayole were displaced by city *askaris* or city council guards (*kanjo*) in a private land fight lasting eleven years.[34] In 2023 Governor Sakaja approved the redevelopment of most government-owned housing in Eastlands, including the Jericho, Muthurwa, Kaloleni, Makongeni, Starehe, and Kariokor estates, putting the residents on notice of eviction. In 2024 there were demolitions across the city, including homes along the river in Mukuru wa Njenga during the April floods, that displaced thousands with no warning.

Again. Still. Once more.

CORRUPTION, DOCUMENTATION, AND THE POLITICS OF LAND BROKERAGE

If people are not to be displaced from their long-term homes for the sake of building public infrastructure, what are the alternatives? The government needs to provide services—water, roads, and schools—and to provide space for housing and commerce. The dialectic of development and demolition by which it seeks to meet these needs is built on anti-urbanism. This has meant that housing planning is always out of sync with the needs of actual urban populations. Dealing with a population considered temporary and out of place calls for different kinds of planning than accommodating permanent residents.

Development of city infrastructure is likewise out of sync with the needs of the current population, as it necessarily involves planning for a hypothetical future population. In Nairobi, because of the lack of planning, action, and maintenance during the fiscal strains of the 1990s, current governments face further challenges and constraints. Nevertheless, unless anti-urbanism is directly addressed, demolitions, dispossessions, and displacements will be repeated again and again.

KURA has a mandate to build throughways for commuters coming into the center of town. Decisions about which roads to build are made by officials at all levels of government. In the face of budget constraints, however, KURA (and subagencies) must decide what they can afford to build. Decisions to redesign, scale down, renegotiate project parameters, or to prioritize particular aspects of a project all have social, economic, and legal consequences for the community.

In modern Nairobi, as in colonial times, urban planning gives preference to the car-owning residents of the outskirts of the city rather than to the pedestrian residents at the center. I am reminded of the 1950 film *Nairobi*, celebrating Nairobi's new status as a city, showing the cars driving into the city at the beginning of the day and driving out at the end.[35] After sixty years of independence, movement in and out of the city is still prioritized over movement within the city. Finance, business, and transportation are prioritized over housing and residential life. And the colonial idea of removing unwanted, out-of-place urban residents to serve these objectives persists.

Corruption adds significantly to the problem: it influences the selection of contractors, the construction of the roads and buildings, the placement of the roads, and the acquisition and disbursement of funds (especially just before elections). Corruption is at work in the Lands Office, in the allotment of land, in the gazetting of change, in the titling of property. Corruption affects every choice made and increases the cost of every part of a project. The use of land as a tool of political patronage was notorious in the 1990s. Jeremia Njeru observes, for example, that "faced with declining donor support and serious economic hardship, the regime 'privatized' Karura Forest to raise funds to support the re-election of [President Daniel arap] Moi in 1997. The Moi regime then creatively used the discourse of privatization (and associated need for safeguarding private property rights) to mask the patronage connections underpinning the selling of a key public urban forest."[36] Land allocations and brokerage from the 1990s and beyond continue to affect the city's development and redevelopment.

Corruption also makes it hard for the public to believe the government when officials make statements about a lack of funding. The public is asked to sacrifice on behalf of a government that has dismissed them as unimportant to its vision of the future. Moreover, the need for sacrifice in the first place stems from the government's failure to address the presence, extent, and damage of corruption within its systems.

Working against the land grabs at City Park made me keenly aware of the many different kinds of land fiddles possible in government. Even if specific agencies try to work against corruption, it is likely to crop up in others. Such corruption is often actively or tacitly supported by politicians. The political scientist Kathleen Klaus argues that in situations of land inequality and tenure insecurity, politicians can present themselves as land patrons in order to gain votes. Elections are seen as "a rare window of opportunity to gain and secure land, and equally, a moment to lose."[37] Title deeds, or the lack thereof, are at the center of this kind of political land brokerage.

Even beyond the obvious problem of corruption, policies in Nairobi are often implemented in a way that reflects a total disdain and disregard for residents living in the way of demolition. Development is premised on the idea that the future is more important than the present, and there is no place in that future for current residents. How would this change if we imagined Nairobi as home and planned accordingly?

The 2020 demolitions in Kariobangi North caused an uproar from the general public as well as from legislators. The Kariobangi North MCA (member of the county assembly) Julius Maina Njoka condemned the demolitions and accused the government of treating citizens inhumanely during the pandemic but regretted there was not much he could do.[38] A few days later, he announced that Governor Mike Sonko would provide food for five hundred people—a fraction of those affected. Nairobi Senator Johnson Sakaja called the demolitions inhuman, ill-advised, and executed at the wrong time.[39] He did not suggest when might be the right time. He went on to state that "as much as we support the repossession of public land, proper humane methods must be used. Those affected by these demolitions are the most vulnerable in society and deserve protection from the government."[40] Indeed, during his 2022 campaign for governor, Sakaja promised that he would not demolish structures if elected.

All three of these politicians set themselves up as solutions to these and future demolitions. The poor get their houses demolished and their lives destroyed, to be "rescued" by the very politicians who rendered them vulnerable in the first place.

Again. Once more. Still.

In May 2022, Sakaja declared that if he were elected governor, "no one will leave a home in the morning and come back to no home in the evening. Or sleep in a home and get a rude awakening of their home being demolished at night."[41] This simple declaration reflects how central demolition has become to life in Nairobi. But it also demonstrates the ubiquity and consequences of being out of place. It indicates the way demolitions take place: unpredictably, without warning, and often at night—in a sense, out of time. It hints at the precarity of interactions with the state, whether legitimate or illegitimate. The politician does not seek to permanently alter the terms by which people can be at home, or not, in the city. Rather he (it is usually a *he*) suspends the consequences of their being out of time or place for as long as it is politically expedient for him to do so. Thus each election cycle renews the threat to any sense of belonging and the meaning of home.

This kind of political land brokerage has a long history in Nairobi. It has blurred the line between squatters and tenants, between legitimate and illegitimate owners, between formal and informal settlement, and between law and politics. The urban economist and development sociologist Philip Amis argues that the combination of population growth, lack of housing options, and unequal distribution of land has produced blurred and fuzzy conditions of land rights that are exploited by government officials.[42] He uses the example of Kibera, an area encompassing about two hundred thousand low-income people living in mainly rented housing.[43]

The name Kibera is derived from the Nubian word *kibra*, meaning "forest," as the area once lay at the edge of Nairobi and the Ngong Road Forest. In 1902, 4,197 acres were awarded as a military reserve to Nubian Sudanese soldiers so that they would be within call of the colonial government in Nairobi if needed. At Independence in 1963, the Nubians living on the reserve remained there in lieu of being repatriated to Sudan by the British.[44] However, it was only in 2017 that their rights to land in Kibera were even partially recognized by the Kenyan government: they gained a title deed for 116 hectares (288 acres) as a community trust.

Nubians were long able to maintain some spatial and economic control over land in Kibera, where they (especially women) rented out extensions to their houses. However, this situation changed in 1974, when the local administration decided to intervene in the unauthorized housing market though "formalization," which consisted of requiring permission to build in Kibera and threatening to demolish any new unpermitted buildings. No single area of Nairobi has experienced more demolitions and displacements than Kibera. As Amis argues, the informal practice of local government officials allocating "protection" for new construction in Kibera opened up a very lucrative space for corruption. The local administration and those higher up can pay back favors, consolidate clients indebted to them, and enrich friends and fellow ethnic group members by giving out free land for urban development. These practices have also concentrated land that was protected from demolition (regardless of legal title) in the hands of local administrative functionaries, who in the 1970s were predominantly Kikuyu.[45] The high concentration of tenement housing held by Kikuyu landlords during the 1990s is a result, reflection, and repetition of these formalization practices in Kibera and beyond.

ANCESTRAL LANDS AND THE CONSEQUENCES OF ANTI-URBANISM

Kibera residents again faced demolition and displacement in 2004, when some two thousand houses were demolished (for being built on public land) while the inhabitants were at church. In 2005 more houses were demolished for the building of the Southern By-Pass. In 2018 four hundred residents were displaced for road construction, and another thirty thousand residents were displaced for the construction of the Southern By-Pass Road just a few months later.[46]

In July 2018, homes, churches, clinics, and schools were demolished at six o'clock in the morning.[47] While some residents said they had no warning, other residents had seen a posted notice dated July 3 that all structures must be removed before July 16.[48] According to Ghetto Radio, "The residents said they received notices last month, [but] they did not know where to move to."[49] Wilson Lundu, a resident who managed to move his belongings before his house was demolished, said, "Most people did not heed the call to vacate because they lacked the money to help them start new lives elsewhere. The Government promised to compensate us last week, but we have yet to receive even a single coin."[50] Josephine Munee asked, "At sixty-five years old, where would they expect me to go?"[51] Ms. Akoth asked, "Where do I go? Just yesterday I had made arrangements to transport my belongings and my family upcountry as I look for alternative shelter, but now I have nothing left."[52]

Though the government clearly considered these people temporary and out of place, Kibera was their home. One resident, Halima, said, "I was raised on my paternal grandfather's land—this land that they have just evicted me from." Halima's grandfather, Marjan Sakar, was among the first Nubian soldiers to be settled at Kibera. Munee, who was born in Kibera, had faced demolition before: "I've spent all my life in Kibera, I know no other home. In all of my 65 years, we grew up being threatened by demolitions and evictions, but we fought back and we survived. Somehow, the past governments would perhaps think twice and have mercy on us."[53]

The Nubian community in Kibera took the government to court regarding the Southern By-Pass in 2016.[54] In the 2016 court petition *Abdulmajid Ramadhan v KURA*, the community accused KURA, the attorney general, the National Land Commission (NLC), the National Environment Management Authority (NEMA), and the contractor H. Young Company Ltd. of threatening their property rights, violating their right to adequate and accessible housing and dignity, diverting the lines on the original survey map, and not carrying out their duties as government authorities to marginalized communities.[55] They petitioned for the court to compel NEMA to "discharge its lawful statutory and constitutional obligations," to prohibit all from altering the original survey map, and to protect them against illegal eviction and the threat of demolition. In addition, they contended that Kibera was their ancestral land and challenged the logic of eviction by contradicting the idea that they had other homes to go to.

The government responded that the petitioners had no title to the land and thus no right to compensation. John Cheboi, the KURA communication officer, stated, "We will however give out something 'small' to help the residents relocate. They will also be allowed to carry their structural materials."[56] The court case was decided in April 2017. However, as the Kenyan government finally recognized Nubian rights to land in Kibera only in June 2017, the residents could not produce a title deed to their ancestral lands. The judge therefore could not determine whether the government should compensate them for their loss of property. The judge stated, however, that people living on the land should have been consulted and halted all evictions and demolitions until all parties could agree on a resettlement plan.

Through this lawsuit, after almost fifty years of having to deal in the currency of protection against demolitions, Nubians in Kibera mobilized strategies to gain official recognition as urban people and lands as their ancestral home. It is not surprising that Nubians, of all the residents of Kibera, were the ones to sue. They were emboldened in the lawsuit because in the eyes of the state they had the longest recorded history of being "in place" in that part of Nairobi. Like a few other Kenyan groups who are predominantly urban, especially Asian Kenyans, Nubians trouble the anti-urban argument that no one can belong to Nairobi because everyone has a home elsewhere.

This perception is one of the strongest colonial legacies of government urban policy across eastern and southern Africa, often upheld by citizens and government alike. The Kenyan version of anti-urbanism allows the government to take the position that there is no such thing as homelessness. Since everyone is temporary in Nairobi, everyone has a home to go to somewhere else. As a consequence, the government accepts no real responsibility to those evicted in the name of development.

The Nubian community challenged this position by claiming Kibera as their ancestral lands in their lawsuit. This phrase has resonances from different eras: it may connote one's rural home, one's place of origin, the colonial notion of where Africans properly belong, or a pure place uncontaminated by the Western world. If Kibera is Nubian ancestral land, then Nubians belong in the city. By mobilizing their ancestrality, they call on a higher moral authority than the state. Like the graves in rural Kenya, the graves in the Nubian Muslim Military Cemetery at Kibera help residents legitimate their claim to ancestral land.

For Nubians and Asian Kenyans (among others), recognition of their ownership and title to land is a recognition not only of ancestral claims to a home in Nairobi but also of their membership in the nation.[57] Much as the grave of Pio Gama Pinto in City Park identifies him as belonging to Kenya rather than Portuguese Goa, in calling their land in Kibera ancestral, the Nubian community made claims to their place in Kenya. Their articulation of the problem perfectly encompasses the effects of anti-urbanism in government policy and the inherent cruelty of demolition as a tool of development.

Nevertheless, the Nubians and other residents of Kibera faced the prospect of demolition again in 2018. KURA did not comply with the judge's order to consult with the residents until July 13, 2018, three days before the posted deadline to relocate. Along with the residents and much of the public, Amnesty International in Kenya condemned the demolitions because no resettlement action plan was in place prior to the eviction.[58] Still. Again. Once more.

In January 2024, *The Standard* newspaper reported that the residents who were evicted in Kariobangi North in 2020 were to be resettled in the same place, following a reallotment of the land by Governor Sakaja and the Nairobi City County Government.[59] What then was the point of the demolitions? Were people compensated? Is this another kind of land brokerage? What happened to the plans for the sewage treatment plant? Will the same residents actually get to resettle back in Kariobangi? The proof, as they say, is in the pudding.

Demolitions have been a primary tool for implementing anti-urbanist policy in Nairobi ever since the colonial era. They were first used to limit African residence and permanence in the city, then to dislodge successful Asian and African businesses under the pretext of public health, then to maintain racial segregation, then to contain insurgency during the Emergency, then to maintain rural ethnic political bases and prevent urban class mobilization, then to police and control the poor. Today these measures also serve to sustain property prices, contain social protest, amass resources, and control political constituencies.

What these demolition campaigns have in common is the lack of legal procedure, the endless back-and-forth between residents and the state, and the assumption of the illegality of the residents. The result has been bad-faith negotiations, minimal or no warning of demolitions, political land brokerage, and a latent belief that everyone in Nairobi has somewhere else to go to if they are displaced and their property demolished. This is how belonging is understood in an anti-urbanist city. Part of the punishment of being out of place and time is the uncompensated loss of property.

Judging by newspaper reports, books, and articles from the last hundred years, between 160,000 and 500,000 people (5–13 percent of the current population) have been evicted through demolitions in Nairobi since its founding. Evictions and demolitions are quintessential aspects of the city's dynamics. Demolitions are not the tool of anti-urbanism alone, but they make real the anti-urbanist presumption that there is no place like home in Nairobi. Still. Again. Once more.

Epilogue

Civil Twilight

As I write this epilogue in May 2024, Nairobi faces both flooding and demolition. In April 2024 the long rains produced torrential downpours, setting single-day records for rainfall and causing floods that killed over two hundred people and left over ninety missing across the country.[1] The news and social media outlets were full of stories and pictures of flooding in low-lying areas of Nairobi, where roads became rivers, houses were flooded, and property was destroyed. Blame flew in all directions. The government was too slow to react. People had built on riparian land. The problem was climate change.

In April 2024, in an address to the public, Nairobi Governor Johnson Sakaja stated that sixty thousand people had been affected in Nairobi, all the city's rivers had burst their banks, bridges had been swept away, and roads had been destroyed, creating a humanitarian crisis.[2] He announced that the government would be clearing buildings along the rivers, no matter how long they had been there. He asked everyone to move and not wait to be moved. He assured residents that the city would provide food, water, and supplies to those affected. Finally, he said the city had halted all excavations of building sites and all pending building approvals.

T. J. Kajwang', the MP for Ruaraka, responded to Sakaja's speech thanking him for the promised interventions but pointing out that "it is the implementation that will make the difference." He called for local and national government to give people what they want: "Human dignity, carefulness to the Constitution, and making sure people are respected."[3]

And then, in May, came Cyclone Hidaya, the first cyclone in history to threaten Nairobi. As the storm moved up the coast of Tanzania, Kenya's President William Ruto gave people living within thirty meters of the wetland corridor of the Nairobi

River twenty-four hours to evacuate.[4] Ostensibly because of this new cyclone threat, and despite a week of negotiations to enumerate residents and identify space for relocations, the government demolished the neighborhood of Mukuru wa Ruben before the twenty-four hour evacuation period was up, rendering thirty thousand people homeless. They were people out of time, and now definitely out of place.

Despite Sakaja's campaign promises against demolitions, especially surprise demolitions, the BBC reported that people came home after work to find their houses gone.[5] Although wealthier, higher-elevation neighborhoods like Runda were also inundated by floodwaters, only the poorer area of Mukuru was demolished. Despite Kajwang's plea for dignity, constitutionalism, and respect, people were left in shock and pain, with nowhere to go. The climate may have changed, but not much else.

Perhaps even with all good intentions it is not that easy to change.

The disasters of the floods—and the floods themselves—are products of the way we have shaped the story of Nairobi so far. They are products of accepting anti-urbanism as the foundation on which the city is built. Anti-urbanism is a durable structure, outlasting and overshadowing good intentions and actions. But it does not have to be this way. The narrative can change, and with it, the ways we think about, plan for, act in, and live in the city.

The long-term presence of people in the city, both the living and the dead, illuminates both the persistence of and the challenge to anti-urbanism in Nairobi. It evokes both what is and what could have been. This book has investigated the ways that the city is claimed, imagined, storied, and understood. It has argued that the stories we tell of and about the city, as well as the ways stories get legitimized, matter to people's lives in the city. In retelling the story, we also have to reimagine the narrator. The process demands a closer look at who is imagining what, and for whom.

It is not enough to recognize anti-urbanism's legacy. To give weight to alternative visions, we must acknowledge and challenge the power embedded in the dominant narrative.[6] A new story will need to imagine time and space differently. This book has tried to show how new stories have been and could be imagined.

Spaces can conjure up permanence and act as a call to realize dreams. Remnants evoke a sense of permanence: memories of childhood adventure, of beauty, of sound, or of home can disrupt categories of temporal and spatial displacement, such as native and detribalized native, Asian, and poor. Social halls, dance, and music have claimed and professed a self-determined modernity in the face of accusations of backwardness. Gravesites and family homes evoke generational continuity and continuity across life and death, claiming a lasting place in the city despite the ubiquitous presence of bulldozers. The presence of the dead can inspire the building of new communities. Nairobi's rivers connect neighborhoods separated by anti-urbanism, showing us how, in the context of climate change, transformation of one area affects another. Demolition narratives highlight how both colonial and neoliberal governments and entities have sought to deal with needed but unwanted city populations.

How should we think about the city in relation to the countryside, or the older parts of the city in relation to the new? Positing the concept of home as a challenge to anti-urbanism has allowed me to understand what is at stake in the creation and destruction of spaces, in growing old, in envisaging futures that never happened and forgotten pasts that did. Framing the city as home also allows for different futures built through practice, place-making, protest, and advocacy by ordinary people as well as planning by experts. If we saw Nairobi as home for everyone who lives there, what would we do differently? What would change?

We would need a new urbanism with an understanding of permanence as well as mobility, an understanding of childhood, youth, aging, and generational change. We would need to build for the living and the dead as well as those to come. We would need spaces designed for work, leisure, and rest. We would need to build playgrounds, parks, and retirement housing, cemeteries as well as office buildings and roads. Visions of the past as much as the future would shape the present.

A new urbanism would see water and greenery as foundational. It would take into account the history and future of the watersheds and hinterlands of rivers, not just their floodplains. It would trace the paths of underground waterways through the city, understanding how water use and flow in one neighborhood affect residents downstream.

A new urbanism would discard demolition as a tool of governance, whether in crisis or for regeneration, and look to the root causes of flooding, overcrowding, housing shortages, traffic congestion, and structural instability. And it would take for granted that urban Africans are fully at home in the city, in their rightful place and time.

Urbanism is a form of dreaming. We need to ask, Who is dreaming? For whom, why, and how? How will our dreams determine what kind of Nairobi we build? Realizing dreams is a political as much as a scientific or engineering project. It needs consultation, participation, and negotiation as much as it needs designing, planning, and building.

The ethical and moral questions that arise in trying to realize dreams must be addressed through public debate. We must debate the legacies of colonialism, anti-urbanism and the kinds of policies that reinscribe it, how individuals should tread their own paths, the public good, and the nature and purpose of development. We should start from the principle that people belong to Nairobi and don't necessarily have (or want) anywhere else to go, rather than pretending that long-term residents do not exist. And the debate, although these questions are national and global in scope, should start locally.

A few years ago, on a sunny February day, I accompanied my eighty-two-year-old father on one of his daily walks to Don Bosco Church and back. My dad always

FIGURE 20. My father's walking route. Photo by author.

told us that that was his route. Once a man who walked the length of downtown Nairobi daily as a break from his office work, he now walked the one kilometer to the church and back. We walked in the middle of the street—the old new road, no longer the dirt road of my childhood. The road is now four lanes wide and divided by a concrete barrier. It has painted speed bumps and zebra (pedestrian) crossings. But everyone walks in the road because there are no sidewalks.

We walked slowly, my father with care and I with trepidation. I was fearful he wouldn't hear the few cars that come speeding down this road. Carefully looking both ways before crossing, he had to twist his whole body to see properly. A lifetime of urban living in Nairobi automatically guided his actions. Then he stepped out boldly, even if he lacked the speed with which he used to traverse Nairobi's streets.

At every gate my father paused to greet the guards (*askaris*). They greeted him back: "Habari Babu. Say hello to Mama." "Babu, you have come far today." Or "Habari Babu, we have not seen you in a while. It is good to see you again." Slowly we made our way back down the hill, passing flats I had seen being built on a vacant lot when I was a child. I remember the architect saying that if he had known he would have to live in those flats, he would have built them differently. We pass houses whose workers and guards have gray hair like their employers.

This route is a complex combination of new roads, changed landmarks, familiar sights, elderly residents, jacaranda trees, hills, and whizzing cars. The old is layered beneath the very new, but its remnants are still visible. Each layer tells a different story of the neighborhood. Each layer is disturbed by the occasional eruptions of the layers beneath it, which, like tree roots under a tarmacked path, lift, twist, bump and deform the surface, because there is nowhere else for them to go.

This book has tried to reveal the multiple and varied layers of life in Nairobi and their moments of eruption into the present, reminding us of the histories, people, and dreams that came before. We need to ask new questions so that we don't need to fear for our elders walking down the road.

My father passed on three years ago. A few days before his final journey, he was still walking up the middle of the road, past the double roundabouts, past Michael's fruit stand, in sight of, but not reaching, Don Bosco Church. He walked with his grandson, now an adult returned from college, greeting the gray-haired *askaris* on the way. "Habari Babu. Say hello to Mama." "Babu, you have come far today." These same *askaris* later came to the house to ask after him, as they had not seen him for a few days. When I think of Nairobi, I like to think back on that sunny day in February, when I was walking with my dad on the streets of my childhood, each changed space sparking a memory of home and stimulating dreams of alternative futures.

INTRODUCTION: DAWN

1. Pseudonyms for interviewees are used throughout the book.

2. Kenya became independent from Britain in 1963 and became a republic a year later, in 1964.

3. For local versions, see Njoroge, "Down Memory Lane," and Médard, "City Planning."

4. Bigon, "Garden Cities;" King, "Exporting 'Planning;'" Njoh, "Experience and Legacy."

5. Robinson, *Ordinary Cities*.

6. For example, new cities in China, Democratic Republic of the Congo, Cameroon, Rwanda, and Kazakhstan.

7. Guyer, "Describing Urban 'No Man's Land.'"

8. See Fair, *Reel Pleasures*; Callaci, *Street Archives*; Mabandla, *Lahla Ngubo*; Jean-Baptiste, *Conjugal Rights*; Nuttall and Mbembe, *Johannesburg*; Spronk, *Ambiguous Pleasures*; Smith, *Nairobi in the Making*; Morton, *Age of Concrete*; Murray, *Taming the Disorderly City*.

9. Callaci, *Street Archives*; Jean-Baptiste, *Conjugal Rights*; Morton, *Age of Concrete*; Smith, *Nairobi in the Making*; Slater, *Shaking Up the City*.

10. Robinson, *Ordinary Cities*; Simone, "On the Worlding."

11. Phrasing derived from Moore-Pewu, "Digital Mapping."

12. Mbembe and Nuttall, "Introduction;" Myers, *Seven Themes*; Médard, "City Planning;" King, "Exporting 'Planning.'"

13. See, for instance, Fontein et al., *Nairobi Becoming*; Myers, "A World-Class City;" Murray, "Taming the Disorderly City;" Naidoo, Nair, and Ngcobo, "A Critique;" Nuttall and Mbembe, *Johannesburg*; Mamdani, *Citizen and Subject*.

14. West-Pavlov, *Temporalities*; Fabian, *Time and the Other*.

15. In this book the term *African* is a racial category for individuals of any citizenship (Kenyan, Somali, etc.), referencing heritage from Africa. Such individuals were mostly

classified by the colonial administration as "native" (lowercased), with the exceptions of some Somalis, Nubians, and Swahili (due to their religion and their relationship to the colonial government).

16. Lonsdale, "Town Life;" Anderson, "Corruption."

17. Lonsdale, "Town Life;" De Boeck and Plissart, *Kinshasa.*

18. De Boeck, "Inhabiting Ocular Ground."

19. Kenya National Bureau of Statistics, *2019 Population and Housing Census,* vol. 3.

20. See for instance Spronk, *Ambiguous Pleasures;* Schmidt, *Migrants and Masculinity.*

21. Gitonga, *Nairobi Half Life.*

22. Hood, *Tsotsi.*

23. Callaci, *Street Archives;* Lonsdale, "Town Life;" Morton, *Age of Concrete.*

24. Callaci, *Street Archives,* 182.

25. See for instance Martinez-Muños, "Vertical Urbanization;" Conn, *Americans Against the City;* Miles, *Paradoxical Urbanism;* Stavrides, "Contested Urban Rhythms."

26. Mbembe and Nuttall, "Introduction," 11.

27. See also Gordon, "The Resurgent City," and Miles, *Paradoxical Urbanism.*

28. These two differently applied ideas of the garden city illuminate the question of for whom the policy functions.

29. For discussions of this framing see, for instance, King, "Exporting 'Planning;'" Mbembe and Nuttall, "Introduction."

30. See for instance, King, "Exporting 'Planning;'" Naidoo, Nair, and Ngcobo, "A Critique."

31. Njoh, "Experience and Legacy."

32. Although it is now customary to capitalize the word *Native* with reference to Indigenous peoples, in this book I frequently use the uncapitalized form, reflecting colonial usage, to avoid anachronism when discussing policies and documents from the colonial period.

33. Mabandla, *Lahla Ngubo;* Teppo, *Making of a Good White;* Robinson, *Ordinary Cities;* Njoh, "Experience and Legacy;" Callaci, *Street Archives;* Morton, *Age of Concrete;* Quayson, *Oxford Street;* Jean-Baptiste, *Conjugal Rights.*

34. Callaci, *Street Archives;* Jean-Baptiste, *Conjugal Rights;* Quayson, *Oxford Street.*

35. For instance, Fontein et al., *Nairobi Becoming,* starts with entry into the city.

36. De Boeck and Plissart, *Kinshasa*: Smith, *Nairobi in the Making.*

37. Watson, "Planned City;" Smith, *Nairobi in the Making;* Slater, *Shaking Up the City.*

38. In a general newspaper search the word *homeless* is rarely used with reference to demolitions or evictions in Nairobi, except as a consequence of natural disasters.

39. De Boeck, "Inhabiting Ocular Ground."

40. Watson, "Planned City;" Watson, "African Urban Fantasies;" Slater, *Shaking Up the City.*

41. De Boeck and Plissart, *Kinshasa;* De Boeck, "Inhabiting Ocular Ground;" Watson, "Planned City;" Watson, "African Urban Fantasies;" Morton, *Age of Concrete.*

42. Robinson, *Ordinary Cities.*

43. Simone, "On the Worlding;" De Boeck, "Inhabiting Ocular Ground;" McDonald, *World City Syndrome.*

44. See King, "Exporting 'Planning,'" and Mbembe and Nuttall, "Introduction," for discussion of this marginalization. Many (if not most) studies of cities and urbanity don't even mention African cities.

45. Martinez-Muños, "Vertical Urbanization."

46. Bigon, "Garden Cities;" King, "Exporting 'Planning;'" Njoh, "Experience and Legacy."

47. Bigon, "Garden Cities."

48. King, "Exporting 'Planning.'"

49. Harrison and Croese, "The Persistence."

50. Njoh, "Experience and Legacy."

51. Moore-Pewu, "Digital Mapping."

52. Ng'weno, "Growing Old;" Mutongi, *Matatu*; Mabandla, *Lahla Ngubo*; Smith, *Nairobi in the Making*; Morton, *Age of Concrete*; Ese and Ese, *City Makers*; Jean-Baptiste, *Conjugal Rights*; Callaci, *Street Archives*.

53. In this book the term *Railways* refers to the entity called at various times the Uganda Railway, the East African Railways and Harbours (EAR&H), and the Kenya Railways. The Uganda Railway became the EAR&H after World War I. After the collapse of the East African Community, the part of the railway network in Kenya became the Kenya Railways in 1977. The main line between Mombasa and Nairobi was replaced in 2017 as part of a proposed multinational railway network known locally as SGR (Standard Gauge Railway).

54. While there is a growing literature on Nairobi that looks at sexuality and youth (for instance, Spronk, *Ambiguous Pleasures*, and Schmidt, *Migrants and Masculinity*), transportation (for instance, Mutongi, *Matatu*), and specific neighborhoods (for instance, Smith, *Nairobi in the Making* and Ese and Ese, *City Makers*) that pushes beyond the usual antiurbanist descriptions of Nairobi to demonstrate place-making practices, there are no works structured around the water and the Railways. This study is different from studies that focus on a single neighborhood or culture in Nairobi. Rather, it focuses on the processes that produced long-term residents in Nairobi, including the development of water and Railways infrastructure.

55. Hay, "Shauri ya Serakali."

1. THE RAIN AT HOME

1. Today, ID cards are required for everyone eighteen and over.

2. Colonial chiefs were Africans working at the most local level of the colonial administration. Some of them were coopted traditional authorities; others were inventions of the British, to facilitate rule where no such institution existed. Today they fall under the Office of the President as the lowest level of government administrator.

3. Osborn, "Chiefs."

4. Aiyar, *Indians in Kenya.*

5. Osborn, "Chiefs."

6. Aiyar, *Indians in Kenya.*

7. Osborn, "Chiefs."

8. See Mamdani, *Citizen and Subject.*

9. Myers, "A World-Class City."

10. Quoted in Robertson, *Trouble Showed the Way*, 17 (my emphasis).

11. Aiyar, *Indians in Kenya*; Patel, *Challenge to Colonialism.*

12. In this book the term *Asian* refers to individuals of any citizenship (Kenyan, Indian, British, etc.), mainly of Indian, Pakistani, Iranian, and Afghan heritage. As a racial category it can be a subset of geographical categories such as *African* or *Kenyan.*

13. Hyde, "Nairobi General Strike."

14. Hyde, "Nairobi General Strike."

15. Aiyar, *Indians in Kenya*; Frenz, "*Swaraj*."

16. Nairobi's numerous ethnic groups include the Athi, Bajuni, Baganda, Digo, Embu, Luhya, Luo, Kamba, Kalenjin, Kikuyu, Kipsigis, Maasai, Meru, Nandi, Nubian, Nyamwezi, Samia, Seychellois, Somali, Sukuma, Swahili, and Taita peoples.

17. Robertson, *Trouble Showed the Way*; Morgan, "Agricultural Land."

18. Robertson, *Trouble Showed the Way*.

19. White, *Comforts of Home*; Ogot and Ogot, *History of Nairobi City*; Anderson, "Corruption at City Hall."

20. Ogot and Ogot, *History of Nairobi City*, 32.

21. Ochieng, *History of Kenya*.

22. Anderson, "Corruption at City Hall;" Macharia, "Nairobi's Changing Skyline."

23. In this book the term *Somali* is an ethnic category for individuals of any citizenship (Kenyan, Somali, etc.), referencing Somali heritage. As Muslims, Somalis posed a problem for colonial racial classifications and were exempt from "native" status.

24. Lonsdale, "Town Life," 211.

25. Because of the way anti-urbanism affected gender ratios in Nairobi, it wasn't until 2019 that there were almost equal numbers of men and women in the city.

26. Appelbaum, "Whitening the Region;" Pagden, *Fall of Natural Man*; Said, *Orientalism*; Cooper, "Conundrum of Race."

27. Cooper, "Conundrum of Race."

28. Aiyar, *Indians in Kenya*; Appelbaum, "Whitening the Region;" Appelbaum et al., *Race and Nation*; Decker and McMahon, *Idea of Development*.

29. West-Pavlov, *Temporalities*; Fabian, *Time and the Other*.

30. See Pagden, *Fall of Natural Man*, on Latin America, and Said, *Orientalism*, on the Middle East and Asia.

31. Scott, *Conscripts of Modernity*.

32. Aiyar, *Indians in Kenya*, 24.

33. Home, "Colonial Township."

34. Home, "Colonial Township."

35. Okoth-Ogendo, *Tenants of the Crown*.

36. Robertson, *Trouble Showed the Way*; Macharia, "Slum Clearance."

37. Aiyar, *Indians in Kenya*.

38. Home, "Colonial Township Laws," 190.

39. "In 1915, the Crown Lands Ordinance imposed a veto on the sale or lease of property in the highlands from Europeans to Indians or Africans." Murunga, "Cosmopolitan Tradition," 479.

40. Aiyar, *Indians in Kenya*.

41. Herzig, *South Asians in Kenya*.

42. Kenya Gazette, "Indians in Kenya," 967.

43. Home, "Colonial Township," 186.

44. Although *township* has today taken on the connotation, originating in South Africa, of inner-city or slum, across British colonial Africa it referred to a self-governing municipality, suburb, or neighborhood.

45. These ideas were not particular to Africa. As Appelbaum shows in "Whitening the Region," they were alive and well in Colombia in the nineteenth century.

46. Much of the political rhetoric of postcolonial Kenya was concerned with combatting "tribalism," construed as the practice of thinking and acting narrowly along ethnic rather than national lines. In particular people were and are concerned about the awarding of power, recourses, or political, economic, and social favor to members of one's own ethnic group and about the increase of violent ethno-nationalism. The concept of tribalism borrows heavily from colonial notions of *native* and *detribalized native*, framed by the idea of *tribe* as a static, self-contained spatial and moral social world.

47. Spanning most of the 1950s, the Mau Mau is often described as either a war waged by the British state against the Kenya Land and Freedom Army or as a violent conflict among Kikuyu populations split by allegiances and antagonisms to the colonial order. The term *Mau Mau* encompasses an array of concerns, including general resistance to the imperial political economy, the rebelliousness of African youth, and anxieties over shifting urban/rural demographics.

48. Wipper, "Kikuyu Women."

49. Cohen and Odhiambo, *Burying SM.*

50. In this book the term *Nubian* refers to Sudanese veterans and their descendants who were settled in the Kibera area before Independence in lieu of repatriation to Sudan.

51. White, *Nairobi.*

52. Parsons, "Kibra."

53. Golla, "Rich Man's Road."

54. See for instance Appelbaum et al., *Race and Nation.*

55. Murunga, "Inherently Unhygienic," 102.

56. Kenya Gazette, "Indians in Kenya;" Aiyar, *Indians in Kenya.*

57. Patel, *Challenge to Colonialism.*

58. Murunga, "Cosmopolitan Tradition."

59. Murunga, "Cosmopolitan Tradition."

60. Murunga, "Refugees at Home."

61. Freeman, *City of Farmers,* 24.

62. Lindsay and Martens, "Malaria."

63. Fastring and Griffith, "Malaria Incidence."

64. Lindsay and Martens, "Malaria."

65. Fastring and Griffith, "Malaria Incidence," and Lindsay and Martens, "Malaria," both point out that the military encampments of the First and Second World Wars caused epidemics in highland areas of Kenya, where the population had low functional immunity.

66. Freeman, *City of Farmers.*

67. Robertson, *Trouble Showed the Way.*

68. Aiyar, *Indians in Kenya.*

69. Kenya Gazette, "Indians in Kenya," 696.

70. White, *Comforts of Home.*

71. Martin and Bezemer, "The Concept and Planning."

72. Martin and Bezemer, in "The Concept and Planning," note that in 1910, the Railways replaced the original clay- and-iron-covered buildings with stone ones. My father remembers Muthurwa as consisting of two sections, Landhi Mabati (corrugated-iron Landhi) and

Landhi Mawe (stone Landhi). Landhi Mawe still stands and is today considered separate from Muthurwa.

73. Martin and Bezemer, "The Concept and Planning," 618.

2. GROWING OLD IN A NEW CITY

A version of this chapter was first published in 2018 in *City* 22, no. 1, as "Growing Old in a New City: Time, the Post-colony and Making Nairobi Home."

1. Structural adjustment was a set of economic reforms pushed by the International Monetary Fund and the World Bank that included reducing government spending, liberalizing markets, devaluing currencies, cutting public-sector employment, privatizing state-owned enterprises, deregulating industries, and improving tax collection.

2. JG, discussion with author, Nairobi, 2013.

3. JM, discussion with author, Nairobi, 2013.

4. Anderson, "Corruption at City Hall," 141.

5. As a result, there are Landhies Roads in cities in both India and Pakistan.

6. Grillo, *African Railwaymen*.

7. Achola, "Colonial Policy."

8. Grillo, *African Railwaymen*.

9. JK, discussion with author, Nairobi, 2014.

10. Lonsdale, "Town Life," 16.

11. DA, discussion with author, Nairobi, 2013; JHO discussion with author, Nairobi, 2013.

12. Likimani, *Fighting without Ceasing*; Likimani, *Passbook*.

13. Frederiksen, "African Women."

14. LO, discussion with author, Nairobi, 2013.

15. DA, discussion.

16. Hilary Ng'weno, discussion with author, Nairobi, 2013.

17. DA, discussion.

18. "The Emergency" refers to the state of emergency declared by the British colonial administration in response to land and freedom struggles between 1952 and 1958. These anticolonial struggles became known as the Mau Mau.

19. Smyth, "Grierson."

20. Hilary Ng'weno, discussion with author.

21. Hyde, "Nairobi General Strike," 241.

22. *Satrose Ayuma and 11 Others v Registered Trustees of the Kenya Railways Staff.*

23. Owuor and Mbatia, "Nairobi."

24. "Retired Staff of Kenya Railways."

25. Kamotho, "Nairobi 72 Acre."

26. Macharia, "Nairobi's Changing Skyline."

27. Kamau, "Analysis of Sustainability."

28. Kamotho, "Nairobi 72 Acre."

29. MaVulture, "Once upon This Space."

30. Kamotho, "Reclaiming Muthurwa."

31. Kamotho, "Reclaiming Muthurwa."

32. Nairobi City County, *Final Report*.

33. Government of Kenya, *Nairobi Metro 2030*, 29.

34. Owuor and Mbatia, "Nairobi."

35. Olick, "Nairobi Governor."

36. Kagai, "Kenya Seeks Wealthy Investors."

37. Otuki, "Mega Sh217bn Railway."

38. Bayside Realty, "Nairobi Railway City."

39. Kenya Railways Corporation, "Nairobi Railway City" (my emphasis).

40. Kenya Railways Corporation, "Nairobi Railway City."

41. Kenya National Bureau of Statistics, *2019 Population and Housing Census*, vol. 3.

42. Kenya National Bureau of Statistics, *2019 Population and Housing Census*, vol. 3.

43. De Boeck, "Inhabiting Ocular Ground;" Watson, "African Urban Fantasies."

44. Simone, *City Life*, 7–8.

45. Guyer, Denzer, and Agbaj, "Preface," xi.

46. Scott, *Conscripts of Modernity*, 29, 44.

47. Watson, "African Urban Fantasies," 225.

48. Simone, *City Life*, 9.

49. Guyer, Denzer, and Agbaj, *"Preface;"* Simone, *City Life*.

50. *Satrose Ayuma and 11 Others v Registered Trustees of the Kenya Railways Staff*.

51. Albrecht et al., "Solastalgia;" Galway et al., "Mapping."

52. Achebe, *No Longer at Ease*.

53. Huyssen, "Present Pasts."

54. Huyssen, "Present Pasts," 34.

3. ONE HUNDRED YEARS OF SEGREGATION

1. Murunga, "'Inherently Unhygienic Races.'"

2. Aiyar, *Indians in Kenya*; Murunga, "Cosmopolitan Tradition."

3. Murunga, "Refugees at Home."

4. These included the Somali Exemption Ordinance (1919), the Definition of the Term "Native" Ordinance (1921), the General Revision Ordinance (1925), and the Interpretation (Definition of Native) Ordinance (1934). See Murunga, "Cosmopolitan Tradition."

5. Murunga, "Refugees at Home." Many current residents of Nairobi would consider Eastleigh as becoming a Somali area only after 1990, following the civil war in Somalia that caused a huge influx of refugees to Kenya. The new arrivals sought to settle in a place that already had a Somali presence. This influx of Somalis pushed out the remaining Asian Eastleigh residents.

6. Ogot and Ogot, *History of Nairobi City*, 34.

7. Anderson, "Corruption at City Hall."

8. White, *Comforts of Home*.

9. Murunga, "Cosmopolitan Tradition."

10. Jainsamaj, "Jains in Nairobi," notes that the Digamber Jain Mumukshu Mandal was established in Nairobi on June 4, 1950.

11. Noronha, "Interesting Timeline."

12. The Legislative Council, modeled on the Westminster system of governance, was the legislature of Kenya between 1907 and 1963. Initially it consisted of appointed members,

exclusively European. From 1920 some of its members were elected, and in 1924 Asian members were admitted. The first African member was nominated in 1944. In 1957 the first eight elected Africans joined the LegCo.

13. Murunga, "Cosmopolitan Tradition."

14. In this book the term *Goan* refers to people with heritage from Goa, India, who until India's takeover of Goa from Portugal were considered Portuguese citizens.

15. Hart, "Art Deco Houses."

16. Patel, *Challenge to Colonialism*. Jeevanjee's family became the second Asian family to move into the formerly all-white area, following the photographer John Kamarli and his family.

17. Murunga, "Cosmopolitan Tradition," 477.

18. Wanjiku and Iwatani, *A Brief Tour*; Hart, "Art Deco Houses."

19. Morgan, *Reflection*, 101.

20. Macharia, "Slum Clearance."

21. Morgan, *Reflection*, 101.

22. Morgan, *Reflection*, 101, 102.

23. Morgan, *Reflection*, 102, 103.

24. Makwaro and Mireri, "Public Open Spaces." In 1900 Nairobi was only 18 square kilometers in area. Its boundaries were extended in 1927 to 25 square kilometers, in 1948 to 78 square kilometers, and in 1963 to its current area of 696 square kilometers.

25. Kamau, "How Muthaiga Estate."

26. Awori, *Riding on a Tiger*, 74.

27. Awori, *Riding on a Tiger*.

28. Robertson, *Trouble Showed the Way*.

29. The "Asian question" in Kenya was always a version of Europe's "Jewish question." Both reflect racial ideas that are tied up with class and economic competition as well as xenophobia. In Nairobi these two questions sometimes overlapped. For instance, before Independence, no Asians, Jews, or Africans could be members of the Muthaiga Club. According to a Muthaiga Club member, even after Independence, while Africans were allowed to be members, the club continued to exclude Asians and Jews. This has now changed up to a point.

30. Lonsdale, "Town Life."

31. Hyde, "Nairobi General Strike."

32. Hyde, "Nairobi General Strike."

33. Robertson, *Trouble Showed the Way*, 129.

34. Robertson, *Trouble Showed the Way*.

35. Hyde, "Nairobi General Strike;" Robertson, *Trouble Showed the Way*. This situation differed starkly and ironically from the situation after World War II, when returning African soldiers from the colonial forces were refused business licenses by the government. Using their remittances, they set up Burma Market near Pumwani, the name commemorating their service in Burma.

36. Morange, "Street Trade," 252.

37. Meerkotter, *Vagrancy-Related Provisions*.

38. By 2023 the civil service was mostly made up of Kikuyu, Kalenjin, and Luhya employees, reflecting the national political landscape.

39. Aiyar, *Indians in Kenya*.

40. Aiyar, *Indians in Kenya*; Robertson, *Trouble Showed the Way.*

41. Frenz, "Swaraj," sees this change as an inversion of colonial categories of racial segregation between Native and non-Native. I argue rather that the categories shifted but retained temporal and spatial restrictions.

42. Klopp, "Pilfering the Public."

43. Aiyar, *Indians in Kenya*, argues that because of decisions to resell the bought-out lands, between 1964 and 1967, more than half of the farms were reacquired by Europeans.

44. Kimani, "Structure of Land Ownership."

45. Klopp, "Pilfering the Public."

46. Aiyar, *Indians in Kenya.*

47. Robertson, *Trouble Showed the Way.*

48. Aiyar, *Indians in Kenya.*

49. Aiyar, *Indians in Kenya.*

50. Ng'weno and Aloo, "Irony of Citizenship."

51. Médard, "City Planning."

52. Kimani, "Structure of Land Ownership."

53. Aiyar, *Indians in Kenya.*

54. Awori, *Riding on a Tiger*, 82.

55. Awori, *Riding on a Tiger*, 85, 86.

56. Kimani, "Structure of Land."

57. According to Kimani, "Structure of Land," in the 1970s, half of the land owned by Africans was in formerly European areas of the northwest, probably obtained after Independence.

58. Kimani, "Structure of Land Ownership."

59. Site and service is a form of housing development that provides a wet core (water and sewage services) around which owners build a house.

60. Robertson, *Trouble Showed the Way.*

61. Macharia, "Slum Clearance."

62. Callaci, *Street Archives*; Morton, *Age of Concrete.*

63. Macharia, "Slum Clearance," 229; Médard, "City Planning."

64. Macharia, "Slum Clearance," 229.

65. Morange, "Street Trade."

66. Klopp, "Pilfering the Public."

67. Mwau, "Rise of Nairobi's Concrete."

68. Mwau, "Rise of Vertical Slums."

69. Maina and Mwau, "Nairobi," 217.

70. Mugambi, "Vertical Slums."

71. Schmidt, *Migrants and Masculinity.*

4. DANCING TO THE SOUND OF NAIROBI

A version of this chapter was first published in *Music and Dance in Eastern Africa*, edited by Kahithe Kiiru and Maina wa Mutoya (Nairobi: IFRA, 2020).

1. ML, discussion with author, Nairobi, 2013.

2. See for instance, Plageman, "Recomposing;" Plageman, *Highlife*; Moorman, *Intonations*; Callaci, "Dancehall Politics;" Chikowero, *African Music.*

3. See also Quayson, *Oxford Street.*

4. Mutongi, *Matatu*, 66.

5. The film project *Last Dance in Kaloleni* is ongoing. More information can be found at https://lastdanceinkaloleni.co.ke.

6. The McMillan Memorial Library, modeled on the Carnegie libraries, was endowed by a wealthy British settler.

7. Burton, "Townsmen," 348.

8. Chikowero, *African Music.*

9. Frederiksen, "Making Popular Culture," 9.

10. Frederiksen, "Making Popular Culture," 9.

11. Muchugu, "Pumwani Social Hall."

12. White, *Comforts of Home*; Muchugu, "Pumwani Social Hall," 1.

13. Myers, *Verandahs of Power.*

14. Anderson, "Corruption at City Hall."

15. Odhiambo, "Kula Raha."

16. SW, discussion with author, Nairobi, 2014.

17. White, *Comforts of Home.*

18. MOO, discussion with author, Nairobi, 2014.

19. MOO, discussion.

20. NM, discussion with author, Nairobi, 2013.

21. Frederiksen, "African Women," 229.

22. Owen, "Lands of Leisure."

23. HJO, discussion with author, Nairobi, 2016.

24. MOO, discussion.

25. Frederiksen, "African Women."

26. Rumba is an Afro-Cuban style of music that was taken up in ballroom dancing. It is referred to as rhumba in the United States. Since both styles influenced Kenyan music, I retain the Cuban spelling throughout.

27. HJO, discussion.

28. Owen, "Lands of Leisure."

29. HJO, discussion.

30. HJO, discussion.

31. Frederiksen, *Making Popular Culture.*

32. SMO, discussion with author, Nairobi, 2015.

33. HJO, discussion.

34. Among manual laborers, engineers, and firemen (the men who shoveled fuel on locomotives) were among the highest paid because they earned overtime wages on long-distance hauls.

35. Hilary Ng'weno, discussion with author, Nairobi, 2013.

36. Craig, *Sorry I Don't Dance.*

37. Callaci, *Street Archives*, 367.

38. Burton, "Introduction."

39. Burton, "Townsmen in the Making."

40. Tsuruta, "Popular Music."

41. Callaci, *Street Archives*, 367.

42. Low, "History;" Odhiambo, "Kula Raha."

43. Nyairo, "'Zilizopendwa.'"

44. Nyairo, "'Zilizopendwa,'"50.

45. Stapleton and May, *African All-Stars.*

46. Chikowero, *African Music.*

47. Stapleton and May, *African All-Stars.*

48. Nairobi City Council, *Nairobi*; ML, discussion with author, Nairobi, 2013; HBN, discussion with author, Nairobi, 2013.

49. AO, discussion with author, Nairobi, 2014.

50. Gerhard, "Neo-traditional Popular Music," 92.

51. Ketebul Music, *Shades of Benga.*

52. Eagleson, "Between Uptown and River Road."

53. NM, personal communication, 24 April 2024. NM studied under Mohamed Absura at Starehe Boys School.

54. SMO, discussion.

55. DA, discussion with author, Nairobi, 2013; Cpt. O, discussion with author, Nairobi, 2015.

56. Ketebul, *Shades of Benga.*

57. Hilary Ng'weno, discussion with author, Nairobi, 2013.

58. Ondieki, Ogama, and Achieng'Akuno, "Zilizopendwa."

59. Low, "History."

60. Stapleton and May, *African All-Stars.*

61. Low, "History," 21.

62. Eagleson, "Between Uptown and River Road."

63. Eagleson, "Between Uptown and River Road."

64. Low, "History."

65. Low, "History;" "Odhiambo, "Kula Raha;" Stapleton and May, *African All-Stars.*

66. Low, "History," 19; HJO discussion with author, Nairobi, 2016.

67. Stapleton and May, *African All-Stars.*

68. Low, "History;" Stapleton and May, *African All-Stars.*

69. Low, "History."

70. Wilkinson, "The BBC."

71. Frederiksen, *Making Popular Culture*, 28.

72. Amour, "The BBC."

73. Amour, "The BBC;" Soja, *Geography.*

74. Harvey, "Jambo."

75. Odhiambo, "Kula Raha."

76. Sykes, "Peter Colmore," 1.

77. Sykes, "Peter Colmore."

78. Tsuruta, "Popular Music," 212.

79. Ally Sykes's father, Abdullah Kleist Sykes, known as Kleist Sykes, was born in Pangani, Tanganyika, to Sykes Mbuwane, a Zulu mercenary working for the German authority. Mbuwane died at war after Kleist was born. Kleist fought for Germany in World War I, joining as a twelve-year-old. He later worked on the Tanganyika Railway and became a successful businessman and politician in Dar es Salaam. His son Ally was also an excellent businessman, music producer, and politician.

80. Callaci, *Street Archives.*
81. Sykes, "Peter Colmore."
82. Odidi, "Golden Years."
83. Eagleson, "Between Uptown and River Road."
84. Eagleson, "Between Uptown and River Road," 31.
85. East African Railways & Harbours, *Annual Report.*
86. Grillo, *African Railwaymen,* 29.
87. Frederiksen, *Making Popular Culture.*
88. Eagleson, "Between Uptown and River Road."
89. There continues to be a controversy over the copyright to the song "Malaika," as various artists claim credit for its composition, although it was first recorded by Fadhili William. Miriam Makeba contributed to the controversy by crediting it as a Tanzanian folk song, despite singing it along with Fadhili William on stage at Kenya's Independence celebrations.
90. Low, "History."
91. Eagleson, "Between Uptown and River Road," 26.
92. Goldsworthy, *Tom Mboya.*
93. Parkin, *Cultural Definition,* 239.
94. Goldsworthy, *Tom Mboya,* 113.
95. Ketebul Music, *Shades of Benga.*
96. Ondieki, Ogama, and Achieng'Akuno, "Zilizopendwa," 50.
97. Eagleson, "Between Uptown and River Road," 31.

5. REMNANT OF A GREEN CITY IN THE SUN

1. Friends of City Park, *City Park,* 8.
2. *Upland* refers to areas at higher elevations than the coast but below the highlands, which are generally thought to start at Nairobi, about five hundred kilometers from the coast. In colloquial parlance, *up-country* is anywhere higher than you.
3. Friends of City Park, *City Park.*
4. Smith, *Nairobi in the Making,* 133.
5. Trouillot, *Silencing the Past.*
6. See discussions of colonial town planning and garden cities in King, "Exporting 'Planning;'" Myers, "The Afterlife."
7. Anderson, *Imagined Communities*; Myers, "The Afterlife."
8. Kenyatta, "We're Committed;" Wood, *Green City.*
9. Freeman, *City of Farmers*; Myers, "The Afterlife."
10. Freeman, *City of Farmers.*
11. Freeman, *City of Farmers*; Aiyar, *Indians in Kenya.*
12. Freeman, *City of Farmers.*
13. Bigon, "Garden Cities."
14. Pastor, Canniffe, and Jiménez, "Learning from Letchworth;" Edwards, "Further Criticism."
15. Conn, *Americans Against the City.*
16. Bigon, "Garden Cities," 477.
17. Conn, *Americans Against the City.*
18. For instance, Bigon, "Garden Cities," 480, states that "the white residential area in Antananarivo (Madagascar) is described there as a 'satellite garden-suburb'; in Thiès (east

of Dakar) it is described as 'a real Garden City'; in Elisabethville (Belgian Congo) 'a large Garden City with greenery creates all the charms' and even in Beira (Portuguese Mozambique) the white area is characterized as a desirable 'Garden City.'"

19. Freeman, *City of Farmers.*

20. White, Silberman, and Anderson, *Nairobi.* When I was growing up, the minimum plot size in the Lang'ata area of Nairobi was five acres. This limit, which was justified by the lack of a piped water supply, was not changed until the 1990s.

21. Martin and Bezemer, "Concept and Planning."

22. Martin and Bezemer, "Concept and Planning," 619.

23. Martin and Bezemer, "Concept and Planning."

24. Awori, *Riding on a Tiger*, 382.

25. AH, discussion with author, Nairobi, 2016.

26. BKK, discussion with author, Nairobi, 2016.

27. Bissell, "Engaging Colonial Nostalgia," 236.

28. Writing this in Hawaii, I see these yellow Nandi flames every so often along the roadsides and imagine just how far this innovation traveled.

29. Makwaro and Mireri, "Public Open Spaces."

30. Discussion with Friends of City Park, Nairobi, 2016.

31. Mensah, "Urban Green Spaces," 8.

32. Friends of City Park, "Highland Forest."

33. AKTC, *Rehabilitation of Nairobi.*

34. Hilary Ng'weno, discussion with author, Nairobi, 2012.

35. Submission to Friends of City Park essay competition, Nairobi, 2013. *Tarmacking* is a colloquial expression meaning to pound the pavement in search of work. The reference to Caesar alludes to the biblical quotation "Render unto Caesar the things that are Caesar's." Here, it means not being able to pay taxes because of having no job.

36. BK, discussion with author, Nairobi, 2021.

37. Revive Consulting Solutions, *Conceptual Integrated Design.*

38. CG, retired Bamburi Cement employee, discussion with author, Nairobi, 2022.

39. Mensah, "Urban Green Spaces," 1.

40. Slater, *Shaking Up the City.*

41. Njeru, "'Donor-Driven' Neoliberal Reform."

42. World Health Organization, *Urban Planning.*

43. AKTC, *Rehabilitation.* Although Nairobi National Park is an important and beloved part of Nairobi's green space and only a short distance from the city center, its nature makes it inaccessible and unsuitable for walking or casual public recreation. Because it is home to potentially dangerous wild animals, entry is permitted only by motor vehicle. This limits access to those with private cars, those who can afford to rent a car, and organized groups.

44. AKTC, *Rehabilitation.*

45. CN, discussion with author, Nairobi, 2016.

46. Manji, "Nairobi Arboretum."

47. Manji, "Nairobi Arboretum." In 2021 the cost of entry to the arboretum went up twice and now stands at around 70 shillings, or 70 US cents. In 2023 a fee for electronic payment—the only accepted form of payment—was added to the entrance fee, almost doubling the cost of a single entry.

48. See for instance Hoffman et al., "Do Free Goods Stick?;" Ashraf, Berry, and Shapiro, "Can Higher Prices Stimulate Product Use?;" Cohen and Dupas, "Free Distribution."

49. Larson, "Imagining Social Justice," 397.

50. Larson, "Imagining Social Justice," 399.

51. CN, as told to Friends of City Park, Nairobi, 2016.

52. Médard, "City Planning."

53. Friends of City Park, *City Park*.

54. CN, discussion with author. 2017

55. Revive Consulting Solutions, *Conceptual Integrated Design*; Ng'weno, *City Park Initiative*.

56. Majanja, "A Park Called Freedom."

6. REMAINS OF AN UNREALIZED YESTERDAY

1. Balakrishnan, "Archives in Stone," 6.

2. Adebanwi, *Yoruba Elites*; Adebanwi, "Burying 'Zik;'" Mpofu, "Ruling;" Fontein, *The Politics of the Dead*; Mataga, "Unsettled Spirits."

3. Adebanwi, *Yoruba Elites*; Mpofu, "Ruling."

4. Adebanwi, "Burying 'Zik.'"

5. Adebanwi, *Yoruba Elites*, 72.

6. Trouillot, *Silencing the Past*, 29.

7. Commonwealth War Graves Commission, "Nairobi (Forest Road)."

8. Kariokor was once a predominantly Asian part of town, but the name commemorates the Africans who served in the Carrier Corps in World War I. The area could now be termed inner-city as a result of decline, population change, and age.

9. Other communities whom the British found difficult to classify included the Swahili, the Somalis, the Greeks, the Balochis, and the Seychellois.

10. Balakrishnan, "Building."

11. Commonwealth War Graves Commission, "Nairobi Park Cemetery."

12. Karanja, "Comparative Analysis."

13. Graves maintained by the Commonwealth War Graves Commission in Kenya include those at the Nairobi War Cemetery, which holds 1,952 burials from World War II (some of them African); the Kariokor World War II Commonwealth War Graves Cemetery, which holds 59; the Muslim (Quarry Road) Cemetery, which holds 33 world war dead; and the Nairobi South Cemetery, which holds 155 World War I and 2 World War II dead.

14. Quoted in Hay and Burke, *Report of the Special Committee*, 8.

15. Hay and Burke, *Report of the Special Committee*, 6.

16. Hay and Burke, *Report of the Special Committee*, 6, 48.

17. Hay and Burke, *Report of the Special Committee*.

18. Ng'weno, "Inheriting Disputes."

19. Interview with Emma Gama Pinto (Pio's wife) by Frederick Noronha, reprinted in Durrani, *Pio Gama Pinto*.

20. Rothmyer, *Joseph Murumbi*.

21. Donovan, "Joseph Murumbi." Donovan claims that Murumbi "was probably Africa's greatest private collector of art, books, postage stamps, artifacts, textiles, jewelry and everything African, including 50,000 documents on Africa."

22. Donovan, "Joseph Murumbi."

23. Durrani, *Pio Gama Pinto.*

24. Wanga-Odhiambo, "Challenge to African Democracy."

25. Wanga-Odhiambo, "Challenge to African Democracy."

26. Wanga-Odhiambo, "Challenge to African Democracy."

27. De Souza, *Forward to Independence.*

28. Pinto, quoted in Durrani, *Pio Gama Pinto*, 35.

29. De Souza, *Forward to Independence*, 253.

30. Durrani, *Pio Gama Pinto*, 350.

31. Going through my father's office in 2020 as we organized the donation of his papers to Moi University, I came across a receipt for my parents' donation to the fund for resettling Pinto's family in Canada.

32. Wanga-Odhiambo, "Challenge to African Democracy."

33. The other heroes honored by stamps were Tom Mboya, Oginga Odinga, and Ronald Ngala. Frenz, "Swaraj," points out that Pinto is the only non-African Kenyan honored in this way.

34. Goodman, "Remembering Mzee."

35. Mataga, "Unsettled Spirits;" Fontein, *Politics*; Mpofu, "Ruling."

36. Walibora Waliaula, "Remembering."

37. Murray, *Commemorating and Forgetting*, iii.

38. Commonwealth War Graves Commission, "Nairobi Park Cemetery."

39. Anderson and Lane, "Unburied Victims," 16.

40. Coombes, "Monumental Histories," 210.

41. Adewanwi, in *Yoruba Elites*, argues that in Nigeria the posthumous political life of the Yoruba politician Olafemi Awolowo was due to his cultivation of community while he was alive, along with Yoruba elites' investment in and maintenance of his project after death, created through ethnic identification. Neither applied to Pinto.

42. Pinto was in detention on Manda Island when his father died and could not participate in the decision about where he should be buried.

43. Fernandes, *Yesterday.*

44. See also see Balakrishnan, "Building," on graves as claims to land and ancestrality.

45. These centers include the Kayole Social Justice Center, the Mathare Social Justice Center, the Mukuru Social Justice Center, Kamkunji Human Rights Defenders, and the Githurai Human Rights Net.

46. SD, personal communication, August 2, 2024.

47. Missing Voices website, www.missingvoices.or.ke.

48. Okune, Matathia, and Mutonga, "Scholarly Memory." According to Waweru and Balhorn, "Kenya's First Socialist Library," activists included the Mwakenya Movement, Vita Books, and the Mau Mau Research Center.

49. Bombaa, Zhu, and Omondi, *Until Everyone Is Free.*

50. Adebanwi, *Yoruba Elites*; Adebanwi, "Burying 'Zik;'" Adebanwi, "Death."

51. Mwangi and Maghanga, *Pio Gama Pinto*, 40.

52. Mwangi and Maghanga, *Pio Gama Pinto*, 20.

53. Walibora Waliaula, "Remembering."

54. Smith, *Nairobi in the Making*.

55. Walibora Waliaula, "Remembering," argues that names commemorate the dead, so that they live on through new generations rather than through graves or marked monuments.

56. Walibora Waliaula, "Remembering."

7. PLACE OF SWEET WATER

1. "10 Dead, 134 Injured."

2. Obulutsa, "Death Toll."

3. "10 Dead, 134 Injured."

4. BBC, "Nairobi Building Collapse."

5. "10 Dead, 134 Injured."

6. "At Least Three Killed."

7. Mutambo, "History of Collapsed Buildings."

8. "10 Dead, 134 Injured."

9. Guguyu, "Ministry Seeks Cabinet Action;" Mutambo, "History of Collapsed Buildings."

10. Kilimani means "at, on, or in the hills."

11. Guguyu, "Ministry Seeks Cabinet Action."

12. Agutu, "Sonko Lists Grabbed Properties."

13. Dzuya, "Court Declines to Stop Demolition;" Kakah, "Stop NEMA Bulldozers."

14. Dzuya, "Court Declines to Stop Demolition."

15. Ombaka, "Demolitions."

16. Ogina, "Ukay Center Owners."

17. Calculated from Kenya National Bureau of Statistics, *2019 Kenya Population and Housing Census*, vol. 3.

18. The altitude of Karen is 6,100 feet (1,860 meters) and of Kikuyu 6,450 feet (1,964 meters). The altitude at Wilson Airport is 5,500 feet (1,682 meters), at Huruma 5,457 feet (1,663 meters), and at Dandora sewage pools 4,921 feet (1,500 meters).

19. Mukuru means "valley" (Kikuyu), Ziwani means "at the lake" (Swahili), and Ngara means "the last watering place" (Maasai).

20. Only three relatively flat sections of Nairobi are laid out in a grid—the central business district, Parklands, and Eastleigh. Parklands and Eastleigh have numbered avenues, which are rare in the rest of the city.

21. Freeman, *City of Farmers*.

22. Mwathane, "There Is Need."

23. Maina and Mwau, "Nairobi."

24. Gertz, *Kenya's Trade Liberalization*.

25. Macrotrends, "Kenya Inflation Rate."

26. Amis, "Squatters or Tenants?"

27. Médard, "City Planning."

28. Maina and Mwau, "Nairobi."

29. Maina and Mwau, "Nairobi."

30. Huchzermeyer, "Tenement City," 715.

31. Ochieng, "Built to Fail."

32. Kenya National Bureau of Statistics, *2019 Kenya Population and Housing Census*, vol. 3.

33. Kenya Engineer, "Technical Audit."

34. Huchzermeyer, "Tenement City."

35. Huchzermeyer, "Tenement City."

36. Slater, *Shaking Up the City.*

37. Ben Teresa, quoted in Slater, *Shaking Up the City*, 67.

38. Huchzermeyer, "Tenement City," 719.

39. Huchzermeyer, "Tenement City."

40. Smith, "Collapse."

41. Kenya Engineer, *Technical Audit.*

42. Willstone Homes, "Why Buildings Collapse."

43. Kamau, "Building Collapse."

44. Smith, "Collapse," 15.

45. Kenya Engineer, *Technical Audit.*

46. Wakaya, "Nairobi's Condemned Buildings."

47. Ochieng, "Built to Fail." This workload would entail inspecting at least one building project per day. Travel distances and threats of violence hamper the inspectors' ability to work at this pace.

48. Willstone Homes, "Why Buildings Collapse."

49. Steven Oundo (architect), discussion with author, Nairobi, 2022.

50. Kamau, "Analysis of Sustainability."

51. Kamau, "Why the Mlolongo Building Collapsed;" Kamau, "Building Collapse."

52. Singh, "How to Construct Foundation."

53. Fulzele, Ghane, and Parkhe, "Study of the Structures."

54. Mishra, "Study on Engineering Behavior."

55. Ingold and Simonetti, "Introducing Solid Fluids," 22.

56. Oundo, discussion.

57. Singh, "How to Construct Foundation."

58. Oundo, discussion; Fulzele, Ghane, and Parkhe, "Study of the Structures."

59. Neelawani and Patil, "Behavior," 116.

60. Fulzele, Ghane, and Parkhe, "Study of the Structures."

61. Ingold and Simonetti, "Introducing Solid Fluids," 13.

62. Juma, "Kenya—Flash Floods."

63. Abuje et al., "Vulnerability of Nairobi."

64. Krhoda and Kwambuka, "Impact of Urbanization."

65. Abuje et al., "Vulnerability of Nairobi," 40.

66. Hirst, *Struggle for Nairobi.*

67. The years 2011 and 2012 saw some of the highest-ever rainfall accumulations on the Muthaiga rain gauge.

68. Juma, "Kenya—Flash Floods."

69. "Billions Lost."

70. Karisa, "Negotiated Framework;" Kakonge, "Nairobi River Basin;" Kenya Rivers and Water Resources, *Master Plan.*

71. Kakonge, "Nairobi River Basin."

72. Kenya Rivers and Water Resources, *Master Plan.*

73. Kakonge, "Nairobi River Basin;" Karisa, "Negotiated Framework."

74. Karisa, "Negotiated Framework."

75. Kakonge, "Nairobi River Basin."

76. Kahongeh, "Kenya."

77. Urban Pathways, "Nairobi Is Kick-Starting."

78. Kimari and Parish, "What Is a River?"

79. Slater, *Shaking up the City,* 80 (emphasis in original).

80. Coates, "Infrastructural Events," 2.

81. Hasan, "Why Karachi Floods."

8. NO PLACE LIKE HOME

1. The legal concept of surrendering land exists to allow residents to contribute to neighborhood improvements. In theory this raises property values and benefits all residents while reducing the costs to individual landholders. Typical improvements for which land may be surrendered include upgrading sewer lines or laying cables. Surrender is voluntary, as opposed to compulsory acquisition, by which the government compels the sale of land for the public good (usually development projects) and compensates landowners. Surrender and compulsory acquisition are two of the pillars of private-property regimes: they guarantee that property will not be expropriated by the state without fair compensation and that individual landowners will not stand in the way of the public good. Thus when KURA asked landowners to surrender land, it was on the assumption that the road constituted a benefit to the landowners and the neighborhood.

2. Kinyanjui, "5,000 Evicted;" Kinyanjui, "State Halts Kariobangi North Demolitions."

3. Imende, "State Probing Kariobangi North Evictions."

4. Igadwah, "Nairobians Pay for Sins."

5. Maombo, "Kariobangi Residents."

6. Kinyanjui, "5,000 Evicted."

7. Maombo, "Kariobangi Residents."

8. Kinyanjui, "5,000 Evicted."

9. Kinyanjui, "5,000 Evicted."

10. Murunga, "Inherently Unhygienic Races," 113.

11. These practices are particularly well documented for North and South America. See for instance, Appelbaum, Macpherson, and Rosenblatt, *Race and Nation.*

12. White, *Comforts of Home;* Ogot and Ogot, *History of Nairobi.*

13. Ogot and Ogot, *History of Nairobi.*

14. Mudhune et al., "Clinical Burden."

15. Murunga, "Inherently Unhygienic Races."

16. Awori, *Riding on a Tiger,* 383.

17. Slater, *Shaking Up the City,* 64.

18. A curfew was also decreed during the 1917 influenza pandemic, restricting Africans to native locations.

19. Manyibe, "President Uhuru Apologizes."

20. Slater, *Shaking Up the City,* 24.

21. Koech, "State to Build Wastewater Plant."

22. Kinyanjui, "State Halts Kariobangi North Demolitions."

23. Koech, "State to Build Wastewater Plant."

24. Koech, "State to Build Wastewater Plant;" Okoth-Ogendo, *Tenants of the Crown.*

25. Coray, "Kenya Land Commission."

26. Kinyanjui, "5,000 Evicted."

27. Slater, *Shaking Up the City*, 56.

28. Médard, "City Planning."

29. Amis, "Squatters or Tenants."

30. Médard, "City Planning."

31. Médard, "City Planning."

32. Advisory Group on Forced Evictions, UN-Habitat, *Forced Evictions*; Habitat International Coalition, "Launch."

33. Amnesty International, "Legislation Urgently Required."

34. Kiplagat, "Kayole Evictees;" Gumbihi, "President Moi."

35. Nairobi City Council, *Nairobi.*

36. Njeri, "'Donor-driven' Neoliberal Reform," 75.

37. Klaus, *Political Violence*, 7.

38. Kinyanjui, "5,000 Evicted."

39. Kinyanjui, "State Halts Kariobangi North Demolitions."

40. Siele, "Sakaja Responds."

41. Capital News, "Sakaja."

42. Amis, "Squatters or Tenants;" see Médard, "City Planning," for a similar argument. While Nubians actively maintained a "non-native" status so that they could retain privileges such as land ownership, they did not necessarily want to be repatriated to Sudan. According to Parsons, "'Kibra Is Our Blood,'" their long period of residence in Kenya and their mixed ethnic heritage made them feel they would be strangers in Sudan. Parsons argues that they used the impossibility of repatriation to Sudan as a means for securing land in Kenya.

43. Kenya National Bureau of Statistics, *2019 Kenya Population and Housing Census*, vol. 2. There is extensive debate about the size of the population of Kibera—see, for instance, Desgroppes and Taupin, "Kibera"—as its numbers are often inflated to facilitate NGO and aid organization fundraising. Despite being stereotyped as Africa's biggest slum and rumored to have over one million residents, according to the national census it had a population of 185,768 people in 2019.

44. Parsons, "Kibra."

45. Amis, "Squatters or Tenants."

46. Obura, "Over 20,000 Families."

47. Ghetto Radio, "Hundreds of Families;" Okinda, "Lobbies, Residents Protest."

48. Kahura, "Road to Hell;" Mutavi, "Stop Inhumane Kibera Demolition;" Juma, "Notice of Massive Demolition."

49. Ghetto Radio, "Hundreds of Families."

50. Thiong'o, "Plight of Kibera."

51. Kahura, "Road to Hell."

52. Thiong'o, "Plight of Kibera Residents."

53. Kahura, "Road to Hell."

54. Kahura, "Road to Hell."

55. *Abdulmajid Ramadan and 3 Others v Kenya Urban Roads Authority and 4 Others.*

56. Obura, "Over 20,000 Families."

57. Balaton-Chrimes, "Indigeneity."

58. Ndonga, "Amnesty International;" Okinda, "Lobbies, Residents Protest."

59. Ng'enoh, "Plans to Resettle Kariobangi Residents."

EPILOGUE: CIVIL TWILIGHT

1. Nkonge and Lasteck, "Kenya Floods."

2. "Governor Sakaja."

3. "Governor Sakaja."

4. Philips, "Kenya Orders Flood Evacuations."

5. Nkonge and Lasteck, "Kenya Floods."

6. Trouillot, *Silencing the Past.*

"10 Dead, 134 Injured as 6-Story Building Collapses in Heavy Rain in Kenyan Capital." *Los Angeles Times*, April 30, 2016.

Abuje, Sunday Julius, Bernard Moirongo Otoki, Bernard Mugwima Njuguna, and Gerryshom Munala. "The Vulnerability of Nairobi to the Effects of Climate Change between 1984 and 2016." *Landscape Architecture and Regional Planning* 5, no. 2 (2020): 38–45.

Abdulmajid Ramadhan and 3 Others v Kenya Urban Roads Authority and 4 Others [2017]. eKLR Petition no. 974 of 2016.

Achebe, Chinua. *No Longer At Ease*. 2017 London: Penguin Books. 1960.

Achola, Milcah. A. "Colonial Policy and Urban Health: The Case of Colonial Nairobi." *Azania*, 36–37, no. 1 (2001): 119–37.

Adebanwi, Wale. "Burying 'Zik of Africa:' The Politics of Death and Cultural Crisis." *Contemporary Studies in Society and History* 6, no. 1 (2021): 41–71.

Adebanwi, Wale. "Death, National Memory and the Social Construction of Heroism." *Journal of African History* 49, no. 3 (2008): 419–44.

Adebanwi, Wale. *Yoruba Elites and Ethnic Politics in Nigeria: Olafemi Awolowo and Corporate Agency*. New York: Cambridge University Press, 2014.

Advisory Group on Forced Evictions, UN-Habitat. *Forced Evictions: Towards Solutions?* Nairobi: UN-Habitat, 2005.

Agutu, Nancy. "Sonko Lists Grabbed Properties in City Hall Reclamation Plan." *The Star*, August 9, 2018.

Aiyar, Sana. *Indians in Kenya: The Politics of Diaspora*. Cambridge, MA: Harvard University Press, 2015.

AKTC (Aga Khan Trust for Culture). *Rehabilitation of the Nairobi City Park*. Nairobi: Aga Khan Trust for Culture and Aga Khan Development Network, 2013.

Albrecht, Glenn, Gina-Maree Sartore, Linda Connor, Nick Higginbotham, Sonia Freeman, Brian Kelly, Helen Stain, Anne Tonna, and Georgia Pollard. "Solastalgia: The

Distress Caused by Environmental Change." *Australasian Psychiatry* 15, no. 1 (2007): S95–S98.

Alushula, Patrick and Sam Kiplagat. "Supreme Court's Danial Arap Moi Land Ruling Sends Banks, Buyers into a Panic." *Business Daily*, June 19, 2023.

Amis, Philip. "Squatters or Tenants: The Commercialization of Unauthorized Housing in Nairobi." *World Development* 12, no. 1 (1984): 87–96.

Amnesty International. "Legislation Urgently Required to Halt Devastating Forced Evictions." Amnesty International. October 07, 2013. www.amnesty.org/en/wp-content/uploads/2021/06/preo15212013en.pdf.

Amour, Charles. "The BBC and the Development of Broadcasting in British Colonial Africa, 1946–956." *African Affairs* 83, no. 332 (1984): 359–402.

Anderson, Benedict. *Imagined Communities*. London: Verso, 1991.

Anderson, David M. "Corruption at City Hall: African Housing and Urban Development in Colonial Nairobi." *Azania* 36–37, no. 1 (2001): 138–54.

Anderson, David M,. and Paul J. Lane. "The Unburied Victims of Kenya's Mau Mau Rebellion: Where and When Does the Violence End?" In *Human Remains in Society: Curation and Exhibition in the Aftermath of Genocide and Mass-Violence*, edited by Jean-Marc Dreyfus and Elisabeth Anstett, 14–37. Manchester: Manchester University Press, 2016.

Appelbaum, Nancy. "Whitening the Region: Caucano Mediation and 'Antioqueño Colonization' in Nineteenth–Century Colombia." *Hispanic American Historical Review* 79, no. 4 (1999): 631–68.

Appelbaum, Nancy, Anne S. Macpherson, and Karin Alejandra Rosenblatt. *Race and Nation in Modern Latin America*. Chapel Hill: University of North Carolina Press, 2003.

Ashraf, Nava, James Berry, and Jesse M. Shapiro. "Can Higher Prices Stimulate Product Use? Evidence from a Field Experiment in Zambia." *American Economic Review* 100, no. 5 (2010): 2383–2413.

"At Least Three Killed After Residential Building Collapses in Kenya." Reuters, December 6, 2019.

Awori, Moody. *Riding on a Tiger: an Autobiography*. Nairobi: Moran (E.A.), 2017.

Balakrishnan, Sarah. "Archives in Stone: Cemeteries, Burial, and Urban Ownership in Late Colonial Ghana." *Journal of Urban History*. (2024): 1–16.

Balakrishnan, Sarah. "Building the Ancestral Public: Cemeteries and the Necropolitics of Property in Colonial Ghana." *Journal of Social History* 56, no. 1 (2022): 1–25.

Balaton-Chrimes, Samantha. "Indigeneity and Kenya's Nubians: Seeking Equality in Difference or Sameness?" *Journal of Modern African Studies* 51, no. 2 (2013): 331–54.

Bayside Realty Ltd. "The Nairobi Railway City Development Plan: The Future of Nairobi, Kenya." Bayside Realty Ltd. 2020. www.youtube.com/watch?v=935Y-PMNlQ8&theme Refresh=1.

BBC. 2017. "Nairobi Building Collapse: People Missing as Residents Join Search." BBC. June 13, 2017.

Bigon, Liora. "Introduction: Garden Cities and Colonial Planning: Transnationality and Urban Ideas in Africa and Palestine." In *Garden Cities and Colonial Planning: Transnationality and Urban Ideas in Africa and Palestine*, edited by Liora Bigon and Yossi Katz, 1–32 Manchester: Manchester University Press, 2016.

"Billions Lost as Nairobi Regeneration Downs Buildings." *Business Today*, August 8, 2018.

Bissell, William Cunningham. "Engaging Colonial Nostalgia." *Cultural Anthropology* 20, no. 2 (2005): 215–48.

Bombaa, Stoneface, April Zhu, and Felix Omondi. *Until Everyone Is Free.* Podcast. Episode 7, "*Shujaa.*" July 2, 2022. https://untileverypod.com/Episode-7-Shujaa.

Burton, Andrew. "Introduction: Urbanisation in Eastern Africa: An Historical Overview, c. 1750–2000." *Azania* 36, no. 1 (2001): 1–28.

Burton, Andrew. "Townsmen in the Making: Social Engineering and Citizenship in Dar es Salaam, c. 1945–1960." *International Journal of African Historical Studies* 36, no. 2 (2003): 331–65.

Callaci, Emily. "Dancehall Politics: Mobility, Sexuality and Spectacles of Racial Respectability in Late Colonial Tanganyika, 1930–1961." *Journal of African History* 52, no. 3 (2011): 365–84.

Callaci, Emily. *Street Archives and City Life: Popular Intellectual in Postcolonial Tanzania.* Durham, NC: Duke University Press, 2017.

Capital News. "Sakaja: I Will Not Demolish Structures If Elected Nairobi Governor." Capital News, May 12, 2022.

Chikowero, Mhoze. *African Music, Power, and Being in Colonial Zimbabwe.* Bloomington: Indiana University Press, 2015.

Coates, Robert. "Infrastructural Events? Flood Disaster, Narratives and Framing under Hazardous Urbanism." *International Journal of Disaster Risk Reduction* 74 (2022): 1–12.

Cohen, David William, and E. S. Atieno Odhiambo. *Burying SM: The Politics of Knowledge and the Sociology of Power in Africa.* Nairobi: East African Educational Publishers, 1992.

Cohen, Jessica, and Pascaline Dupas. "Free Distribution or Cost-Sharing? Evidence from a Randomized Malaria Prevention Experiment." *Journal of Economics* 125, no. 1 (2010): 1–45.

Commonwealth War Graves Commission. "Nairobi (Forest Road) Cemetery." n.d. www .cwgc.org/visit-us/find-cemeteries-memorials/cemetery-details/12207/NAIROBI %20(FOREST%20ROAD)%20CEMETERY.

Commonwealth War Graves Commission. "Nairobi Park Cemetery." n.d. www.cwgc.org /visit-us/find-cemeteries-memorials/cemetery-details/2085702/nairobi-park-cemetery.

Conn, Steven. *Americans Against the City: Anti-Urbanism in the Twentieth Century.* Oxford: Oxford University Press, 2014.

Coombes, Annie E. "Monumental Histories: Commemorating Mau Mau with the Statue of Dedan Kimathi." *African Studies* 70, no. 2 (2011): 202–23.

Cooper, Elizabeth. "The Conundrum of Race: Retooling Inequality." In *The Caribbean: A History of the Region and Its People*, edited by Stephan Palmie and Francisco A. Scarano, 385–97. Chicago: University of Chicago Press, 2011.

Coray, Michael. "The Kenya Land Commission and the Kikuyu of Kiambu." *Agricultural History* 52, no. 1 (1978): 179–93.

Craig, Maxine. *Sorry I Don't Dance: Why Men Refuse to Move.* Oxford, Oxford University Press, 2014.

De Boeck, Filip. "Inhabiting Ocular Ground: Kinshasa's Future in the Light of Congo's Spectral Urban Politics." *Cultural Anthropology* 26, no. 2 (2011): 263–86.

De Boeck, Filip, and Marie-Francoise Plissart. *Kinshasa: Tales of the Invisible City.* Leuven: Leuven University Press, 2004.

De Souza, Fitzval. *Forward to Independence: My Memoirs.* Independently published, 2019.

Decker, Corrie, and Elisabeth McMahon. *The Idea of Development in Africa: A History.* Cambridge: Cambridge University Press, 2020.

Dennie, Garrey. "The Standard of Dying: Race, Indigence, and the Disposal of the Dead Body in Johannesburg, 1886–1960." *African Studies* 68, no. 3 (2009): 310–30.

Desgroppes, Amelie, and Sophie Taupin. "Kibera: The Biggest Slum in Africa?" *Les Cahiers de l'Afrique de l'Est* (2011): 23–34.

Donovan, Alan. "Joseph Murumbi Peace Memorial Garden." Friends of City Park. n.d. https://friendsofcitypark.org/things-to-do/joseph-murumbi-peace-memorial-garden.

Donovan, Alan. "Murumbi Legacy." African Heritage House. n.d. https://africanheritage house.info/portfolio-item/murumbi-legacy.

Durrani, Shiraz. *Pio Gama Pinto: Kenya's Unsung Martyr, 1927–1965*. Nairobi: Vita Books, 2018.

Dzuya, Walter. "Court Declines To Stop Demolition of Ukay Centre." *Citizen Digital*, August 9, 2018. https://citizentv.co.ke/news/court-declines-to-stop-demolition-of-ukay -centre-209307.

Eagleson, Ian. "Between Uptown and River Road: The Making and Undoing of Kenya's 1960s 'Zilizopendwa.'" *World of Music* 3, no. 1 (2014): 25–45.

East African Railways and Harbours. *Annual Report for East African Railways and Harbours 1959*. Nairobi: East African Railways and Harbours, 1960.

Edwards, Trystan. "A Further Criticism of the Garden City Movement." *Town Planning Review* 4, no. 4 (1914): 312–18.

Ese, Anders, and Kristin Ese. *The City Makers of Nairobi: An African Urban History*. New York: Routledge, 2020.

Fabian, Johannes. *Time and the Other: How Anthropology Makes its Object*. New York: Columbia University Press, 1983.

Fair, Laura. *Reel Pleasures: Cinema Audiences and Entrepreneurs in Twentieth-Century Urban Tanzania*. Athens: Ohio University Press, 2018.

Fastring, D. R., and J. A. Griffith. "Malaria Incidence in Nairobi, Kenya, and Dekadal Trends in NDVI and Climatic Variables." *Geocarto International* 24, no. 3 (2009): 207–21.

Fergus, Devin. *Land of the Fee: Hidden Costs and the Decline of the American Middle Class*. Oxford: Oxford University Press, 2018.

Fernandes, Cyprian. *Yesterday in Paradise: 1950–1974*. Bloomington, IN: Balboa Press, 2016.

Fontein, Joost. *The Politics of the Dead in Zimbabwe, 2000–2020: Bones, Rumors and Spirits*. Cambridge: Boydell and Brewer, 2022.

Fontein, Joost, Tessa Diphoorn, Peter Lockwood, and Constance Smith, eds. *Nairobi Becoming: Security, Uncertainty, Contingency*. Punctum Books, 2024.

Frederiksen, Bodil Folke. "African Women and Their Colonisation of Nairobi: Representations and Realities." *Azania* 36, no. 1 (2001): 223–34.

Frederiksen, Bodil Folke. *Making Popular Culture from Above: Leisure in Nairobi, 1940–60*. Calcutta: Centre for Studies in Social Sciences, 1994.

Freeman, Donald. *A City of Farmers: Urban Agriculture in the Open Spaces of Nairobi, Kenya*. Montreal: McGill-Queen's University Press, 1991.

Frenz, Margret. "Swaraj for Kenya, 1949–1965: The Ambiguities of Transnational Politics." *Past and Present*, no. 8 (2013): 151–77.

Friends of City Park. *City Park: The Green Heart of Nairobi*. Nairobi: Friends of City Park, 2012.

Friends of City Park. "Highland Forest." Friends of City Park, n.d. https://friendsofcitypark .org/discover-city-park-plants-and-other-wildlife/highland-forest.

Fulzele, U. G., V. R. Ghane, and D. D. Parkhe. "Study of the Structures in Black Cotton Soil." *International Journal of Advances in Science Engineering and Technology* 4, no. 4 (2016): 136–40.

Galway, Lindsay P., Thomas Beery, Kelsey Jones-Casey, and Kirsti Tasala. "Mapping the Solastalgia Literature: A Scoping Review Study." *International Journal of Environmental Research and Public Health* 16, no. 15 (2019): 2662.

Gerhard, Kubik. "Neo-traditional Popular Music in East Africa Since 1945." *Popular Music* 1 (1981): 83–104.

Gertz, Geoffrey. *Kenya's Trade Liberalization of the 1980s and 1990s: Policies, Impacts and Implications.* Background paper on the impact of Doha Round on Kenya. Carnegie Endowment for International Peace, 2008.

Ghetto Radio. "Hundreds of Families Left Homeless in Kibera Demolitions." Ghetto Radio, June 21, 2018.

Gitonga, David T., dir. *Nairobi Half Life.* Nairobi: One Fine Day Films, 2012. 96 minutes.

Golla, Rajiv. "'The Rich Man's Road:' Nairobi Slum Demolished for Highway." *The Guardian*, August 20, 2018.

Goldsworthy, David. *Tom Mboya: The Man Kenya Wanted to Forget.* London: Heinemann, 1982.

Goodman, Edward. "Remembering Mzee: The Making and Re-making of 'Kenyatta Day,' 1958–2010," In *The Politics of Historical Memory and Commemoration in Africa: Essays in Honor of Jan-Georg Deutsch*, ed. Cassandra Mark-Thiesen, Moritz A Mihatcsch and Michelle M. Sikes, 77–106. Berlin: De Gruyte Oldenbourg, 2022.

Gordon, Ian. "The Resurgent City: What, Where, How and Whom?" *Planning Theory and Practice* 5, no. 3 (2004): 371–79.

Government of Kenya. *Nairobi Metro 2030: A World-Class African Metropolis.* Nairobi: Government of Kenya, 2008.

"Governor Sakaja Finally Breaks Silence over Crazy Floods Being Witnessed in Nairobi!" Kenya Digital News, April 24, 2024.

Grillo, Ralph D. *African Railwaymen: Solidarity and Opposition in an East African Labour Force.* Cambridge: Cambridge University Press, 1973.

Guguyu, Otiato. "Ministry Seeks Cabinet Action over Unsafe Buildings in Nairobi." *The Nation*, June 17, 2015.

Gumbihi, Hudson. "President Moi Gave Us Land, Insist Nyama Villa Residents." *The Standard*, n.d. (2019). www.standardmedia.co.ke/entertainment/county-nairobi/article /2001310748/president-moi-gave-us-land-insist-nyama-villa-residents.

Guyer, Jane. "Describing Urban 'No Man's Land' in Africa." *Africa* 81, no. 3 (2011): 474–92.

Guyer, Jane, LaRay Denzer, and Adigun Agbaje. "Preface." In *Money Struggles and City Life: Devaluation in Ibadan and Other Urban Centers in Southern Nigeria, 1986–1996*, edited by Jane Guyer, LaRay Denzer and Adigun Agbaje, ix–xvi. London: Heinemann, 2002.

Habitat International Coalition. "Launch: Campaign Against Forced Evictions in the Informal Settlements in Nairobi." 2007. www.hic-net.org/launch-campaign-against-forced -evictions-in-the-informal-settlements-in-nairobi.

Harrison, Philip and Croese, Sylvia. "The Persistence and Rise of Master Planning in Urban Africa: Transnational Circuits and Local Ambitions." *Planning Perspectives* 38, no. 1 (2023): 25–47.

Hart, Thomas. "The Art Deco Houses of Parklands." *Kenya Past and Present*, 36 (2006): 73–79.

Harvey, F. "Jambo (East Africa)." In *Continuum Encyclopedia of Popular Music of the World: Performance and Production*, vol. 1, *Media, Industry and Society* edited by John Shepherd, David Horn, David Laing, Paul Oliver, and Peter Wicke. London: Continuum, 2003.

Hasan, Arif. "Why Karachi Floods." *Dawn*. September 19, 2020. www.dawn.com/news /1578061.

Hay, Alison, and Richard Harris. "'Shauri ya Sera Kali:' The Colonial Regimes of Urban Housing in Kenya to 1939." *Urban History* 34, no. 3 (2007): 504–30.

Hay, George, and John Burke. *Report of the Special Committee to Review Historical Inequalities in Commemoration*. Maidenhead, UK: Commonwealth War Graves Commission, 2021.

Herzig, Pascale. *South Asians in Kenya: Gender, Generation and Changing Identities in Diaspora*. London: Transaction Publishers, 2006.

Hirst, Terry. *The Struggle for Nairobi*. Nairobi: Mazingira Institute, 1994.

Hoffmann, Vivian, Christopher B. Barrett, and David R. Just. "Do Free Goods Stick to Poor Households? Experimental Evidence on Insecticide Treated Bednets." *World Development* 37, no. 3 (2009): 607–17.

Home, Robert. "Colonial Township Laws and Urban Governance in Kenya." *Journal of African Law* 56, no. 2 (2012): 175–93.

Hood, Gavin, dir. *Tsotsi*. London: UK Film and TV Production Company, 2005. 95 minutes.

Huchzermeyer, Marie. "Tenement City: The Emergence of Multi-Storey Districts Through Large-scale Private Landlordism in Nairobi." *International Journal of Urban and Regional Research* 31, no. 4 (2007): 714–32.

Huyssen, Andreas. "Present Pasts: Media, Politics, Amnesia." *Public Culture* 12, no. 1 (2000): 21–38.

Hyde, Dave. "The Nairobi General Strike (1950): From Protest to Insurgency." *Azania* 36, no. 1 (2001): 235–53.

Igadwah, Lynet. "Nairobians Pay for Sins of Poor Land Planning." *Business Daily*, October 1, 2020.

Imende, Benjamin. "State Probing Kariobangi North Evictions, says Oguna." *The Star*, June 17, 2020.

Ingold, Tim and Cristian Simonetti. "Introducing Solid Fluids." *Theory, Culture, and Society* 39, no. 2 (2022): 3–29.

Jainsamaj. "Jains in Nairobi." Jainsamaj. n.d. www.jainsamaj.org/content.php?url=Jains _Associations_-_Nairobi.

Jean-Baptiste, Rachel. *Conjugal Rights: Marriage, Sexuality, and Urban Life in Colonial Libreville, Gabon*. Athens: Ohio University Press, 2014.

Juma, Bernard. "Kenya—Flash Floods in Nairobi After 3 Hour Storm." *Floodlist*, April 29, 2016. https://floodlist.com/africa/Kenya-flash-floods-nairobi-storm-april-2016.

Juma, Christinus. "Notice of Massive Demolition Issued in This Area, Nairobi." Pulse Live, July 4, 2018, www.pulselive.co.ke/news/local/state-issues-demolition-notice-in-kibera -for-road-construction-id8576541.html.

Kagai, Danson. "Kenya Seeks Wealthy Investors to Build Nairobi Railway City." *Kenya Construction Business Review*, June 3, 2014. www.constructionkenya.com/2122/nairobi -railway-city-development.

Kahongeh, James. "Kenya: Inside a Government Project to Save Nairobi's Polluted Rivers." *The Nation*, April 10, 2021.

Kahura, Dauti. "Road to Hell: The Kibera Evictions and What they Portend for Human Rights and 'Development.'" The Elephant, August 10, 2018. www.theelephant.info/fea tures/2018/08/10/the-road-to-hell-the-kibera-evictions-and-what-they-portend-for -human-rights-and-development.

Kakah, Maureen. "Stop NEMA Bulldozers, Ukay Center Owners ask Nairobi Court." *The Nation*, August 9, 2018.

Kakonge, John O. "Nairobi River Basin Rehabilitation and Restoration: Succeeding by Building on Lessons from Past Failure." *Pambazuka News*, May 31, 2017.

Kamau, Francis Gichuhi. "Analysis of Sustainability of Nairobi CBD Land Prices Apprecia-tion." A4Architect. March 18, 2014. www.a4architect.com/2014/03/analysis-of-sustain ability-of-nairobi-cbd-land-prices-appreciation.

Kamau, Francis Gichuhi. "Building Collapse in Kenya: Problems and Solutions." A4Archi-tect. January 7, 2015. www.a4architect.com/2015/01/building-colapse-kenya-problems -solutions.

Kamau, Francis Gichuhi. "Why the Mlolongo Building Collapsed." A4Architect. June 14, 2012. www.a4architect.com/2012/06/why-the-mlolongo-building-collapsed.

Kamau, John. "How Muthaiga Estate of 1920s Fought Not to Become Another Eastleigh." *The Nation*, April 7, 2024.

Kamotho, Patrick. "Nairobi 72 Acre Century-Old Estate up for Grabs: How it Started." Baraza la Taifa, July 12, 2012. http://barazalataifa.blogspot.co.uk/2012/07/nairobi-72-acre -century-old-estate-up.html.

Kamotho, Patrick. "Reclaiming Muthurwa Dallas Social Hall." *Pambazuka: Pan African Voices for Freedom*, January 18, 2012. www.pambazuka.net/en/category/advocacy/79207 %20www.flickr.com/photos/barazalataifa/with/12405316405.

Karanja, Ndung'u Joseph. "A Comparative Analysis of Planning and Management of Cemeteries in Nairobi." MA thesis, University of Nairobi, 2015.

Karisa, Charles. "A Negotiated Framework for Rehabilitation of Riparian Zones in Nairobi City: The Case of Mathare River Valley." 46th ISOCARP Congress, Nairobi, September 19–23, 2010.

Kenya Engineer. *Technical Audit of Buildings as a Tool for Disaster Risk Reduction*. Kenya Engineer, October 10, 2016. www.kenyaengineer.co.ke/technical-audit-of-buildings-as -a-tool-for-disaster-risk-reduction.

Kenya Gazette. "Indians in Kenya: Memorandum Presented to Parliament by Command of His Majesty the King." *Official Gazette of the Colony and Protectorate of Kenya* 25, no. 899 (August 17, 1923): 691–97.

Kenya National Bureau of Statistics. *2019 Kenya Population and Housing Census*, vol. 2, *Dis-tribution of Population by Administrative Units*. Nairobi: Kenya Bureau of Statistics, 2019.

Kenya National Bureau of Statistics. *2019 Kenya Population and Housing Census*, vol. 3, *Distribution of Population by Age and Sex*. Nairobi: Kenya Bureau of Statistics, 2019.

Kenya Railways Corporation. "Nairobi Railway City." Kenya Railways Corporation, n.d. https://krc.co.ke/nairobi-railway-city-2.

Kenya Railways Corporation. "Nairobi Railway City: A Place for People." Kenya Railways Corporation, n.d. https://krc.co.ke/nairobi-railway-city-3.

Kenya Rivers and Water Resources. *Master Plan for Rehabilitation and Restoration of Nairobi River Basin*. Kenya Rivers and Water Resources blog, November 8, 2016. https://kenyari

versandwaterresources.wordpress.com/2016/11/08/master-plan-for-nairobi-river
-basin.

Kenyatta, Uhuru. "We're Committed to the Restoration of Nairobi's 'Green City in The Sun'
Status, President Kenyatta Assures." President of the Republic of Kenya. December 24,
2020. www.president.go.ke/2020/12/24/were-committed-to-the-restoration-of-nairobis
-green-city-in-the-sun-status-president-kenyatta-assures.

Ketebul Music. *Shades of Benga: The Story of Popular Music in Kenya, 1946–2016*. Nairobi:
Ketebul Music, 2017.

Kimani, Samson M. "The Structure of Land Ownership in Nairobi." *Canadian Journal of
African Studies* 6, no. 3 (1972): 379–402.

Kimari, Wangui, and Jessica Parish. "What Is a River? A Transnational Meditation on the
Colonial City, Abolition Ecologies and the Future of Geography." *Urban Geography* 41,
no. 55 (2020): 643–56.

King, Anthony D. "Exporting 'Planning:' The Colonial and Neo-colonial Experience."
Urbanism Past and Present, no. 5 (Winter 1977–78): 12–22.

Kinyanjui, Maureen. "5,000 Evicted in Kariobangi Even As Covid-19 Cases Rise in City."
The Star, May, 2020.

Kinyanjui, Maureen. "State Halts Kariobangi North Demolitions after Uproar." *The Star*,
May 8, 2020.

Kiplagat, Sam. "600 Embakasi Landowners Face Eviction in Way-Leave Row." *Business
Daily*, January 2, 2020.

Kiplagat, Sam. "Kayole Evictees in Court to Seek Compensation from City Tycoon." *Nairobi
News*, January 11, 2019.

Klaus, Kathleen. *Political Violence in Kenya: Land, Elections, and Claim-Making*.
Cambridge: Cambridge University Press, 2020.

Klopp, Jacqueline M. "Pilfering the Public: The Problem of Land Grabbing in Contemporary Kenya." *Africa Today* 47, no. 1 (2000): 7–26.

Klopp, Jacqueline M. "Remembering the Destruction of Muoroto: Slum Demolitions, Land
and Democratization in Kenya." *African Studies* 67, no. 3 (2008): 295–314.

Koech, Gilbert. "State to Build Wastewater Plant on Reclaimed Kariobangi Land." *The Star*,
May 7th, 2020.

Krhoda, George Okoye, and Alice Monene Kwambuka. "Impact of Urbanization on the
Morphology of Motoine/Ngong River Channel, Nairobi River Basin, Kenya." *Journal of
Geography and Regional Planning* 9, no. 4 (2016): 36–46.

Larson, Scott. "Imagining Social Justice and the False Promise of Urban Park Design."
Environment and Planning A: Economy and Space 50, no. 2 (2018): 391–406.

Lee, Rebekah. "Death 'on the Move:' Funerals, Entrepreneurs and the Rural-Urban Nexus
in South Africa." *Africa: Journal of the International African Institute* 81, no. 2 (2011):
226–47.

Likimani, Muthoni. *Fighting Without Ceasing*. Nairobi: Noni's Publicity, 2005.

Likimani, Muthoni. *Passbook Number F.47927: Women and Mau Mau in Kenya*. Nairobi:
Noni's Publicity, 1998.

Lindsay, S. W., and W. J. M. Martens. "Malaria in the African Highland: Past, Present and
Future." *Bulletin of the World Health Organization* 17, no. 1 (1998): 33–45.

Lonsdale, John. "Town Life in Colonial Kenya." *Azania* 36–37, no. 1 (2001): 206–22.

Low, John. "A History of Kenyan Guitar Music: 1945–1980." *African Music* 6, no. 2 (1982): 17–36.

Mabandla, Nkululeko. *Lahla Ngubo: The Continuities and Discontinuities of a South African Black Middle Class*. Leiden: African Studies Center, 2013.

Macharia, Joel. "Nairobi's Changing Skyline: Commercial Real Estate on the Rise." *Ventures: Nothing Ventured Nothing Gained*, September 7, 2014. www.asaaseradio.com/nairobi-s -changing-skyline-commercial-real-estate-on-the-rise.

Macharia, Kinuthia. "Slum Clearance and The Informal Economy of Nairobi." *Journal of Modern African Studies* 30, no. 2 (1992): 221–36.

Macrotrends LLC. "Kenya Inflation Rate 1960–2024." n.d. www.macrotrends.net/global -metrics/countries/KEN/kenya/inflation-rate-cpi.

Maina, Miriam, and Baraka Mwau. "Nairobi: The Socio-political Implications of Informal Tenement Housing in Nairobi, Kenya." In *The Routledge Handbook on Informal Urbanization*, edited by Roberto Rocco and Jan van Ballegooijen, 215–25. New York: Routledge, 2018.

Majanja, Lutivini. "A Park Called Freedom." *The Elephant*, August 9, 2019. www.theele phant.info/culture/2019/08/09/a-park-named-freedom.

Makwaro, Micah and Caleb Mireri. "Public Open Spaces in Nairobi City, Kenya, Under Threat." *Journal of Environmental Planning and Management* 54, no. 8 (2011): 1107–23.

Mamdani, Mahmood. *Citizen and Subject: Contemporary Africa and the Legacy of Late Colonialism*. Princeton, NJ: Princeton University Press, 1996.

Manji, Ambreena. "Nairobi Arboretum, Green Inequality and Social Justice." *The Star*, September 10, 2016.

Manyibe, Ezra. "The President Apologizes over Police Brutality." *Kenyans*, April 1, 2020. www.kenyans.co.ke/news/51542-president-uhuru-apologises-over-police-brutality?fb _comment_id=3000167740022014_3000221863349935&page=23.

Maombo, Sharon. "Kariobangi Residents Left Homeless as Houses Demolished." *The Star*, May 4, 2020.

Martin, Aurora M., and Pauline M. Bezemer. "The Concept and Planning of Public Native Housing Estates in Nairobi, Kenya, 1918–1948." *Planning Perspectives* 35, no. 4 (2020): 609–34.

Martinez-Muños, Adrian. "Vertical Urbanization: The Territorial Crisis of a Universal Model." *IOP Conference Series: Materials Science and Engineering* 1203, no. 2 (2021): 1–10.

Mataga, Jesmael. "Unsettled Spirits, Performance and Aesthetics of Power: The Public Life of Liberation Heritage in Zimbabwe." *International Journal of Heritage Studies* 25, no. 3 (2019): 277–97.

MaVulture. "Once Upon a Time This Space Was a Neat, Homely Estate Called Muthurwa." *MaVulture*, September 30, 2013. http://mavulture.com/special-features/space-neat -homely-estate-called-muthurwa.

Mbembe, Achille, and Nuttall, Sarah. "Introduction: Afropolis." In *Johannesburg: The Elusive Metropolis*, ed. Sarah Nuttall and Achille Mbembe, 1–33. Durham, NC: Duke University Press, 2008.

McDonald, David. *World City Syndrome: Neoliberalism and Inequality in Cape Town*. London: Routledge, 2007.

Médard, Claire. "City Planning in Nairobi: The Stakes, the People, the Sidetracking." In *Nairobi Today: The Paradox of a Fragmented City*, ed. Hélène Charton-Bigot and Rodriguez-Torres, Deyssi, 25–60. Nairobi: Mkuki na Nyota.

Meerkotter, Anneke. *Vagrancy-Related Provisions in Various Criminal Laws and Criminal Procedure Laws in Africa*. Southern Africa Litigation Center, 2018. https://icj-kenya.org/news/vagrancy-related-provisions-in-various-criminal-laws-in-africa.

Mensah, Collins Adjei. "Urban Green Spaces in Africa: Nature and Challenges." *International Journal of Ecosystem* 4, no. 1 (2014): 1–11.

Miles, Malcolm. *Paradoxical Urbanism: Anti-urban Currents in Modern Urbanism*. Singapore: Palgrave Macmillan, 2021.

Mishra, Brajesh. "A Study on Engineering Behavior of Black Cotton Soil and Its Stabilization by Use of Line." *International Journal of Science and Research* 1, no. 11 (2015): 290–94.

Missing Voices. "Missing Voices: Shining Light on Extrajudicial Killings Since 2019." n.d. Accessed August 15, 2020. https://missingvoices.or.ke.

Moore-Pewu, Jamila. "Digital Mapping the Black Atlantic: Spatial Imagination and the Politics of Reappropriation Between Africa and the US." PhD diss., UC Davis, 2014.

Moorman, Marissa J. *Intonations: A Social History of Music and Nation in Luanda, Angola from 1945 to Recent Times*. Athens: Ohio University Press, 2008.

Morange, Marianne. "Street Trade, Neoliberalisation and the Control of Space: Nairobi's Central Business District in the Era of Entrepreneurial Urbanism." *Journal of Eastern African Studies* 9, no. 2 (2015): 247–69.

Morgan, Frank H. P. *A Reflection of Twelve Decades*. Durham, CT: Eloquent Books, 2010.

Morgan, W. T. W. "Agricultural Land Use." In *Nairobi: City and Region*, ed. W. T. W Morgan 78–89. Nairobi: Oxford University Press, 1967.

Morton, David. *Age of Concrete: Housing and the Shape of Aspiration in the Capital of Mozambique*. Athens: Ohio University Press, 2019.

Mpofu, Shepherd. "Ruling from the Grave? The Political Instrumentalization of Robert Mugabe's Corpse in Contemporary Zimbabwean Politics." *Journal of Asian and African Studies* 59, no. 3 (2024): 673–91.

Muchugu, Frank. "Pumwani Social Hall Gets New Lease of Life." *The Star*, March 7, 2016.

Mudhune, Sandra A., Emelda A. Okiro, Abdisalan M. Noor, Dejan Zurovac, Elizabeth Juma, Sam A. Ochola, and Robert W. Snow. "The Clinical Burden of Malaria in Nairobi: A Historical Review and Contemporary Audit." *Malaria Journal* 10, no. 138 (2011): 1–10.

Mugambi, Hassan. "Vertical Slums: How New Crop of Apartments in Kilimani, Kileleshwa is Affecting Nairobi's Infrastructure." *Citizen Digital*, April 30, 2023. www.citizen.digital/news/vertical-slums-how-new-crop-of-apartments-in-kilimani-kileleshwa-is-affecting-nairobis-infrastructure-n318936.

Mungai, Allan. 2020. "Residents Lose Bid to Stop Fresh Demolitions on Disputed City Land." *The Standard*, May 27, 2020.

Murray, Martin. *Commemorating and Forgetting: Challenges for the New South Africa*. Minneapolis: University of Minnesota Press, 2013.

Murray, Martin. *Taming the Disorderly City: The Spatial Landscape of Johannesburg after Apartheid*. Ithaca: Cornell University Press, 2008.

Murunga, Godwin Rapando. "The Cosmopolitan Tradition and Fissures in Segregationist Town Planning in Nairobi, 1915–23." *Journal of Eastern African Studies* 6, no. 3 (2012), 463–86.

Murunga, Godwin Rapando. "'Inherently Unhygienic Races:' Plague and the Origins of Settler Dominance in Nairobi, 1899–1907." In *African Urban Spaces in Historical Perspective*, edited by Steven J. Salm and Toyin Falola, 98–130. Rochester, NY: University of Rochester Press, 2005.

Murunga, Godwin Rapando. "Refugees at Home? Coping with Somali Conflict in Nairobi, Kenya." In *African Studies of Geography from Below*, edited by Michael Ben Arrous and Lazare Ki-Zerbo, 198–232. Dakar: Codesria, 2009.

Mutambo, Aggrey. "History of Collapsed Buildings in Nairobi." *The Nation*, May 2, 2016.

Mutavi, Lillian. "Stop Inhumane Kibera Demolition, KNCHR tells KURA." *The Star*, July 24, 2018.

Mutongi, Kenda. *Matatu: A History of Popular Transportation in Nairobi*. Chicago: University of Chicago Press, 2017.

Mwangi, Nicolas, and Lewis Maghanga. *Pio Gama Pinto: Kenyan Organic Intellectuals' Reflections on the Legacy*. Nairobi: Daraja Press, 2021.

Mwathane, Ibrahim. "Daniel Arap Moi Land Ruling Portends Unintended Consequences to Investments." *Business Daily*, June 8, 2023.

Mwathane, Ibrahim. "There is Need for Clarity of Land Rights on Riparian Reserves." Mwathane blog, December 31, 2012. http://ibrahimmwathane.com/index.php/front page/entry/there-is-need-for-clarity-of-land-rights-on-riparian-reserves.

Mwau, Baraka. "The Rise of Nairobi's Concrete Tenement Jungle." *International Institute for Environment and Development*, July 2019. www.iied.org/rise-nairobis-concrete-tene ment-jungle.

Mwau, Baraka. "The Rise of Vertical Slums in Nairobi." The Age of Zinc blog, October 10, 2019. https://ageofzinc.wordpress.com/2019/10/10/the-rise-of-vertical-slums-in-nairobi.

Myers, Garth Andrew. "The Afterlife of the Lanchester Plan: Zanzibar as Garden City of Tomorrow." In *Garden Cities and Colonial Planning: Transnationality and Urban Ideas in Africa and Palestine*, ed. Liora Bigon and Yossi Katz, 98–120. Manchester: Manchester University Press, 2014.

Myers, Garth Andrew. *Seven Themes in African Urban Dynamics*. Uppsala: Nordiska Afrikainstitutet, 2010.

Myers, Garth Andrew. *Verandahs of Power: Colonialism and Space in Urban Africa*. Syracuse, NY: Syracuse University Press, 2003.

Myers, Garth Andrew. "A World-Class City-Region? Envisioning the Nairobi of 2030." *American Behavioral Scientist* 59, no. 3 (2015): 328–46.

Naidoo, Chloe, Jaclyn Nair, and Lindokuhle Ngcobo. "A Critique of the Modernist Approach to Post-Apartheid Housing Delivery and Urban Design," *Journal of Inclusive Cities and Built Environment* 1, no. 1 (2021): 25–37.

Nairobi. Colonial Film Unit, 1950. 8 min. www.colonialfilm.org.uk/node/1698.

Nairobi City Council. *Nairobi: City in the Sun, 1955/57*. Nairobi: Nairobi City Council, 1957.

Nairobi City County. *Final Report: The Project on Integrated Urban Development Master Plan for the City of Nairobi in the Republic of Kenya*. Nairobi: Government of Kenya, 2014.

Ndonga, Simon. "Amnesty International Condemns Demolitions at Kibera." Capital News, July 24, 2018. www.capitalfm.co.ke/news/2018/07/amnesty-international-condemns -demolitions-at-kibera.

Neelawani, Mahantesh, and Prasanna Patil. "Behavior of Fully and Partially Encased Stone Column in Black Cotton Soil." In *Recent Advances in Civil Engineering: Select Proceedings of CTCS 2021*, edited by L. Nandagiri et al., 115–133. Singapore: Springer Nature Singapore, 2023.

Ng'enoh, Pkemoi. "Plans to Resettle Kariobangi Residents Evicted During Covid Period." *The Standard*, January 18, 2024.

Ng'weno, Bettina. *The City Park Initiative: A Park for the People*. Nairobi: Friends of City Park, 2016.

Ng'weno, Bettina. "Growing Old in a New City: Time, the Post-colony and Making Nairobi Home." *City* 22, no. 1 (2018): 26–42.

Ng'weno, Bettina. "Inheriting Disputes: The Digo Negotiation of Meaning and Power Through Land." *Journal of African Economic History* 25 (1997): 59–77.

Ng'weno, Bettina, and L. Obura Aloo. "Irony of Citizenship: Descent, National Belonging and Constitutions in the Postcolonial African State." *Law and Society Review* 53, no. 1 (2019): 141–72.

Njeru, Jeremia. "'Donor-driven' Neoliberal Reform Processes and Urban Environmental Change in Kenya: The Case of Karura Forest in Nairobi, Kenya." *Progress in Development Studies* 13, no. 1 (2013): 63–78.

Njoh, Ambe J. "The Experience and Legacy of French Colonial Urban Planning in Sub-Saharan Africa." *Planning Perspective* 19, no. 4 (2004): 435–54.

Njoroge, Josephine. "Down Memory Lane of Nairobi's Initial Beauty and Lost Glory." *The Nation*, March 30, 2024.

Nkonge, Anita, and Alfred Lasteck. "Kenya Floods: Nairobi Homes Demolished as Cyclone Hidaya Approaches." BBC News, May 5, 2024.

Noronha, Frederick. "Interesting Timeline: Goans in Africa (Kenya)." *International Goan Convention*, July 12, 2008. www.mail-archive.com/goanet@lists.goanet.org/msg32025.html.

Nuttall, Sarah, and Achille Mbembe, eds. *Johannesburg: The Elusive Metropolis*. Johannesburg: Witwatersrand University Press, 2008.

Nyairo, Joyce. "'Zilizopendwa:' Kayamba Afrika's Use of Cover Versions, Remix and Sampling in the (Re)membering of Kenya." *African Studies* 64, no. 1 (2005): 29–54.

Obulutsa, George. "Death Toll From Building Collapse in Kenya Rises to 16." *Reuters*, May 1, 2016.

Obura, Frederick. "Over 20,000 Families Left Homeless in Kibera Demolition." *The Standard*, July 23, 2018.

Ochieng, Andrew. "Built to Fail: The Ravaged Landscape of Construction Corruption." *Journalists for Transparency*, n.d. https://j4t.org/toolkit/stories/built-to-fail-construction-danger-kenya.

Ochieng, William R. *A History of Kenya*. London: Macmillan, 1985.

Odhiambo, E. S. Atieno. "Kula Raha: Gendered Discourses and the Contours of Leisure in Nairobi, 1946–63." *Azania* 36, no. 1 (2001): 254–64.

Odidi, Bill. "The Golden Years of Kenya's Music." *The Daily Nation Online*, August 12, 2013.

Ogina, Sam. "Ukay Center Owners Want Ksh. 2.3 B Compensation over Demolition." Citizen Digital, February 3, 2019. https://citizentv.co.ke/news/ukay-centre-want-ksh-2-3b-compensation-over-demolition-229663.

Ogot, Bethwell A., and Madara Ogot. *History of Nairobi City, 1899–2000: From a Railway Camp and Supply Depot to A World Class African Metropolis*. Kisumu: Anyange Press, 2020.

Okinda, Brian. "Lobbies, Residents Protest as Houses in Kibera Demolished." *Daily Nation*, July 24, 2018.

Okoth-Ogendo, Hastings W. O. *Tenants of the Crown: Evolution of Agrarian Law and Institutions in Kenya*. Nairobi: ACTS Press, 1991.

Okune, Angela, Trevas Matathia, and Syokau Mutonga. "Scholarly Memory in Nairobi, Kenya: Care for Sites and Sources." In Innovating STS Digital Exhibit, curated by Aalok Khandekar and Kim Fortun. Society for Social Studies of Science, 2019. https://stsinfra structures.org/content/scholarly-memory-nairobi-kenya-care-sites-and-sources /essay.

Olick, Felix. "Nairobi Governor Evans Kidero Unveils City Master Plan." *Standard Digital*, May 28, 2014.

Ombaka, Rachel. "Demolitions at Ukay Center in Nairobi Begin." Citizen Digital, August 10, 2019. https://citizentv.co.ke/news/demolitions-at-ukay-centre-begin-after-court-declined -to-stop-orders-209326.

Ondieki, Donald Otoyo, Sylvester Otieno Ogama, and Emily Achieng'Akuno. "Zilizopendwa: The Ramifications for Development and Revival." *World of Music* 3, no. 1 (2014): 47–62.

Osborn, Michelle. "Chiefs, Elders, and Traditional Authority." In *The Oxford Handbook of Kenyan Politics*, edited by Nic Cheeseman, Karuti Kanyinga, and Gabrielle Lynch, 297–309. Oxford: Oxford University Press, 2020.

Otuki, N. "Mega Sh217 bn Railway Cities a Step Closer to Reality." *The Daily Nation*, October 2, 2016.

Owen, Caleb Edwin. "Lands of Leisure: Recreation, Space, and the Struggle for Urban Kenya: 1900–2000." PhD Diss, Michigan State University, 2016.

Owuor, Samuel, and T. Mbatia. "Nairobi." In *Capital Cities in Africa: Power and Powerlessness*, edited by Goran Therborn and Simon Bekker, 128–140. Cape Town: Human Science Research Council, 2012.

Pagden, Anthony. *The Fall of Natural Man: The American Indian and the Origins of Comparative Ethnology*. Cambridge: Cambridge University Press, 1987.

Parkin, David. *The Cultural Definition of Political Response: Lineal Destiny Among the Luo*. London: Academic Press, 1978.

Parsons, Timothy. "'Kibra Is Our Blood:' The Sudanese Military Legacy in Nairobi's Kibera Location, 1902–1968." *International Journal of African History* 30, no. 1 (1997): 87–122.

Pastor, Antonio Blanco, Eamonn Canniffe, and Carlos Jesus Rosas Jiménez. "Learning from Letchworth and Welwyn Garden City: Garden Cities' Policies of the Development of Existing Settlements in the Contemporary World." *Land Use Policy* 132 (2023): 1–15.

Patel, Zarina. *Challenge to Colonialism: The Struggle of Alibhai Mulla Jeevanjee for Equal Rights in Kenya*. Nairobi: Zand Press, 1997.

Philips, Aleks. "Kenya Orders Flood Evacuations as It Warns Dams Could Spill." BBC News, May 5, 2024.

Plageman, Nate. *Highlife Saturday Night: Popular Music and Social Change in Urban Ghana*. Bloomington: Indiana University Press, 2013.

Plageman, Nate. "Recomposing the Colonial City: Music, Space, and Middle-Class Building in Sekondi, Gold Coast, 1900–1920." *Interventions* 22, no. 8 (2020): 1013–1031.

Quayson, Ato. *Oxford Street, Accra: City Life and the Itineraries of Transnationalism*. Durham. NC: Duke University Press, 2014.

Rahedi, Ivy. 2020. "State Has Trampled on Human Rights in City Slum Evictions." *The Standard*, August 12, 2020.

"Retired Staff of Kenya Railways Paid Sh 278m." *The Nation*, July 14, 2011.

Revive Consulting Solutions Ltd. *Conceptual Integrated Design for the Restoration of Kibagare River Within City Park, Nairobi*. Report presented to Friends of City Park. Nairobi: Revive Consulting Solutions, 2017.

Robertson, Claire C. *Trouble Showed the Way: Women, Men and Trade in the Nairobi Area, 1890–1990*. Bloomington: Indiana University Press, 1997.

Robinson, Jennifer. *Ordinary Cities: Between Modernity and Development*. London: Routledge, 2006.

Rothmyer, Karen. *Joseph Murumbi: A Legacy of Integrity*. Nairobi: Zand Graphics, 2018.

Said, Edward W. *Orientalism*. New York: Random House, 1978.

Satrose Ayuma and 11 Others v Registered Trustees of the Kenya Railways Staff Retirement Benefits Scheme and 2 others [2011]. KEHC 3992 Kenya Law Reports, Republic of Kenya Petition 65 of 2010.

Schmidt, Mario. *Migrants and Masculinity in High-Rise Nairobi: The Pressure of being a Man in an African City*. London: James Curry, 2024.

Scott, David. *Conscripts of Modernity: The Tragedy of Colonial Enlightenment*. Durham. NC: Duke University Press, 2004.

Siele, Martin. "Sakaja Responds After Coming Under Fire over Demolitions." Kenyans, May 17, 2020. www.kenyans.co.ke/news/53332-exclusive-sakaja-responds-after-coming-under-fire-over-demolitions-hypocrisy.

Simone, AbdouMaliq. "On the Worlding of African Cities." *African Studies Review* 44, no. 2 (2001): 15–41.

Simone, AbdouMaliq. *City Life from Jakarta to Dakar: Movements at the Crossroads*. New York: Routledge, 2010.

Singh, Sanjay. "How to Construct Foundation in Black Cotton Soil." Civil Engineering Web, August 30, 2020. www.civilengineeringweb.com/2020/08/construction-of-foundation-in-black-cotton-soil.html.

Slater, Tom. *Shaking Up the City: Ignorance, Inequality, and the Urban Question*. Berkeley: University of California Press, 2021.

Smith, Constance. "Collapse: Fake Buildings and Gray Development in Nairobi." *Journal of Global and Historical Anthropology* 86 (2020): 11–23.

Smith, Constance. *Nairobi in the Making: Landscapes of Time and Urban Belonging*. Nairobi: Twaweza Communications, 2019.

Smyth, Rosaleen. "Grierson, the British Documentary Movement, and Colonial Cinema in British Africa." *Film History* 25, no. 4 (2013): 82–113.

Social Justice Centre Working Group. "Social Justice Community" n.d. www.sjc.community. Accessed August 15, 2022.

Soja, Edward W. *The Geography of Modernization in Kenya: A spatial Analysis of Social, Economic and Political Change*. Syracuse, NY: Syracuse University Press, 1968.

Spronk, Rachel. *Ambiguous Pleasures: Sexuality and Middle Class Self-Perceptions in Nairobi*. New York: Berghahn Books, 2012.

Stapleton, Chris, and Chris May. *African All-Stars: the Pop Music of a Continent*. London: Quartet Books, 1987.

Stavrides, Stavros, "Contested Urban Rhythms: From the Industrial City to the Post-industrial Urban Archipelago." *Sociological Review* 6, no. S1 (2013): 34–50.

Sykes, Ally. "Peter Colmore: The Man with the Midas Touch." *The East African*, February 16, 2004.

Teppo, Annika. *The Making of a Good White: A Historical Ethnography of the Rehabilitation of Poor Whites in a Suburb of Cape Town*. Helsinki: Helsinki University Press, 2004.

Thiong'o, Josphat. "Plight of Kibera Residents Worsens as Demolitions Begin." *The Standard*, July 24, 2018.

Thornton White, L. W., L. Silberman, and P. R. Anderson. *Nairobi: Master Plan for a Colonial Capital*. London: His Majesty's Stationery Office, 1948.

Trouillot, Michel-Rolph. *Silencing the Past: Power and the Production of History*. Boston: Beacon Press, 1995.

Tsuruta, Tadasu. "Popular Music, Sports, and Politics: A Development of Urban Cultural Movements in Dar es Salaam, 1930s–1960s." *African Study Monographs* 24, no. 3 (2003): 195–222.

Urban Pathways. "Nairobi Is Kick-Starting Urban Regeneration Programme with Support from UN-Habitat." Urban Pathways, July 14, 2021. www.urban-pathways.org/urban-regeneration-programme.html.

Wakaya, Jeremiah. "Nairobi's Condemned Buildings Stand Tall as Collapse Claims 3 in Huruma." Capital News, June 3, 2018.

Walibora Waliaula, Ken. "Remembering and Disremembering in Africa." *Thoughtful Museum* 55, no. 2 (2012): 113–27.

Wambugu, Benson. "Runda Estate Homes to be Pulled Down." *The Nation*, May 18, 2013.

Wanga-Odhiambo, Godriver. "Challenge to African Democracy: The Activism and Assassination of Pio Gama Pinto." In *A Tapestry of African Histories: With Longer Times and Wider Geopolitics*. edited by Nicholas K. Githuku. Washington, DC: Rowman and Littlefield, 2021.

Wanjiku, Evelyne, and Yuko Iwatani. *A Brief Tour of the Buildings of Nairobi*. Nairobi: Yuko Iwatani, 2011.

Watson, Vanessa. "African Urban Fantasies: Dreams or Nightmares?" *Environment and Urbanization* 26, no. 1 (2013): 215–31.

Watson, Vanessa. "'The Planned City Sweeps the Poor Away…:' Urban Planning and 21st Century Urbanization." *Progress in Planning* 72 (2009): 151–93.

Waweru, Kimani, and Loren Balhorn. "Kenya's First Socialist Library," Rosa Luxemburg Schiftung, 12 September 2019. www.rosalux.de/en/news/id/41361/kenyas-first-socialist-library.

West-Pavlov, Russell. *Temporalities*. London: Routledge, 2013.

White, Luise. *The Comforts of Home: Prostitution in Colonial Nairobi*. Chicago: University of Chicago Press, 1990.

Wilkinson, J. F. "The BBC and Africa." *African Affairs* 71, no. 283 (1972): 176–85.

Wilks, Tammy. 2022. "Bypassing the Bulldozer: The Materiality of State Violence on Religion in Kibera, Nairobi." In *Material Perspectives on Religion, Conflict and Violence: Things of Conflict*, edited by Lucien van Liere and Erik Meinema, 73–93. Leiden: Brill.

Willstone Homes. "Why Buildings Collapse in Kenya." Willstone Homes blog, March 13, 2021. https://willstonehomes.co.ke/why-buildings-collapse-in-kenya.

Wipper, Audrey. "Kikuyu Women and the Harry Thuku Disturbances: Some Uniformities of Female Militancy." *Africa* 59, no. 3 (1989): 300–336.

Wood, Barbara. *Green City in the Sun.* New York: Turner Publishing, 2012.

Woods, Clyde. 2017. *Development Drowned and Reborn: The Blues and Bourbon Restorations in Post-Katrina New Orleans.* Edited by Laura Pulido and Jordan T. Camp. Athens: University of Georgia Press.

World Health Organization. *Urban Planning, Environment and Health: From Evidence to Policy Action.* World Health Organization, 2010. www.euro.who.int/__data/assets/pdf_file/0004/114448/E93987.pdf?ua=1.

World Peace Foundation. 2020. *Justifying and Resisting Evictions in Kenya: The Discourse of Demolition During a Pandemic.* https://sites.tufts.edu/reinventingpeace/2020/09/21/justifying-and-resisting-evictions-in-kenya-the-discourse-of-demolition-during-a-pandemic.

Abdulmajid Ramadhan v KURA
(2016 court petition), 164
Abidjan, 97
Absura, Mohamed, 78
Abuje, Sunday Julius, 142
Accra, 46
Achebe, Chinua, 49
Addis Ababa, 97
Adebanwi, Wale, 110
Afghanistan, 21
African and Asian populations, 28–30, 52, 164;
building of recreational facilities and the
prescribing of recreational activities to
control, 71; burial/non-burial in City Park of,
112, 124–25; colonial overcrowding of, 153–54;
as consumers, 81; development and, 132, 137;
garden city vision and areas of settlement of,
92, 98, 174n28; migration to Nairobi of, 62;
political mobilizations of, 55. *See also*
Asian Kenyans; population
African Development Bank (ADB), 158
African Elected Members Organization
(AEMO), 85
African Gramophone Stores (AGS), 79
African Heritage House, 115, 117. *See also* art
Africanization, 34, 85; African traders as part of,
65; of commerce, 63
Agade, George, 82
Aga Khan Trust for Culture (AKTC), 103
Aga Khan University, 52

Agbaje, Adigun, 47
Agence Française de Développement (AFD), 158
aging, 10–13, 45. *See also* elderly
agriculture, 22, 88; clearing of the forest for
settlement and, 29; urban, 91
Albrecht, Glenn, 49
Amin, President Idi, 64
Amin, S. G., 63
Amis, Philip, 162–63
Amnesty International, 165
Amunga, David, 79, 85
ancestrality, 110, 125, 165
Anderson, David M., 122
Anditi, Olima, 80
Angola, 120–21
anticolonialism, 60, 62, 80, 124.
See also Independence
anti-urbanism, 4–10, 35, 122, 132–33, 140, 152–54;
ancestral lands and the consequences of,
163–66; children as challenge to colonial, 40;
in colonial and postcolonial cities, 9–10, 32,
52; dance and music as means of undoing
the structures of, 76, 86; of dialectic of
development and demolition, 137, 160; as
form of urbanism, 3, 9; garden city concept
and interventions of, 92, 174n28; and gender
ratios, 176n25; graves and cemeteries of City
Park as challenge to, 109–10, 113, 128; lack of
burial spaces for Africans as a reflection and
reinforcement of, 113; long-term presence

anti-urbanism (*continued*)
of people in the city as challenge as, 168; positing the concept of home as a challenge to, 169; practices of containment and curfew of, 155; regular people and their everyday existence as challenge to, 89; rustication as, 18, 22–23; social halls as challenge to, 70–71; surviving green spaces as challenge to, 105; temporal and spatial aspects of, 58. *See also* colonialism; rustication; urbanism
Arabic, 81
Arboretum, 100–102; cost of entry to the, 185n47; demolitions in a riparian area near the, 134*fig.* *See also* Nairobi
architecture, 56, 170; of social halls, 74; urban planning and, 40. *See also* art; urban planning
art: modern African, 115–17; and styles of the social hall, 71. *See also* architecture; African Heritage House
Art Deco, 56
Asian Kenyans, 52–55, 175n12; exodus of, 64; main businesses in Nairobi as run by, 28, 63; as majority of the visible elderly, 45; as "migrant races," 60; movement to Parklands of, 53–56; oldest permanent residents of Nairobi as, 25; as politicians, 63–64; presence in Pangani of, 54. *See also* African and Asian populations
Asian question, 60–64, 180n29; as Africanization, 62–64
askaris (guards), 160, 170–71
Athi, 20–21
Athi River plains, 136
Australia, 113
Awori, Moody, 59, 65, 93, 154
Ayuma, Satrose, 41–42, 45, 48

Balakrishnan, Sarah, 109–10
Belafonte, Harry, 79–80, 84
benga, 80. *See also* music
Bezemer, Pauline, 30–31, 92–93
Bigon, Liora, 14, 92
Bissel, William Cunningham, 95
Botswana, 155
boxers, 43, 72–73
Brazil, 146
Britain, 14, 63, 82–83, 90, 113; Commonwealth of, 94; garden cities in, 92; tenement housing and overcrowding in industrial cities of, 92
British Commonwealth Development Corporation, 66

bubonic plague, 91. *See also* disease
buildings: black cotton soil and, 141–42, 147; colonial racial segregation of, 24; government audit of, 140–41; hasty construction of, 140–41; high-rise, 19; residential collapses of, 138–42. *See also* demolitions; housing
bulldozers, 135, 150–51, 157; in Upper Hill neighborhood, 157*fig.*; ubiquitous presence of, 168. *See also* demolitions
bureaucracy, 17–18
burial: colonial burial of Africans and Asians, 22; countryside, 113, 127; detribalized, 22; Kenyan burial traditions that allow for forgetting, 122, 127. *See also* cemeteries
Burma, 78
Business Today, 145

Callaci, Emily: *Street Archives and City Life*, 7–8, 76, 82
Canada, 113, 121, 187n31
Cape Town, 46, 153. *See also* South Africa
capitalism: development as idea of progress fueled by, 152; Indian traders as agents of "civilization and progress" by virtue of their participation in, 21. *See also* modernity
Capitol Music Stores (CMS), 79
cement industry, 100, 144
cemeteries, 27–28, 32, 90, 107–15; African military, 28; Aga Khan Shia Imami Khoja Ismaili Cemetery, 112; Ahmadiyya Muslim Cemetery, 112; and anti-urbanism, 109–10; Asian Muslim, 112; City Park Cemetery, 107, 109–15, 117, 122–24, 123*fig.*, 127–28; Dawoodi Bohora Cemetery, 112; Detribalized Native Cemetery, 28, 113; European-style efforts of commemoration and, 122; Forest Road Cemetery, 109, 111–15, 112*fig.*, 127–28; Kariokor Cemetery, 95; Lang'ata Cemetery, 32, 113; Nubian Muslim Cemetery, 112, 165; Saaj Shia Cemetery, 112; segregation of, 27–28, 110–13, 124; urban colonial African, 110. *See also* burial; City Park
Central Africa, 79
Central Park, 100, 102. *See also* Nairobi
Ceylon, 78
Chandaria, Manu, 105
chang'aa (moonshine), 74
Cheboi, John, 164
children: limited entertainment and recreation possibilities in colonial Nairobi for African and Asian, 95, 98; Railway estates as places

of, 37–41; as relegated to the countryside, 22; spaces in the city for, 45, 48, 93–95; treasure hunt for, 104; of workers, 16

China, 14, 46

chokora (street urchin), 94, 105

Chokwe, Mwinga, 120

Christians, 27–28; African, 113; British, 111; Goan, 112; Indian, 55

churches, 27; choral styles in music and festivals of, 86; Don Bosco Church, 169, 171

cinema. *See* film

cities: anti-urbanism as concept and ideology underlying the production of, 9; industrialized, 9; new, 173n6; tenements of, 67–68, 137–38; traffic congestion in, 150–51, 156. *See also* urbanism; urban planning

city council guards (*kanjo*), 160

City Park, 87–106, 128, 139; access to green spaces for Asian residents in, 93; bandstand of, 20*fig.*, 77–78, 90, 93–95, 96*fig.*; biodiversity of, 88–89, 98; bougainvillea trees of, 88*fig.*, 90; central garden of, 97, 100, 106, 111; as colonial urban park remnant, 89–91; Commonwealth war graves in, 109–14, 112*fig.*, 122, 123*fig.*, 124; forest of, 87, 89, 94–95, 97–100, 106, 109, 111; illegal allocation of public land in, 103–4, 138; as location with no race restrictions in a segregated city, 90, 93, 95; maze of, 90, 94–95, 104, 131; as microcosm of Nairobi as garden city, 89, 91–93, 106; public entertainments in, 102; rivers of, 100, 106, 111; sculpture garden of, 115, 116*fig.*, 117; survival of, 105–6, 128; wetland plants of, 131. *See also* cemeteries; Friends of City Park; Nairobi; remnant

City Park National Monument, 104

City Park: The Green Heart of Nairobi (guidebook), 87

class: associations of locations and, 54; interacting dynamics of race and, 53, 57–58, 60, 68; white flight and mobility of, 56–58. *See also* race; segregation

climate change, 6, 12, 132; flooding devastation and, 167; rapid urbanization and, 148; as wetter climate for Nairobi, 142–43

Coates, Robert, 146, 148

Cold War, 67, 121, 137, 143

Colmore, Peter, 78, 81–82

Colombia, 148, 177n45

colonial era: attempts to restrict land ownership and residency in the, 28–29; childhood memories of Nairobi in the, 94; constructing

urban accommodations for families in the, 38; demolitions and displacements in Nairobi in the, 153, 165; dry upland forest removed in the, 88; laws that enact racial segregation in the, 24, 29; manicured gardens as remnants of the, 89; spatial and temporal division between work and leisure in the control of the, 71; urban planning in the, 6–7, 29. *See also* colonialism

Colonial Film Unit, 40

colonialism, 23–25, 122; discipline of wage labor and, 41; legacies of, 13; Mboya's use of the popularity of music and dancing in opposition to, 86; Nairobi conceived in terms of urban, 19, 34, 52; as racial project, 62; regulation of race and class in, 52–53. *See also* anti-urbanism; colonial era

Commonwealth War Graves Commission, 111, 113, 122, 186n13

Congo, 79

Conn, Steven: *Americans Against the City*, 8–9

consumerism, 81

Continental Finance Company, 65

Coombes, Anne E., 124

corruption, 67, 145–46; of contractors, 157; expansion of Nairobi and, 140; government stealing of farms and land as, 120; in housing construction, 133; and political patronage, 138, 161; and the politics of land brokerage, 160–63; taxation as process of, 102

COVID-19 pandemic, 1, 140, 152–54, 161

Crown Lands Act (1915), 113, 158, 176n39

Crown Lands Ordinance (1902), 24–25, 158

Crown Lands Ordinance (1925), 25

Cyclone Hidaya, 167–68

Daily Nation, 42, 103

Dakar, 153. *See also* Senegal

Dallas Boxing Club, 43

dancing, 69–86; African clubs for, 76; African traditions of, 76; and freedom, 85–86; Kenyanized ballroom styles of, 75–77; Luo rhythms of, 80; traditional Luhya *sukuma* and *omutibo* rhythms of, 79. *See also* music; rumba; social halls; *twisti*

Dandora Community Justice Centre, 125–27; "Pio Gama Pinto: Reflections in his Struggles for Socialism and Liberation" (presentation), 125

dansi (dances), 76, 82

Dar es Salaam, 7, 76, 81, 183n79. *See also* Tanzania

Darwin, Charles, 23

De Boeck, Filip, 13

decolonization, 89, 152

degeneration theories, 23

demolitions, 13, 18, 51; allocation of public or government lands in legally fuzzy and contestable ways and, 159; as anti-urbanist tools, 67, 165–66, 169; and development, 151–52, 165; disregard for residents living in the way of, 160–64; in downtown Nairobi, 48; as form of urban governance, 152–53, 169; of old residential estates, 48; protection against illegal eviction and the threat of, 164; in riparian areas, 134–35, 134*fig.*, 145–49, 167–68. *See also* buildings; bulldozers; development; homelessness; housing; rivers

Denzer, LaRay, 47

Depression, 60

de Souza, A. C. L., 55–56, 58–59

de Souza, Fitz, 63, 70, 115, 120, 124

detribalization, 26–28, 62, 177n46; colonial-era social halls and native population subject to, 70; unwanted population of natives subject to, 68

detribalized native: as category of temporal and spatial displacement, 62, 168; cemeteries for the, 28; change after Independence in the construct of, 31; class and race after Independence structured on top of and through the category of, 53; post-Independence dichotomy of native and, 62; social halls as outlet under British rule for the excess energy of the, 70; urban youth classified under British rule as, 60. *See also* native

development: aid for, 137; demolitions and, 151–52, 165; high-rise infill, 143; hotels, high-end housing, and shopping malls in, 44; neoliberal city, 148; shrinking of the green spaces in the city on account of, 99–100, 105–6; of vacant land by land-buying companies, 100, 139. *See also* demolitions; infrastructure; Nairobi; neoliberalism; redevelopment

devolution, 11, 124

Digamber Jain Mumukshu Mandal, 54

Digo people, 24, 114

disease: control of, 29, 153–54; Indian Bazaar as reservoir of, 53; influenza pandemic (1917) of, 190n18. *See also* bubonic plague; malaria; public health

disinvestment, 89

Donovan, Alan, 115, 117

Douala, 46

Dubai, 14

Durrani, Shiraz: *Pio Gama Pinto: Kenya's Unsung Martyr, 1927–1965*, 126

East Africa, 15–16; Asians of, 21; British colonies in, 23–24; as Indian settlement, 24; music for, 82, 84; musicians from, 79, 82; Railways neighborhoods in, 37; travel in, 77

East African Association, 27, 72

East African Goan League, 120

East African Protectorate, 21; Land Committee for the, 25

East African Railways & Harbours (EAR&H), 36, 83, 175n53

East African Records, 82

East African Trade Union Confederation (EATUC), 19, 40

Eastlands, 44, 93, 133–34, 136; children of, 105; deadly collapses of six- and seven-story buildings in, 133; general stigma associated with, 154; Jerusalem and Jericho as built by the Israeli government in, 66; redevelopment of most government-owned housing in, 160. *See also* neighborhoods

education, 16, 25, 27

elderly: as Asian Kenyans, 45; as European Kenyans, 45; growing number of African, 45; as homeless, 153, 163; as relegated to the countryside, 22; as relocated from old residential estates, 48. *See also* aging

electricity, 23, 25–26, 53. *See also* infrastructure

Embu, 61

Emergency, The (1952–58), 165, 178n18; City Park cemeteries holding victims of, 109; leaders of the Kenya African Union (KAU) as detained during, 115, 124; music, dance, and film of the social halls subject to restrictions of, 75; Nairobi Sound in the social halls and national political organizing after the, 80; songs that try to address the fear caused by the, 83; war against the Mau Mau during, 122; white exodus from Kenya due to, 60–61; working soldiers with disposable cash during, 77. *See also* Kenya

English: formal Kenyan, 19; radio broadcasts in, 84; songs of urban musicians in, 77

environmental and social impact assessment (ESIA), 157

environmentalism, 91, 101. *See also* pollution

Equator Sound Band, 82

Equator Sound Studios, 82–83

estates and schemes: Bahati estate, 72; Buruburu scheme, 66; Eastleigh estate, 53, 65; Huruma scheme, 66; Jericho estate, 160; Kaloleni estate, 30–31, 41, 69, 72, 74, 160; Kariokor estate, 160; Kayole estate, 66, 139; Madaraka estate, 139; Makongeni estate, 69, 72, 160; Mathare North estate, 139; Muthurwa estate, 31, 36–37, 41–43, 48, 73–74, 154, 160, 177n72; Nyayo estate, 66; Pumwani estate, 69, 73; Shauri Moyo estate, 72; Starehe estate, 30–31, 72, 160; Tobacco Village estate, 72; Umoja scheme, 66; Ziwani estate, 30–31, 72, 75, 85. *See also* housing; neighborhoods
ethnography, 3–5
Europe, 8–9; garden cities in, 92, 174n28
European rural settlers, 26
evictions. *See* demolitions

family, 10, 49, 86; City Park and, 94
fashion, 76, 82, 85; fast, 100
film, 39–40, 74; as circumscribed by colonialism, 74–75; musicals as, 76
flooding, 91, 100, 131, 133, 137, 142–43, 148, 160, 167–68, 189n67
Frankie and Sisters, 79
Frederiksen, Bodil Folke, 71–72, 75, 80
freedom: childhood memories of recreation and, 128; dancing and, 85–86; Nairobi as a place of leisure and, 80; as *uhuru* for all, 120; for workers, 19
Freeman, Donald, 91
Freretown, 22, 27. *See also* Kenya
Friends of City Park, 4, 94–95, 98–99, 101, 103–5, 111, 185n35. *See also* City Park

Gabon, 10
garden city: areas of settlement of African and Asian populations and vision of, 92, 98, 174n28; City Park as microcosm of Nairobi as, 89, 91–93, 106; interventions of anti-urbanism and concept of, 92, 174n28; model of public housing (1929–48) as, 31, 92–93; restriction of colonized peoples and the poor from urban areas in the colonial, 9; segregated use of land and concept of, 92, 137. *See also* Nairobi
gentrification, 14, 18, 48, 159
Ghana, 10, 31. *See also* Kumasi
Ghetto Radio, 163. *See also* radio
Giraffe Center, 100. *See also* Nairobi
Githegi, Dedan, 75
global economic shocks, 35, 143

Goa, 55, 115, 117, 121, 165; Indian military takeover of, 120; opposition to the Portuguese colonial government of, 120. *See also* Goans; India
Goa National Congress, 120
Goan Overseas Association, 55
Goans, 112, 115, 124–25, 128, 180n14. *See also* Goa
Goan Voice, The, 55
golf courses, 100
governance: anti-urbanism as ideology behind urban, 18; colonial, 23; demolition as a standard tool of, 15
gramophone, 77
Great Migration, 8
Greensmith, Peter, 90, 92, 95, 97
group ranches, 31
Gujarati (language), 80, 94
Guyer, Jane, 5, 47–48

Habitat International Coalition, 159
Happy Hour (radio show), 74, 79, 84
harambee (call to pull together), 82–83, 86
Hasan, Arif, 148
hawkers/street vendors, 61; eviction from the central business district of, 43, 159; female, 27, 30
High Fidelity Productions, 82
Hindi, 80
Hirst, Terry: *Struggle for Nairobi*, 143
home, 10, 12, 35, 171; as challenge to anti-urbanism, 169; possible loss of, 48; problem of Nairobi as, 3–6. *See also* housing
homelessness, 41, 48, 159, 164, 168, 174n38; elderly as, 153; Kenyan version of anti-urbanism as the position that there is no such thing as, 164; multiple evictions in low-income areas and, 159–62. *See also* demolitions; housing
hospitals, 25–26
housing: African colonial-era bachelor, 68, 139; construction of low- and mid-income projects of, 139; garden city model (1929–48) of public, 31, 92–93; high-end real-estate sector of, 140; high post-Independence demand for, 64–66; *landhi* concept (1918–29) of public, 30; large tenant-purchase schemes of, 66; long-term residence implied in nuclear family, 93; rise of tenements as, 67–68, 137–38; satellite areas of, 92; for temporary workers, 30–32, 45, 93; urgent demand for, 133, 139–40, 147. *See also* buildings; demolition; estates and schemes; home; homelessness; Nairobi; neighborhoods; Railway estates; slums; townships
Howard, Ebenezer, 92

Huchzermeyer, Marie, 138
Huruma building collapse (2016), 132, 133, 138, 140, 142, 146–47
Huyssen, Andreas, 49
H. Young Company Ltd., 164

ideology: anti-urbanism as foundational, 4, 18, 30–31, 50; of time and space, 3
Idris, Fatuma Amina, 95
immigration, 28; non-African races of, 30
Imperial War Graves Commission, 113
Independence, 1, 15–17, 22, 25, 31, 35, 52–62, 70, 82–86, 105, 109, 115–16, 173n2; accumulation and distribution of land bought from Europeans as part of, 120; broken promises of, 126; historical knowledge of, 124; hoisting the Kenya flag at the top of Mount Kenya at, 124; politics of, 120–21. *See also* anticolonialism; Kenya
India, 21–22, 63, 78, 113, 155; city parks in, 90. *See also* Goa
Indian Ocean, 3, 132, 136
Indigenous peoples. *See* Native peoples
industrialization, 72
inequality, 10; social, 76
infrastructure: development of residential areas without, 68; development of urban, 132, 159–60; development of water and Railways, 175n54; increasing pressure on wastewater, 99; overwhelmed drainage, 143. *See also* development; electricity; Nairobi; roads; sewage
Ingold, Tim, 141–42
international aid agencies, 35, 137
International Monetary Fund (IMF), 137, 178n1
International Union for the Conservation of Nature, 97
Iran, 21

Jainism, 54
Japan, 14
Jeevanjee, Alibhai Mulla, 28–29, 53, 55–56
Jeevanjee Gardens, 101–2. *See also* Nairobi
Jews, 112, 128
Johannesburg, 8. *See also* South Africa
John, Esther, 83–84
"John Brown's Body" (hymn), 83
Joseph Murumbi Peace Memorial Sculpture Garden, 116*fig.*

Kabaka, Daudi, 78, 82–84; "Harambee Harambee" (song), 82, 86

Kabaka, Daudi Chwa II, 78
Kabarnet, 120. *See also* Kenya
Kaggia, Bildad, 124
Kajwang, T. J., 167–68
Kakonge, John O., 145
Kamba, 20–22, 62, 80; British excision of land of the, 120
Kampala, 78. *See also* Uganda
Kamukunji Grounds, 102. *See also* Nairobi
Karachi, 55, 148–49. *See also* Pakistan
Kariuki, Stephen, 133
Karura Forest, 87, 100–102, 161. *See also* Nairobi
Katuga, David, 78
Keen, John, 31
Kental Enterprises Ltd., 135
Kenya: changes to citizenship laws (1985) in, 64; economic situation after the end of the Cold War in, 137–38; Ismaili institutions in, 103; national ID system of, 17–18; nationalist movements of, 27, 55, 60, 62, 74, 80, 85; Nyanza area of, 61, 72; patronage system in, 63, 138, 140, 161; Ukambani areas of, 61, 72; western areas of, 61, 72, 127. *See also* Emergency, The; Freretown; Independence; Kabarnet; Kiambu; Kisumu; Lamu; Manda Island; Mau Mau revolt (1952–58); Mombasa; Nairobi; Nakuru
Kenya African National Union (KANU), 120
Kenya African Union (KAU), 115
Kenya Agricultural Research Organization (KARO), 129
Kenya Breweries, 43
Kenya Broadcasting Service, 80, 82–83
Kenya Forest Research Institute, 106, 128
Kenya Forest Service, 90, 97, 102, 104, 106, 128
Kenya Gazette, 30, 55
Kenya Immigration Bill (1967), 64
Kenyan Federation of Labor (KFL), 83–85
Kenya Railways Corporation, 41–42, 44, 175n53
Kenya Railways Golf Club, 44
Kenya Railways Retirement Benefit Scheme, 41–42, 44
Kenyatta, President Jomo, 62–63, 66, 83, 85, 97, 107, 120–22, 124–25
Kenyatta, President Uhuru, 1, 106, 125, 128, 133, 145
Kenya-Uganda Railway, 37
Kenya Urban Roads Authority (KURA), 4, 51–52, 150–51, 155–56, 160, 164–65, 190n1
Kiambu, 131. *See also* Kenya
Kibagare River, 99, 111, 131–32, 134, 143; and fig tree, 131*fig.*; in flood, 147*fig.*; new main sewer line along the, 145

Kibaki, President Mwai, 35, 70
kibra (forest), 162
Kidero, Governor Evans, 43
Kikuyu, 20–22, 24, 60–62, 80, 89, 131, 136;
    fighters who joined the Mau Mau of the,
    122, 177n47; as landlords, 138, 163; as local
    administrative functionaries, 163; soldiers
    who fought for the British of the, 123
Kimari, Wangui, 146
King, Anthony D., 14
king'ora (siren), 36–37; as tool of colonialism,
    36, 72
King's African Rifles (KAR), 78, 81, 114
kipande (identification document), 17, 19,
    23–24, 27
Kipsigis, 120
Kiruma, Jacob, 133
Kisumu, 44, 75, 80. *See also* Kenya
Klaus, Kathleen, 161
Kodhek, Argwings, 70
Konde, Fundi, 78–79, 84
Krhoda, George Okoye, 143
Kubai, Fred, 19
Kumasi, 97, 100, 149. *See also* Ghana
Kwambuka, Alice Monene, 143

labor: educated Africans as civil service, 61–62,
    72, 76, 180n38; employment of educated
    and skilled Africans as Railway, 60–61, 72;
    Nairobi designed as a city of, 47, 56; Railways
    as attractions for, 15, 21, 25, 35–39, 72, 76;
    retired Railway, 35, 42; salaried African
    urban, 86; single male temporary, 7, 21–22,
    68. *See also* Railways; working class
Lake Victoria, 15, 21–22, 61, 124
Lammy, David, 114
Lamu, 85. *See also* Kenya
Lancaster House conferences, 70, 109, 115
land: African ownership of, 27, 63, 65, 113, 181n57;
    Asian ownership of, 63; demolition of
    buildings sited on riparian, 134–35; European
    ownership of, 63, 181n43; expansion of urban
    communities and industry into rural areas
    seen as grabbing of, 92; garden city concept
    and segregated use of, 92, 137; gentrification
    and scramble for downtown, 48; graves and
    burials to secure, 113; inequities of ownership
    of, 63; legal concept of surrendering, 190n1;
    modernity and ownership of, 31; pastoralism
    and ownership of, 31; problem of public,
    158–60; property transfers of public, 137–38;
    Railways, 138; rapidly increasing prices of, 42;
    redistribution of, 62; unlawful and irregular
    acquisition of, 138; valleys and ridges of, 136.
    See also rivers; townships
landhi (railway worker housing), 30, 36
Lane, Paul J., 122
Larson, Scott, 102
Lasco, Jim, 79
laws: colonial-era racial segregation, 24, 29;
    current riparian, 137; legal challenges to
    racial-segregation, 55
Legislative Council (LegCo), 85, 94
Likimani, Muthoni, 38
loitering, 61
Low, John, 80
Luhya, 21–22, 62, 80
Luo, 21–22, 37, 62, 80

Maasai, 20–22, 24, 115; steady acquisition of the
    land of the, 31–32
Maathai, Wangari, 101
Macharia, Kinuthia, 66–67
Maina, Miriam, 67
Majanja, Lutivini: "A Park Called Freedom," 105
Makeba, Miriam, 84, 184n89
malaria, 28–30, 54; African children as a
    reservoir for, 91; epidemics of, 153–54,
    177n65; European fear of, 137. *See also* disease
Malaya, 90
Malenya, Jackton, 78
Manda Island, 120. *See also* Kenya
Maombo, Sharon, 153
Maputo, 7
Martin, Aurora, 30–31, 92–93
Masengo, Eduard, 79
Mashambani Boys Band, 66
Mashiyane, Spokes, 82
Mashujaa Day (National Heroes Day), 111,
    121–22
Mathare Community Justice Center, 126–27
Mathare River, 109, 131–32, 142–43
Mau Mau revolt (1952–58), 27, 60, 120–22,
    178n18. *See also* Kenya
Mbagathi (Athi) River, 132
Mbatia, T., 43
Mbembe, Achille, 8
mbira (string instrument), 77
Mbotella, Tom, 70
Mboya, Tom, 59, 63, 70, 84–86, 120
McDonald, David, 13
Mensah, Collins Adjei, 97, 100
Meru, 61
Michuki, John, 145

migration: African, 61; detribalization of natives and, 53; of different people across Kenya, 75; of people from lower elevations, 29; of rural people, 60, 140; wartime, 60
Ministry of Environment, 128
miro (countryside person), 40
Mirrors of Africa (British newsreel), 40
Missing Voices Project, 126
modernity, 23–24, 26–27; development as construct of, 152; identification of Kenyatta with, 122; manifestation of international, 56; music, dance, and African, 80–85; neoliberal dreams of, 152, 156; private land ownership and, 31. *See also* capitalism; neoliberalism
Mohan Properties Ltd, 58
Moi, President Daniel arap, 63, 67, 83, 121
Mombasa, 16, 21, 44, 80, 120, 152. *See also* Kenya
Moore-Pewu, Jamila, 14
Morgan, Frank: *A Reflection of Twelve Decades*, 56–57
Morton, David: *Age of Concrete*, 7–8
Mozambique, 8, 10, 66, 120–21
mtego wa panya (the mousetrap), 90, 93
Mugabe, President Robert, 121
Mugambi, Hassan, 68
Mukabi, George, 78–79, 84
multiracialism, 83; protest against royal charter city status as expression of, 20
Munyao, Kisoi, 124
Murray, Martin J., 122
Murumbi, Joseph, 64, 70, 97, 107, 109–10, 121–22, 124; grave in City Park of, 108*fig.*, 109, 111–12, 115, 117, 124; as national hero and art collector, 115–17, 187n21
Murumbi, Sheila, 107, 117; grave in City Park of, 108*fig.*, 115
Murumbi Trust, 115
Murunga, Godwin, 28, 56, 153–54
music: African American, 75; African popular urban, 70, 74, 77–80; American popular dance, 75, 79; as circumscribed by colonialism, 74; East African, 79, 82, 84; general influence of Western, 80; influence of Railways on, 78–79, 85; Kenyan popular, 84; *kwela*, 82; Latin American, 79, 84; Luhya sounds in Nairobi, 79; of military bands, 77; southern African popular, 79. *See also* benga; dancing; Nairobi Sound; radio; *zilizopendwa* (the golden oldies)
Muslims: African, 27, 153; identity of, 82; in Pangani, 54; settlements and peripheral villages of, 21

Muthurwa, 40–43, 65, 69, 71, 78, 93; collapse of the Railways and, 42; dance venues in, 74; evictions in, 48; as Railway estate, 31, 35, 37, 41–42. *See also* neighborhoods; social halls
Mutua, Kisulu, 121
Mwale, John, 79, 84
Mwangaza Music Store, 85
Mwau, Baraka, 67
Mwebe, Expedito, 117
Mwenda, Jean-Bosco, 79
Mwinamo, Isaya, 79

Nairobi: built and natural environment of, 4, 15, 102–4; central business district (CBD) of, 42–44, 98, 133, 188n20; as city of temporary inhabitants, 1, 3, 12, 22, 32; downtown, 46*fig.*; elevations and rivers of, 130*map*; ethnic groups of, 176n16; expansion of, 64–66; as Green City in the Sun, 91–93; Indian Bazaar of, 53, 56, 153–54; long-term residents of, 11, 33, 48, 87, 104–5, 140, 175n54; lost in the city that used to be, 49–50; municipal boundaries of, 59*fig.*; as ordinary city, 13–15; plains area of, 141; postwar development of radio and recording industries in, 79; as railway depot, 21, 36–37; residential areas and locations in, 25–26, 92–93; segregated areas (1948) of, 27*map*; swamps of, 15, 29–30, 91, 137, 153–54; view of, 5*fig. See also* Arboretum; cemeteries; Central Park; City Park; development; garden city; Giraffe Center; housing; infrastructure; Jeevanjee Gardens; Kamukunji Grounds; Karura Forest; Kenya; neighborhoods; Ngong Road Forest; Oloolua Forest; Uhuru Gardens; Uhuru Park; White Highlands
Nairobi (film), 40, 160
Nairobi City Council, 56–57, 59, 65, 67, 72, 74, 103, 121, 139
Nairobi City County Government, 71, 90, 97–98, 165
Nairobi City Government (NCG), 135
Nairobi City Regeneration Programme (NCRP), 145
Nairobi City Water and Sewerage Company, 152–53, 158–59
Nairobi Half Life (film), 7
Nairobi Integrated Urban Development Master Plan, 158
Nairobi Master Plan for a Colonial City (1948), 38, 92
Nairobi Metropolitan Services (NMS), 97–98, 145

Nairobi Metropolitan Services Improvement
Project (NaMSIP), 103; Integrated Urban
Water Management of, 104
Nairobi Metro 2030 strategy, 34, 43–44
Nairobi Museum, 100
Nairobi National Park, 88, 101, 185n43
Nairobi People's Convention Party (NPCP), 85
Nairobi Railway City (NRC), 44
Nairobi River, 132, 142; regeneration of the,
145–46; wetland corridor of the, 167–68
Nairobi River Basin Rehabilitation and
Restoration Programme (NRBP), 145–46
Nairobi Sanitary Commission Report (1913), 29
Nairobi Sound, 71–72, 77–81, 83–86.
See also music
Nakuru, 75. *See also* Kenya
Nation, The, 133
National Archives, 107, 115, 117
National Constitution (2010), 41, 167
National Construction Authority, 134
National Environment Management Authority
(NEMA), 135, 164
nationalism, 90; African, 125; ethnic violence
and, 177n46; freedom fighting and,
124–25; importance of burials to, 122; Kenyan
narratives of race and, 128
National Land Commission (NLC), 104, 164
National Museums and Heritage Act (2006), 104
National Museums of Kenya, 88, 90, 103, 106,
117, 128
National Social Security Fund, 66
National Youth Service (NYS), 135
native: as category of temporal and
spatial displacement, 168; change after
Independence in the construct of, 31; class
and race after Independence structured
on top of and through the category of,
53; colonial category of, 26–27; post-
Independence dichotomy of detribalized
native and, 62. *See also* detribalized native
Native Authority Ordinance (1912), 17
Native Lands Trust and Crown Lands
(Amendment) Ordinance (1908), 25
Native Lands Trust Ordinance (1938), 158
Native peoples, 9, 26, 174n32; areas of residence
for, 30
Native Tribunal Ordinance (1930), 17
Nature Kenya, 103
Nehru, Jawaharlal, 120
neighborhoods, *2map*; Brookside, 99; Buruburu,
31, 66; Dagoretti, 134; Dandora, 126, 132, 136,
139; Doonholm, 65; Eastleigh, 52, 54, 56, 65,
154, 179n5, 188n20; Garden Estate, 134; Gigiri,
31; Githurai, 134; Grogan, 131; High Ridge,
90, 136; Huruma, 31, 132–34, 136, 138–40,
142; Jericho, 1, 13, 65–66; Jerusalem, 65–66;
Juja, 65; Kaburini, 153; Kahawa West, 134;
Kaloleni, 35, 65, 71, 93, 133, 141; Kangemi, 31,
136; Karen, 45, 51–52, 69, 93, 136; Kariobangi,
131, 133–34, 152, 158, 161, 165; Kariokor, 56, 112,
186n8; Kasarani, 134; Kayole, 160; Kibera,
28, 31, 36, 65, 78, 112, 159, 162–65, 191n43;
Kileleshwa, 68, 134, 143, 153; Kilimani, 58,
68, 93, 134, 143; Komarock, 31; Kyuna, 129;
Landhi Mawe, 65; Lang'ata, 31–32, 45, 65, 97,
124, 185n20; Loresho, 69, 99, 129, 131; Loresho
Ridge, 136; Madaraka, 66; Makadara, 17–18,
65–66; Makongeni, 65, 71; Maringo, 65;
Mathare, 65, 126, 131; Mbotela, 65; Mlolongo,
133, 141; Mukuru wa Ruben, 168; Muoroto,
159; Muthaiga, 51–52, 58, 65, 90, 93, 98–99;
Nairobi West, 139; Ngara, 52, 54–55, 65, 90,
93–94, 136; Pangani, 52, 54, 56, 89, 93–94,
109, 131; Pumwani, 71–72, 74, 93, 139; Red
Hill, 136; Ridgeways, 136; Roysambu, 133–34;
Ruaraka, 167; Ruiru, 158; Runda, 31, 159,
168; Shauri Moyo, 93; South B, 139; Spring
Valley, 131, 136; Starehe, 93; Thigiri Ridge,
136; Thome, 134; Umoja, 134; Westlands,
45, 58, 99, 140; Woodley, 65; Zimmerman,
133–34; Ziwani. *See also* Eastlands; estates
and schemes; housing; Muthurwa; Nairobi;
Parklands; Upper Hill
neoliberalism, 44, 101–2, 105, 154; and housing
privatization, 139; and modernity, 152, 156;
and private development, 138; structural
adjustment and, 159. *See also* development;
modernity; structural adjustment
New Njiru Town, 132
newspapers, 83; Indian, 115, 120; Konkani (Goan-
language), 120
New York City, 102–3
New Zealand, 90, 113
Ngei, Paul, 124
Ngong River, 132, 142–43
Ngong Road Forest, 87, 100, 162. *See also* Nairobi
Ngung'u, Gathanga, 126
Ng'weno, Hilary, 38*fig.*, 93, 98, 169–70; walking
route of, 170*fig.*
Njeru, Jeremia, 161
Njoh, Ambe J., 9
Njoka, Julius Maina, 161
Nnaggenda, Francis: *Mother and Child*
(artwork), 117

nostalgia, 50, 105, 109

Nubians, 173n15, 191n42; Christian, 27; established community in Kibera of, 65, 163–65, 177n50; Muslim, 27, 112; as landowners, 66; Sudanese soldiers as, 28, 162, 177n50

Nuttall, Sarah, 8

Nyairo, Joyce, 77

Nyakiongora, Moses, 134

Nyamwezi people, 54

Nyanjiru, Mary Muthoni, 27

nyayo (footsteps), 83

Nyerere, President Julius, 85

Nzenze, John, 79

Obama, President Barack, 35

Obote, President Milton, 35

Odochameny, John, 117

Okoth-Ogendo, Hastings, 24

Old Provincial Commissioner's Office, 115

Oloolua Forest, 87, 100. *See also* Nairobi

Omolo, Gabriel, 82, 84

Ongesa, Elkana, 117

Organic Intellectuals Network, 126

orutu (one-string violin), 75

Otieno, S. M., 32

overcrowding, 53, 77, 92, 154, 169

Owuor, Samuel, 43

Pakistan, 21, 155. *See also* Karachi

Pandit, Lalit, 65

papyrus, 29

Parish, Jessica, 146

Parklands, 45, 52–58, 93, 131, 140, 188n20; creation of the neighborhood of, 89–90; demolition of a mall in, 132, 134; movement of Asians to, 53–56, 65; racial dynamics of, 56–58; rapid construction of high-rise buildings in, 99. *See also* neighborhoods

pastoralist plains, 21, 24, 88

Pichen, Nishil, 82

Pinto, Pio Gama, 64, 70, 115, 117, 120, 124, 187n42; as Asian Kenyan, 124–25; assassination of, 109, 116, 121–22, 125; commemoration on a stamp in stamp series titled "Heroes of Kenya" (2008) of, 121, 187n33; grave in City Park of, 111, 115, 117, 119*fig.*, 121, 124–26, 165; sign to the grave in City Park of, 118*fig.*

plastic waste, 100, 143–45

Police Reforms Working Group, 126

pollution, 106, 143, 145–46. *See also* environmentalism

poor, the: exclusion from the city of, 31, 60–62, 66–67; housing, building, and safety for, 68, 92, 136, 142, 148–49; post-Independence accumulation and distribution of land without concern for the landless and, 120; protests of displacement and takeover of land by the working class and, 41; restriction from urban areas in colonial garden cities of, 9; segregation and the management of populations under colonial classifications of time and space of, 9–10; structuring of Nairobi and the question of, 20; unhygienic space and the control of, 28. *See also* poverty

population, 20–23; unwanted urban, 9, 22–23, 68. *See also* African and Asian populations

Portuguese, 55, 57; colonialism of the, 120

Portuguese Guinea (Guinea-Bissau), 120–21

poverty, 16, 41, 60–62, 77; concentration of, 147; of detribalized natives, 62, 66–67; increase of Kenyans living in, 137. *See also* poor, the

Progressive African Library and Information Activists' group (PALIAct), 126

prostitution, 77

protests, 40–41; containment of social, 165; against inequalities of land and wealth, 125; transformation of social halls into spaces of, 86. *See also* social unrest

public health, 28, 30, 91; as excuse for the displacement of Asian or African businesses and settlements, 28, 165; urban planning and, 92. *See also* disease

Public Health Ordinance (1913), 29

public-private partnership regeneration projects, 65

pumua (breathe, relax), 72

Pumwani Maternity Hospital, 37

Pumwani Memorial Hall, 40

race, 9; African as category of, 173n15; interacting dynamics of class and, 53, 57–58, 60, 68; Kenyan narratives of nationalism and, 128. *See also* class; segregation

racial covenants and conditions of indenture, 58–60

racism, 76; moving to Parklands and encountering, 57; social Darwinism and scientific, 23. *See also* segregation; white supremacy

radio, 74, 79–81, 83, 86; elite urban guitarists appearing in, 80; first regular broadcasts of, 80; music and advertisements on the, 81; Railway workers and customers as closely tied to the, 79, 81, 84. *See also* Ghetto Radio; music; Voice of America radio broadcasts

Railway African Union, 83–84

Railway estates, 22, 26, 31, 36–38, 72, 76, 105; cutting services to, 154; as places of children, 37–41; scheduling for demolition of old pension, 48; wired radios installed in all of the, 79. *See also* housing; Railways

Railways, 15–18, 21–22, 38–39, 60; buying up of land by the, 91; control of time and space of the, 72; countering of popular support for striking Railways workers with propaganda from the, 83; derelict lands of the, 67; long-term workers for the, 50; musicians, rhythms, styles, and sounds brought to Nairobi by the, 78–79, 85; as novel linguistic space, 39; as sign of British imperial power, 21; transformation of the demography of Nairobi by the, 21. *See also* labor; Railway estates

Railway Showboat (radio show), 74, 79, 83–84

real estate. *See* development

redevelopment, 14, 102–3, 148; disinvestment in urban infrastructure creating opportunities for profitable, 159; of government-owned housing, 160. *See also* development; urban planning

remnant, 10; animal species of City Park as, 89; of biodiversity, 88–89; care of City Park as, 95–98; City Park as colonial urban park, 89–91; of green city in the sun, 87–106; plant species of City Park as, 88, 95. *See also* City Park

resettlement, 151, 164, 165

Rhodesia, 31, 77, 79; as settler colony, 71. *See also* Zimbabwe

rivers, 10, 15, 20, 168; banks of, 91; collapse, demolition, and the environment of, 132–35; construction garbage in a Nairobi river, 144*fig.*; pollution of, 99. *See also* demolitions; land; water

Rivers Sewerage Improvement Program, 145

roads, 68, 91; plans to build, 150–51, 155–56; rivers and the names of, 136. *See also* infrastructure

Robertson, Claire, 61, 63

Robinson, Jennifer: *Ordinary Cities: Between Modernity and Development*, 13–14

rumba, 84, 182n26. *See also* dancing

rustication, 68; anti-urbanism as, 18, 22–23. *See also* anti-urbanism

Ruto, President William, 167

Sakaja, Governor Johnson, 160–62, 165, 167–68

Samia, 39

Samoei, Koitalel arap, 124

sanitation, 23, 28, 30; and garbage services, 25; public health and, 153. *See also* sewage

Scott, David, 47

segregation, 6–10, 51–68; City Park as location free from, 90, 93, 95; class, 54, 56, 93; colonial structures of, 114; as enforced through pass laws between the rural and the urban, 23; forms of spatial, 25, 30, 32, 92–93; garden cities as attempts at class, 92, 105; housing, 31, 70, 91–92; as permanent removal of unwanted urban populations, 9, 22–23, 68; plague epidemics and residential racial, 153; postcolonial life and colonial urban, 9–10, 112; racial, 54–56, 91, 93, 122, 165, 181n41; title deeds in the absence of explicit laws of, 59–60. *See also* class; race; racism

Senegal, 153. *See also* Dakar

sewage, 26, 68, 148–49; Athi Water Works Development Agency services regarding, 145; broken lines of, 99–100; facilities for the treatment of, 158, 165; in the Kibagare River, 99. *See also* infrastructure; sanitation

sexuality, 75; and youth, 175n54

Seychelles, 22

Seychellois, 27, 56, 186n9

Shah, Pejul, 135

Sham, Natalie: "A Walk Through Parklands," 52

Shaw, Archibald, 111

Sheng (Nairobi creole), 40

Simone, Abdou Maliq, 13, 47–48

Simonetti, Cristian, 141–42

Simpson Report (1913), 29

Singapore, 14, 18, 92

Singh, Makan, 19, 70

Slater, Tom, 146, 154, 156, 159

slums, 67–68. *See also* housing

Smart, James, 19

Smart, William Henry, 58

Smith, Constance: *Nairobi in the Making*, 89, 127, 140

social Darwinism, 23

social halls, 69–77; dancing in, 74–77, 85–86; and gender imbalance, 72–73; Kaloleni Social Hall, 69, 71–72, 73*fig.*, 74–75, 85; Makongeni Social Hall, 71–72; music played in, 80, 84, 86; Muthurwa Social Hall, 43, 69, 72–74, 78, 84; Ofafa Memorial Hall, 75; Pumwani Social Hall, 71–72, 74; and Railways housing, 74; as spaces of leisure, 71–74; Starehe Social Hall, 72; Sudanese Brass Band, 78; transformation into

social halls *(continued)*
spaces of protest, innovation, and creation of, 86; Ziwani Social Hall, 72. *See also* dancing; music
socialism, 7–10, 66, 120–21, 124–25
Social Justice Working Group, 126
social unrest, 18, 83. *See also* protests
solastalgia, 49–50
Somalia, 22; civil war in, 179n5
Somalis, 27, 52, 54, 173n15, 176n23, 186n9; displacement to Eastleigh of, 54, 65, 179n5; as landowners, 66; property-owning, 53
Sonko, Governor Mike, 135, 146, 148, 155, 161
South Africa, 8–9, 31, 113, 155; anti-urbanism as the postcolonial form of apartheid in, 10; experience in managing Africans from, 24; popular music (*kwela, sinjonjo*, and township jive) of, 79; sonic influences from, 81. *See also* Cape Town; Johannesburg
Ssonko, Charles, 82
Standard, The, 126, 165
Standard Gauge Railway (SGR), 44, 175n53
Star, The, 111, 153
structural adjustment, 89, 100–101, 139–40, 143, 159, 178n1. *See also* neoliberalism
Sudan, 22, 28; Dinka people in, 111
Sudanese Brass Band, 78
Suriname, 84
Swahili (language), 22, 45, 90; as common language of the Railways, 35, 39, 77, 79; radio broadcasts in, 80–81, 84; songs of urban musicians in, 76–77, 79, 83
Swahili (people), 27, 173n15, 186n9; as traders, 22
Swynnerton plan, 31
Sykes, Ally, 78, 81–82, 183n79
Sykes, Kleist, 82, 183n79

Taita, 22
Tanganyika, 54, 76, 79; city parks in, 90; political refugees from, 120; social halls of, 82. *See also* Tanzania
Tanganyika African National Union (TANU), 82
Tanganyika Islamic Jazz Club, 82
Tanzania, 7–8, 10, 66, 85, 167. *See also* Dar es Salaam; Tanganyika
Thuku, Harry, 27
Thuku riots (1922), 27, 55, 72
Time, 85
tourism, 91, 103
townships, 25–26; African housing estates absent from, 26; in British colonial Africa, 176n44; colonial creation of Eastleigh as one of the, 53; colonial creation of Nairobi East as freehold property as one of the, 53; Kileleshwa as former European, 68; Kilimani as former European, 68; native residence in, 30. *See also* housing; land
trade: global secondhand clothing, 100; legal African, 62
trade unions, 60, 86
travel, 74, 77
Trouillot, Michel-Rolph, 89, 110
Truth, Justice and Reconciliation Committee (2013), 121
Tsotsi (film), 7
Tsotsi, Peter, 79, 82
Tuikong, Mathews, 42
tuimbe pamoja ("let's sing together"), 86
turudi mashambani, 66–68
twisti, 79, 82–83; nostalgia for the time of the, 86; rumba and songs of, 84. *See also* dancing
Twitter, 154–55

Uganda, 11, 22, 35, 37; expulsion of Asians from, 64. *See also* Kampala
Uganda Railway, 58, 175n53
Uhuru, 85
Uhuru Gardens, 100. *See also* Nairobi
Uhuru na kazi ("freedom and work"), 63
Uhuru Park, 100–102, 105. *See also* Nairobi
Ukay Center, 134–36, 140, 143; demolition of the, 146–49
Ukombozi Library, 125–26
UN-Habitat, 145–46; Advisory Group on Forced Evictions, 159; United Nations Human Settlements Program, 22
United Kingdom. *See* Britain
United Nations Development Programme (UNDP), 145
United Nations Environment Programme (UNEP), 22, 145
United Nations Office of the High Commissioner for Human Rights, 126
United States, 8–9, 35, 77; garden cities in, 92; sonic influences from, 81; support for predatory new elite from the, 121; white flight and suburbanization in the, 102
Unremembered, The: Britain's Forgotten War Heroes (documentary film), 114
Until Everyone Is Free (podcast), 126
Upper Hill, 44, 58–59, 136; construction work in, 34*fig.*; greenbelts along the railway tracks in, 91, 150; high-rise infill development in, 143. *See also* neighborhoods

Upper Hill Residents Association, 151

urbanism, 12; decolonized, 15; as form of dreaming, 169; water and greenery as foundational to a new, 169. *See also* cities; anti-urbanism

Urban Pathways waste-management projects, 146

urban planning, 4, 18, 28; and anti-urbanist designs, 50, 101, 160; and architecture, 40; "dual cities" as typical of colonial, 92; hydrology as founding principle of, 148; inextricable link between class and race in, 53; as international practice, 92; lament of a lack of African, 4; in Nairobi as water city, 136–40; participant-observation in public, 4; and public health, 92; segregationist, 106. *See also* anti-urbanism; cities; redevelopment

vagrancy, 61

Vagrancy Acts (1902, 1922, 1930, and 1949), 24, 61

veterans, 72, 77; Commonwealth war, 109, 111, 112*fig.*, 114–15

violence, 77; anti-urbanist, 127; police, 154–55; victims of assassination, 127

Voice of America radio broadcasts, 81, 86. *See also* radio

Waliaula, Ken Walibora, 122

wananchi (citizens), 83

Wanga-Odhiambo, Godriver, 121

Wangila, Robert, 43

Wanjira, Mzalendo, 126

water, 25–26, 53, 68; Nairobi as place of sweet water, 129–49. *See also* rivers

Water Resource Management Authority (WRMA), 135

Watson, Vanessa, 47

watu wa kisasa (modern city people), 70

Webuye Paper Mills, 100

West Africa, 100; French colonies of, 9–10

White, Louise, 30

White Highlands, 88; African expulsion from the, 61. *See also* Nairobi

whiteness. *See* white supremacy

white supremacy, 19, 24, 57. *See also* racism

Wildlife Clubs of Kenya, 103

William, Fadhili, 82–84; "Malaika" (song), 84, 184n89; "One for the Road" (song), 82

women: dress for dancing of, 76; male access to intimacy with, 76; male roles as traders in the city for, 61; rustication as removal of unwanted populations including, 22–23, 68

working class, 41, 77; idea of the social hall as a means of pacifying the, 71. *See also* labor

World Bank, 46, 103; site-and-service projects funded by the, 139, 181n59; structural-adjustment loan agreement with the, 137, 178n1

World Health Organization, 101

World War I, 77, 111, 113–14, 127, 183n79; Africans who served in the Carrier Corps in, 186n8

World War II, 30, 38–39, 60, 77–79, 111, 113–14, 127, 180n35

Worrod, Charles, 81–83

Young Kikuyu Association, 27

Zambia, 10, 31

Zanzibar, 95

zilizopendwa (the golden oldies), 85–86

Zimbabwe, 71, 121, 155. *See also* Rhodesia

Founded in 1893,
UNIVERSITY OF CALIFORNIA PRESS
publishes bold, progressive books and journals
on topics in the arts, humanities, social sciences,
and natural sciences—with a focus on social
justice issues—that inspire thought and action
among readers worldwide.

The UC PRESS FOUNDATION
raises funds to uphold the press's vital role
as an independent, nonprofit publisher, and
receives philanthropic support from a wide
range of individuals and institutions—and from
committed readers like you. To learn more, visit
ucpress.edu/supportus.